A Soc...

for International

Development: Prospectus

1984

Ann Mattis, editor

Published by Duke University Press in collaboration
with the Society for International Development
Durham, North Carolina 1983

Library of Congress Cataloging in Publication Data
Main entry under title:

A Society for International Development — Prospectus 1984

(Duke Press policy studies)
Selected proceedings from the 25th anniversary world
conference of the Society for International Development
held in July 1982 in Baltimore, Md.
Includes index
1. Economic development — Congresses. I. Mattis, Ann,
1954–   .   II. Society for International Development.
III. Series.
HD 73.S65   1983   338.9   83–16550
ISBN 0–8223–0561–5   (alk. paper)
ISBN 0–8223–0562–3   (pbk. alk. paper)

ISSN 0020–6555

In memory of the late Barbara Ward

Contents

Book I. Creative "Investment"

Part 1. The Way We Were

Part 2. Workable Dreams—A How-To from Local to Global

Part 3. In the Year 2000

Part 4. We've Got the Power

Book II. Across The Borders

Book III. Insiders' Experiences

Foreword

The twenty-fifth anniversary world conference of the Society for International Development (SID) was planned as a response to the development problems and opportunities within industrialized and Third World countries—capitalist and socialist alike—as well as those within the international framework established following World War II. It also was intended as a stocktaking of development thinking and action at international, national, and local levels with a view to posing these questions: what is the reality of the world today? what have we learned over the past quarter-century? and where do we go from here? Implicit in these concerns is the need to demystify some development issues and to ask two further questions: which nations, structures, groups, and people are part of the problem? and which of them can provide solutions?

In the months since the SID conference took place the global situation has worsened. As a result, major, often cataclysmic problems have emerged in all groups of nations, and a further breakdown in the existing international economic framework has occurred. Yet a clearer diagnosis of the depth and nature of this real crisis—a diagnosis that considers the contradictions, dilemmas, and development alternatives of the pluralistic world as it is—still must be made.

Diagnosing the nature of the crisis, as well as searching for options, is made difficult by the lack of an appropriate intellectual framework. Such a framework should go beyond single discipline analysis and the conventional thinking of both "right" and "left" to encompass a historical/cultural perspective that will view development in wider human terms. Currently, the intellectual processes for change are confused. On the one hand, there is the conservative counterattack against past development policies and strategies in an effort to turn back the clock or simply to do more of the same. On the other hand, there is the debate between progressives of varying shades of opinion who have some understanding of what is wrong but are unable to agree on what can put things right.

The SID conference mainly attempted to sharpen this debate among progressives so as to clarify some of our conceptual confusion, improve our understanding of today's realities, identify various options, and establish a more coherent perspective for future action.

This book, which includes selected proceedings from the conference, is intended to carry the progressives' debate and search for solutions to a wider audience as a matter of utmost urgency. It is not a "gloom and doom" book, nor is it romantically visionary. There is, instead, in its contents a realism tinged with hope that new constituencies may be mobilized in support of *development and international cooperation in new terms* which may lead to an international society with different and better people-to-people, people-to-nature, and people-to-technology relationships.

The conference first identified some critical elements in the present crisis before examining positive and negative lessons to be gleaned from the development experience during the past quarter-century. It then went on to look at a major new trend—development by people and experiments in people's participation and self-reliance—that offers a goal for restructuring society in positive sum terms. There also was an attempt at a stringent evaluation of North-South relations in the aftermath of the failed Cancun Summit and in light of diffused negotiations for a New International Economic Order. Throughout the proceedings there was discussion of seeds of change, from the village through the global order, that may form the basis for a realistic vision of the future. These seeds ranged from a new international framework and better use of resources to the information revolution, the scope of activities among people's organizations, and changes required in the United Nations system.

Thus, A *Society for International Development—Prospectus 1984* is presented to the SID membership in furtherance of SID's development mission. The original concept motivating the Society's founders in the 1950s (and is embodied in SID's Constitution) was the prospect of building pluralistic participatory societies, linked worldwide, for the general well-being of all, not for a few. The book also is presented to people of every social level—whether they be heads of state, policy makers, development technicians, women, students, businessmen, trade unionists, or grass-roots activists—in an attempt to mobilize, raise consciousness, and guide them toward organizing a development movement that can help bring about such a society and provide progressive solutions to a crisis which no longer is emerging but is a reality confronting people everywhere. The Society for International Development invites comments from all such individuals on the ideas put forward in this book. The SID journal, *Development: Seeds of Change, Village through Global Order,* will provide thoughts in progress and a continuing forum for vigorous debate on these critical issues of our times as the process toward a Society for International Development becomes reinforced.

Ponna Wignaraja
Secretary General
Society for International Development

Preface

The Society for International Development (SID) celebrated its twenty-fifth birthday in July 1982 at Baltimore, Maryland, U.S.A. For a nongovernmental organization to have survived for twenty-five years and to have, in addition, developed and grown to new heights is no mean achievement, especially in light of the recent cutbacks in funding experienced by many agencies. Further testimony to the strength of the Society is its growth in the face of indifference to the problems and concerns of the Other in the blind pursuit of self-interest—both at the level of national leadership and at the level of the individual. To cite but one example: Black West Indians recently engaged in a "rebel" cricket tour of South Africa, despite national and international bans on sporting encounters with that country under its present regime and despite the disapprobation of peers and local clubs. The cricketeers' decision has revived in the Jamaican community echos of "Money before Principle," for such a tour was only made possible by the unprecedentedly large sums of money paid to the players.

It is indeed an event to celebrate when an organization of individuals from all walks of life and many nations is able to uphold for twenty-five years the notion of "Principle before Money." The Society too often over the years has pursued its task with inadequate or no funds, yet it managed to bring together in Baltimore over fifteen hundred very busy individuals to join in celebrating not only its own institutional achievement but other achievements in the field of development, the sphere with which SID concerns itself. But the gathering did not simply laud the past; in the SID tradition, it went on to make suggestions for realizing even greater strides in the field of development over the next twenty-five years and beyond.

By "development" we mean a *sustainable* process geared to the satisfaction of the needs of the *majority* of peoples, and not merely to the growth of things or to the benefit of a minority. As summarized in the 1975 Dag Hammarskjöld Report, *What Now,*

> Development is a whole; it is an integral, value-loaded, cultural process; it encompasses the natural environment, social relations, education, production, consumption, and well-being. The plurality of roads to development answers to the specificity of cultural or natural situations; no universal formula exists. Development is endogenous; it springs from the heart of each society, which relies first on its own strength and resources and defines in sovereignty the vision of its future, cooperating with societies sharing its problems and aspirations. At the same time, the international community as a whole has the responsibility of guaranteeing the conditions for the self-reliant development of each society, for

making available to all the fruit of others' experience and for helping those of its members who are in need. This is the very esssence of [a] new international order. . . .

SID is but one actor among many concerned groups and individuals dedicated to bringing order out of the chaos that now characterizes many of the relationships among nations. The task is undertaken in the hope that we may all one day be able to enjoy a more sane, secure, human environment, one that functions in the interest of the human being, who may then be able to say with pride "this is Planet Earth."

The SID community deliberated for four days on the subject "The Emerging Global Village," reviewing twenty-five years of development activity to assess where we were, where we are today, and where we might be in the future. Were one ever to compile a Who's Who in the development field, one would need look no farther than to the list of those present in Baltimore. During the four days of over one hundred panels and plenary sessions, to employ an understatement, a lot was said. Much of what was said was not new, certainly not to the majority of the participants. It was amazing how often one could hear such phrases as, for example, "As we all know," "As you are well aware," and "I don't need to inform an audience such as this."

This volume reflects but certainly does not reproduce the conference deliberations. It does not lay claim to any radical new insights or proposals. It hopes only that—in the words of one of the wise old men of the development field in reply to my impatient accusations of "talk, talk, and nothing *doing*"—if we repeat certain facts and arguments, "maybe somebody will listen." Most important, it hopes that those who will most be encouraged to read it are those who do not "know" and are perhaps not "aware."

Many good ideas were advanced at the formal sessions around the tables and in the corridors of the Baltimore convention center. But if our purpose were solely to search for good ideas, we would need only to point the reader to the numerous other volumes in which these appear. We could then simply provide the reader blank pages on which to note some of these ideas, to play with combinations of ideas in efforts to design an action package, to record his or her own reactions to what was read, or merely to doodle, a yet creative exercise. What we have done, however, is to present ideas, period. Some are untested and their potential therefore difficult to evaluate. Some are tested, and their results bear their own witness. Some are as yet uncrystallized, but we hope the reader may nevertheless find these thought-provoking and stimulating, to the point of giving them further shape and form. We hope that all these ideas may stimulate an uninitiated audience to participate in the struggle for human development and to spur others to action.

The volume is meant for some of the people I have had sitting in my studio while it was being prepared, that is, the young, who are frequently brilliant, well-informed, and intelligent, but all too often unemployed or underemployed. It is even meant for my infant niece, who often helped to "read" the material. It is meant for these people since they all too quickly will be asked to share the responsibility for the management and future of the planet. I would often hear from them in reaction to the conference material, "Hey, this is nice and all that, but is this stuff for real?" Or they would declare, "I wish I knew what these people were talking about—this has nothing to do with anything in that world they never told you existed out there when you were doing your four or five years educational service!" Or they simply complain, "This stuff has no sex appeal... boring." It is meant for those same young people who, in searching for an answer to what ails them, will quickly respond "Reaganomics" if he or she is an American, or, if Jamaican, "Ask Uncle Mike" (Manley, former Prime Minister of Jamaica) or "Check Eddie about that" (referring to Jamaican Prime Minister Edward Seaga). Ronald Reagan, Michael Manley, Edward Seaga, or their counterparts in other regions cannot carry the full burden for the state of the world; such erroneous assignment of responsibility is one of the notions that this book may help to abolish.

Certainly national leaders have contributed, some more than others, to the crises that face individual societies and the international community today, but other forces enter into play. In this volume we explore some of these forces that have shaped the crises of poverty, alienation, unequal economic relations and institutions, and we attempt to demonstrate that there are viable alternatives to the proposals being made by national leaders. Indeed, we would hope that we have not engaged productive energy in laying blame at any one doorstep but, rather, that we have sought and found solutions in many houses.

Many of the solutions we found came in the form of people's initiatives and their organization in response to social, political, and economic assaults threatening a group's or the individual's survival, assaults to which national leadership was either insensitive or consciously ignored. The assaults take many forms, from attacks on the basic civil rights of Black people in the United States that pose a threat to their freedom and ability to live in dignity and to share in the rewards of the land of their birth, to threats to the livelihood and thus to their human survival of poor people in Bangladesh and Latin America posed by closed doors to credit. The various attempts to find solutions bear witness to a power other than that of established authorities, that is, a countervailing people's power, which in the future we may well see exercised increasingly.

We have attempted, while not viewing the world through rose-colored glasses, to avoid ponderous, gloom-and-doom chronicles. Embracing Jim Grant's "tempered optimism," we have chosen to celebrate twenty-five years of development experience. Convinced of the indomitable human spirit and the resolve of peoples all across the globe to survive despite the odds, we have chosen to celebrate the future.

We have paused to ask ourselves, what should the world be like in the year 2000? Do we dare hope that for many it will be different—free from hunger, disease, and the pain of inequalities? Are we already beginning to see shifts toward such a society? And if so, is its future development being threatened— by whom and by what? How do we answer that threat? By "strengthening" military components? Or, might it be possible to lend new meaning to the term "security"? Is it conceivable that our strength may be sought in infinite and often unexploited resources such as culture in an appreciation of the pluralism that characterizes our globe, in increased cooperation between peoples at all levels, in new partnerships between the poor and the traditionally powerful? Do people, whether they sit in parliament, in church, in school, or in their living rooms, have a role in articulating a vision of and the pathways to a society that better satisfies their needs? That is, how do people participate in a process of development that does with surety affect them and that consequently they should control?

And, very important, is all of this economically viable? Is creative investment in people and by people in a project for human development a viable proposal for global management? These are some of the questions this book addresses. Amidst the despair regarding the future of the human family, the book tries to say, "Yes, certainly, hope in a sane, secure tomorrow for the many is justified; yes, humane development policies that assume people the subjects and objects of those policies are possible and viable; yes, it is possible to meet the challenge of innovation to construct a less chaotic, more dynamic, economically viable, sustainable, equitable future." We have the technology, we have the resources, and we have the knowledge. Mass poverty, hunger, inadequate housing and education, poor water systems, a technologically controlled world, poor information systems, inequitable economic relations, violence, armaments on the battleground and in the fields, injustice, these are not situations we *must* live with. With this awareness it may be possible to generate the will for change.

We have entitled the book *A Society for International Development: Prospectus 1984* in the conviction that only by forging a society for human-centered development can the future of this gift we call Planet Earth be assured. As Barbara Ward put it, "We are either going to become a community or we are going to die." We venture in this prospectus some concrete proposals and we draw on real-life experiments for development that would stand the test of political, social, *and* economic viability. Such conditions will be made possible through the cooperation and unencumbered participation of all in a project for international development. Cooperation will be based on mutual respect, shared information, and a willingness to act in the long-term interests of all rather than the short-term gains of the few.

Contributions to this book are at times bold, despite their modest aspirations and proposals, because they recognize that fundamental changes in each of our countries and in relations among nations are imperative; contributions are at the same time modest, recognizing that it has taken centuries for us to reach our present predicament and that thirty or even fifty years is but one sentence in the annals of human development. Finally, all acknowledge that fifteen hundred persons, however eminent, cannot alone chart a path to change the world. And certainly they could not do it in four days!

Several common threads run through all the contributions. First, the human being is mankind's greatest resource. Also common to many of the discussions is the premise that change can result only from clear political vision and deep political commitment. We must strive constantly, therefore, to place the technicalities and the constraints on resources in their proper perspective, that is, that they assume meaning only as they become necessary to realize the architect's vision.

The Baltimore meeting also underscored the reality of interdependence and the imperative that development policies be based on this reality. No one individual, whether leader or disciple, no one nation, at the center or the periphery, can act alone and boast that effective action has been taken. This is not possible now nor will it be true in the future.

The essential of unceasing hope also underlined the deliberations. The specter of despair must never be allowed to transcend that condition. The cases reported on are not held up as inviolable models; rather, they describe experiments that both inform and possibly inspire us to hope that solutions to any given problem are possible and that our dreams are shared by many, some as close as our neighbor and some as distant as the next continent.

Book I, "Creative 'Investment,'" looks at development concepts of the past as well as their contemporary evolution and praxis, highlights the role of popular participation, and draws attention to some priority issues for action now and in the decades on the horizon. Part 1, "The Way We Were," discusses some of the issues and events that have influenced the course of international development over the past three decades. It looks at the decisions taken over those years and how they affected the people of this planet, in the North and the South. It expresses a pride in our accomplishments, a confidence in our capacity to meet present and future challenges and, in large part, an optimism stemming from a faith in the members of the human family to reverse adverse trends and establish a more just, humane, and equitable global society.

Part 2, "Workable Dreams," examines paths to such a future. It looks at a new development and demonstrates the increasing role that people, through their participation in the decision-making process at the local level in their villages and other communities, are playing in shaping and building that new, just, humane, and equitable society. Based on the evidence provided by the examples of people's projects, the contributions here in fact gamble on the future and recommend an investment in the global village as a virtual "sure thing" with potentially infinite returns.

The individual authors in this section discuss from varied perspectives the issues involved in creating that future. Swedish Under Secretary Inga Thorsson helps us look at the critical role disarmament must play if we are to entertain the idea of *any kind* of future, especially one in which we could dare hope for a sane, resource-efficient development. Robert McNamara examines the meaning of interdependence and its effects on the crisis of poverty. He traces the responsibility of international public agencies in the war on poverty, proposes an international central bank as the type of institution to address the challenges posed by interdependence, and stresses the efficiency of involving the poor in development efforts. Andrew Young, Clarence Dias, and Muhammad Yunus point to the successful efforts by people who took the initiative to act in their own behalf, to their own benefit, and who have demonstrated the tremendous power which people, regardless of their social or economic status, have in righting social and economic injustices. Possible strategies and tactics are outlined in the cases discussed: the areas of civil and human rights, law and the legal system, and finance.

Tarzie Vittachi and Robert Moore draw attention to one of the pillars of development, information and communications, and the new scope these must take if people are to participate in a development movement: that is, transforming the *commerce* of communications into communication *services*. Undeniably, such participation will not be possible if information is not freely available and is not comprehensive and effectively communicated. In this field new actors, other than the traditional journalist trained to report events, must be identified to ensure the development of a new kind of information—one that speaks to processes which create the events. Robert Moore proposes that our nations' representatives abroad serve as information/communications agents in addition to their role as goodwill ambassadors. Ulla Ollin explores women's role in development, seeing her as purveyor of a unique approach, planning and programming in a way that tends to be more people-oriented and focused on immediate problems, to be less object-oriented and bent on controlling the future than men may be. Further, she points to women's tendency to plan on a multi-dimensional level—not just income-generating activity, but child-care facilities and broad-based community benefits aimed at improving the quality of life for the public and nuclear family. She ventures the concept of the nation-state as a symbolic family requiring the creation and maintenance of cultural and physical infrastructures—religious institutions, public services, and the like—for its support.

S. N. Leela invites "the world into the classroom" and encourages the increased participation of young people in development by adding new dimensions to curricula. The author discusses one experiment aimed at informing young people about problems such as food shortages and population dynamics and, in general, increasing their awareness of a real world—contrary to the image they are usually presented in the classroom—in which most people are not well fed, clothed, and housed and which, "all things being equal," functions adequately. The classroom is an ideal place to provide information about a world in which all things are *not* equal, and given such an opportunity it challenges our ability to make the seriousness of the problems truly meaningful to all students. In this section, too, Lee Bloom examines the question of the relationship between international business—a traditional power—and Third World countries and their peoples—a potential power. Bloom calls for a renewed and redefined partnership between the two.

Finally in Part 2, we focus on two very important debates for the future. The first is the area of South-South cooperation. Although the Third World remains

a reality, Third World unity in international forums and Third World cooperation in a broader context are somewhat more doubtful. In considering patterns
of development that are different from those of the past, in the North as in the
South, we need to ensure more extensive cooperation among the nations of the
South. The contributors point us to some of these cooperative relationships in
trade, finance, and at the cultural level, for example; they argue their merits
and demerits, as well as suggest concrete areas ripe for further joint action and
in which efforts must be made to strengthen a still shaky but potentially very
powerful instrument for the future social, economic, and cultural development
of the nations of the South.

The second debate focuses on finance capital as it operates in an international system. As the Third World sinks under its burden of debt, its citizens are
exhorted to redouble their toil and increase their productivity, not in order to
use the fruits of those endeavors in their own development and to meet people's
needs, but to service debts and otherwise to participate in a system that does
not serve them in a ratio proportionate to their contribution. Radical measures
incorporating safeguards against future undesirable developments are called for
to resolve a crisis in the international financial system, not now effectively dealt
with by regular debt rescheduling and increased borrowing from private or
multilateral sources. While Third World countries and some Third System
(extragovernmental) bodies have for some time now been calling for a high-level
meeting (like Bretton Woods) to inspect the chasms in the international monetary system, including a reexamination of the institutions that govern it, one is
encouraged to note that reportedly even U.S. Treasury Secretary Donald Regan
has publicly admitted the extent of the crisis and has himself called for just such
a conference.

In Part 3 we have selected a few issues that merit more focused attention in
the years to come. These include food and agriculture, research and research
methodologies, aquatic resources and the Law of the Seas, what we have
termed "monetronics" or electronic money, and one element of the private
sector—small business and its potential contribution to development.

The contributors to Part 4 reinforce for us the notion that "we've got the
power." We have seen evidence of people's power in some of the experiments
discussed in Part 2, and further in references throughout the volume to the
ever-important and effective role being played in the field of development by
Third System extragovernmental bodies. Here, in Part 4, we see that people,
whatever their role in the theater of life, have the power to articulate a vision of
the future and to act to realize that vision. They also have the power to, at any
time, change the script where they see that it is necessary to improve the
production.

Book II, "Across the Borders," takes another look at North-South negotiating
processes and their future. In so doing, we look at, inter alia, perspectives on
this issue by U.N. Secretary General Perez de Cuellar and Canadian Foreign
Minister Mark MacGuigan, who outlines Canada's role in international cooperation for development. The U.S. perspective is also presented. Further, two

dimensions of North-South relations are highlighted: (*a*) a discussion of aid —and its links with the private sector—presently one of the central elements in the relationship between North and South, and (*b*) the concept of bargaining, which lies at the heart of the negotiations to determine the context and the boundaries of the North-South relationship. This concept of bargaining gains in importance as the Third World harnesses its strength and moves to the negotiating table, not as petitioner but as full partner.

Book III, "Insiders' Experiences," provides some national and regional perspectives on twenty-five years of development and in so doing presents some thoughts on what the future may hold for some of these.

The task of preparing this material could not have been completed without the invaluable assistance of the following individuals: SID's indefatigable Secretary General Ponna Wignaraja; Luther Henkel and the crew at NOK, New York; Keith McNeil for services to my sanity; and finally to my niece Tannishia, a.k.a. "Mother" for all her "help," proffered I suspect to hasten the day when we could again "take the plane" and accept the Jamaica Tourist Board's invitation to "make it Jamaica again."

Ann Mattis

Abbreviations

ADB	African Development Bank
ASEAN	Association of South East Asian Nations
COMECON	Council of Mutual Economic Assistance
ECA	Economic Commission for Africa
ECDC	Economic Cooperation among Developing Countries
EEC	European Economic Community
GATT	General Agreement on Tariffs and Trade
GDP	gross domestic product
GNP	gross national product
ICC	International Chamber of Commerce
IDA	International Development Association
IFAD	International Fund for Agricultural Development
IMF	International Monetary Fund
LDC	less developed country
NGO	nongovernmental organization
OAU	Organization for African Unity
OECD	Organization for Economic Cooperation and Development
OPEC	Organization of Petroleum Exporting Countries
SDR	special drawing rights
SELA	Sistema Económico Latinoamericano (Latin American Economic System)
SID	Society for International Development
UNCTAD	United Nations Conference on Trade and Development
USAID	United States Agency for International Development

Dollar figures quoted in this volume refer to United States dollars except where otherwise stated.

Book I

Creative "Investment"

Part 1

The Way We Were

Introduction: Development Then and Now

Ismail Sabri Abdalla

If we reduce development to economic growth, one may say that there has always been development in most societies, and societies that did not "develop" disappeared. Further yet, one could say that under colonial rule there has been development in the colonies. The railway network and the civil service in India, cotton in Egypt—all these things are development if we understand "development" as meaning only economic growth. However, real development is something else. While not entering into a discussion about indicators, a specific example may be valid.

If in a given country a dictator decides to put half of the population in prison, the GNP will grow because the dictator has to build prisons, which requires investment and capital formation. He has to engage jail keepers and he has to provide minimum food and water to keep the prisoners alive. All these goods and services together should normally result in some rate of growth of the GDP or the GNP. Of course, the example is absurd, but it illustrates how unreliable the traditional indicators are and how unrealistic they are when confronted with the facts of most countries of the Third World, whose basic human needs either cannot be met or are simply denied. Accordingly, development, in this restrictive sense, is not always something good. It can be bad, and it has been bad under colonial rule, because underdevelopment has not simply been backwardness. Third World destinies did not rest in the hands of Third World peoples. The development that took place under colonial rule was directed in the service of the colonial power and left the Third World with economies that proved very difficult to handle.

Given this and other experiences with externally stimulated and directed development, Third World nations must see development as being first of all based on the assertion of their cultural identity. They must reject the idea that modernization or equalization is equated to Westernization and must develop while remaining themselves. Third World nations have a long, greatly admired cultural heritage that should not be rejected and considered obsolete because others have developed nuclear power or spy satellites. The Third World has its own cultures, its own values, and must certainly move confidently and with ease into the twenty-first century while retaining and reflecting this heritage. This implies repudiating the idea of Western centralism and embracing the diversity of human culture and the equal exchange among cultures.

We in the Third World, certainly our leaders—those who have or reserve the right to speak in our names—as well as our intellectuals, must accept the responsibility for our recent development history because we were the ones who readily embraced the idea of imitating the Western pattern of civilization and of copying anything that came from abroad, even to the point of cultivating a certain disdain for our culture. We accepted the infamous concept of the stages of growth. When one reads today certain authors who propose as indicators of progress the number of cars per family, and when one then looks to the environmental issue and the costs of the car culture, as well as the problems of the industrialized nations that have been provoked by the car industry, one is truly ashamed ever to have entertained this type of thinking as valid.

Fortunately, however, our peoples are not passive. We do not accept all that our governments do, and we have struggled to obtain political decolonization, a struggle that often takes the shape of a long revolution, a long war of liberation that involves the sacrifice of tens of thousands of human lives. But amazingly enough, once we became independent, the enemy of yesterday became the benefactor of today. We returned to the former colonial powers, asking them, to put it crudely, to develop us. Some leaders in the Third World and some intellectuals recognized this as a mistake as early as the 1960s, and in fact we cannot discuss the development achievement without pointing to the relationships during the last three decades between the developing countries and the developed countries.

The first decade has been, mainly for Asia and Africa, the decade of achieving political independence, while in Latin America the idea of industrialization as a way of rapid development based on import substitution was the common ideology. In fact, Latin America proved to be the testing ground of this development strategy. But as early as 1961 the small group of countries of the nonaligned movement held its first summit conference in Belgrade, where the late President Nasser of Egypt raised the issue of North-South relations. This first summit of nonaligned nations decided to convene a conference of all developing countries to discuss the issue of North-South relations; that conference, held in Cairo in July 1962, issued a document, the Cairo Declaration, which was the first step toward the convening of UNCTAD I. At UNCTAD I, there was no agreement between the North and the South, and the seventy-seven members of the Third World developing countries issued a common resolution that gave birth to the Group of 77, a name that survives despite the growth of the group now to more than 120 members. The idea in the 1960s was more trade and not only aid, already an advancement in the concept of international cooperation and development. Offer us more opportunities of trade, better terms of trade, and we can develop; we can bring in the necessary resources for our own development instead of relying continually on international aid which, in all frankness, is never neutral. Aid is not politically neutral. It is not culturally neutral. It is not economically neutral. In fact, it can be best used only as a supplement to the full mobilization of domestic resources.

The high rates of growth of the industrialized countries in the 1960s allowed, however, for more aid, more investment, and a potential crisis was averted and confrontation postponed. In the 1970s something unprecedented took place. Thirteen Third World countries, very different from each other and coming from three continents, made for the first time in modern history a decision that would affect the whole world economy. The action of thirteen oil-producing nations initiated a power-sharing in the world system, unprecedented in modern global history, which will remain, whatever happens in the future of OPEC. However one may assess OPEC's action, this precedent remains important because it showed the capacity of the Third World to make decisions by itself and even to impose these decisions the world over.

In reaction to that move there have been some attempts at restructuring the international system: witness the Paris North-South Conference and the resolution of the Sixth Special Session of the General Assembly of the United Nations on the New International Economic Order. But very little progress, if any, has in fact taken place in the area of North-South negotiations aimed at evolving a new system of relations. We have had many meetings at all levels, including summit levels, but the outcome of all these endeavors has been very disappointing. In their wake have followed a sense of frustration and a sense of fear and disquiet among the elite of the Third World because they will be the first to pay for the failure of international cooperation on new terms. They will face instability at home, violence, terrorism, whatever it is called, but this is the fact.

In addition, the high rates of growth of the glorious 1960s are no more, and the center of the system is suffering from a recession, an early end to which is difficult to see. Still, I remain optimistic and I believe in the emerging global village. I am optimistic that the marginalization, misery, migration, and population pressures forced by a certain "progress" in the Third World will see a reversal. Very simply, I am optimistic because of all the millions of people of goodwill, millions of people who believe in peace, who believe that there should be no more hunger in the world, people who believe in coexistence, in pluralistic ideologies, in a culturally pluralistic world, and in the human species as a single family. People realize that it is very difficult, if it is possible at all, for any country or a group of countries to unilaterally get out from the recession and the complicated interdependence of today's world while leaving the others to starve. The deep will at the grass-roots level is manifest everywhere, and many governments in the North and in the South are subject to far-reaching critiques at home. This makes me believe that mankind is becoming more and more aware of its unity, of its common interests; maybe, not necessarily tomorrow, but one day soon the global village will emerge as a reality. The present world took many a century to be built. To build the global village, two, three, or even five decades is not really very much time.

Two Steps Backward or One Step Forward?

James Grant

We find ourselves in a *most* difficult time, with recession, unemployment, inflation, and other difficulties deepening and spreading to the great majority of countries, industrialized as well as developing, reaching more intense levels than at any time over the last forty years, and with no early or easy solutions in sight. This crisis has seen a questioning and often a disillusionment with traditional solutions and approaches. The need for serious stock-taking and rethinking is urgent. But in the midst of the crisis we might take a moment to celebrate. For after all, along with the current stalemate and retreat we have experienced forty years of unprecedented economic progress and witnessed the creativity of postwar reconstruction and international cooperation.

The changes were far from perfect. With the notable exception of liberation movements ending colonialism, they were largely worked out among the industrial countries. Many important concerns were neglected, but even so these changes led to four decades of unprecedented progress for the betterment of humankind. Lest we underestimate this progress, we can contrast these achievements with the failures. Five times in this century the world has faced crises of such grand dimensions that they challenged the capacity of people and nations to respond in new and creative ways. Twice we have clearly failed, twice we have largely succeeded—and the fifth crisis is now upon us as we enter the 1980s.

Four Crises—Challenges and Responses

We failed the first challenge and the existing international system collapsed into the conflagration of World War I.

We failed the second challenge as the extraordinary global economic crisis of the late 1920s prompted the nations of the world to choose the path of narrow nationalism and short-run advantage. The result, a worldwide depression and ultimately the carnage of World War II.

The world learned a few lessons with that one, however, including how to respond to the third challenge, the war itself. The very idea of the United Nations was that collective security is preferable to allowing an aggressor nation to take on one country at a time. We learned that coordination and cooperation enable countries to do more together than they could do separately. And, together with the subsequent liberation of the colonies, we learned that people are far more willing to make sacrifices for principles of equity, democracy, and justice than they are for domination, dictatorship, and reversion to barbarism. Indeed, many of these changes were seen as liberation; the giving of the vote to women in France in 1945 was part of this process. So also were freedom from fear, from want, from hunger, which former U.S. President Roosevelt advocated.

The value of those lessons continued beyond the war as a more united world, albeit polarized between East and West, rose to the fourth challenge of rebuilding a devastated Europe and creating a new international political order able to accommodate the hundreds of millions of people emerging from colonial rule. The United Nations, the World Bank, and the IMF spawned at Bretton Woods, as well as many other new institutions, were products of that creativity.

But most importantly, the collective effort of the nations united in war and of peoples in so many parts of this world after the war represented a determination, unprecedented in human history, to advance human well-being: unprecedented in its manifestation of the essential equality of all people and their rights to national embodiment and representation. Unprecedented in the universality of popular subscription to its principles. And unprecedented in the willingness of national governments to work together, collectively, to fulfill the determination.

That determination to support progress in human well-being made possible the emergence of more than one hundred new states in Asia, Africa, and Latin America. The right to national self-determination has become nearly universal in four decades. The determination has also resulted in more progress for more people in the past thirty-five years than in the preceding one hundred years. Life expectancy in low-income countries has increased from 37 to 51 years, and infant mortality has been halved. That determination has made possible extension of the right of participation in the economic process, and of opportunity to derive benefits, to more countries, more families, and more women than ever before. And, finally, that determination has made it possible, limited as it may still be, to embrace more citizens in more countries within the right of equality under law, regardless of sex, race, or creed.

I choose to celebrate these past four decades now because, if certain contrary forces continue, there may soon be little to celebrate.

The Fifth Crisis—Darkening Times

We are now confronted with the fifth great crisis of this century. In the United States, in the United Kingdom, in France, in eastern Europe (as symbolized by Poland), and in a wide range of developing countries as disparate as China, Tanzania, and Mexico, peoples and governments are questioning and challenging many of the basic policies of the past generation.

A recent U.N. study has concluded that "the world community is experiencing greater instability and more severe disruption of steady growth than at any time since the end of the Second World War . . . unless specific steps are taken, the consequences of this adverse external environment will be to increase the numbers of absolute poor (from 800 million) to one billion, before the end of this decade." The industrial countries suffer from the nearly 10 percent unemployment of their work force, and they face the prospect of high unemployment for years to come. In many countries more children will die this year than last, and in all probability the current economic crisis means that during this decade several million more children will die than was expected when it started. In parts of Haiti, as one illustration, the death rate among small children has nearly doubled as one consequence of these darkening times.

There are those who would say that we are facing a crisis arising from the cumulative failures of the past four decades. This may be true in small part. But this crisis arises far, far more from the *successes* of the past generation. The very rapidity of progress has caused a majority of countries, in fact the world community as a whole, to outgrow many of the successful institutions and policies of the past. We have witnessed the world more than treble production in thirty-five years, and, more importantly, per capita consumption has more than doubled in this short period. But, though this is welcome, the disparities in the distribution of goods and of access to necessities both among and within countries challenge the adequacy of the economic institutions of the post-1945 era. The welcome advent of the more than one hundred new nation-states made up largely of the world's poorest people has challenged the adequacy of even the unprecedented rate of change in political and economic institutions of the past four decades. Inadequate attention to the population explosion and the thoughtless exploitation of the planet's resources and its biosphere threaten the very physical environment in which we live.

In this crisis we are threatened by the danger of losing—of abandoning—the very essence of three of the most important lessons revealed to us by the tragic years of the 1930s.

First, cooperation between nations is essential. Lowered trade barriers immediately after 1945 fueled the greatest expansion of trade in history, to the great benefit of all countries. Development cooperation with low-income countries has resulted in their becoming, in one generation, vast and profitable markets for the industrial countries as well as principal sources of inflation-slowing, low-cost raw materials and manufactures.

Second, the world has seen that progress must benefit the many if it is to endure for the few. This is a concept that applies equally among and within countries. The social provisions of the New Deal of the 1930s in the United States made possible the vast expansion of the American mass-market economy after 1945, and the Marshall Plan for assistance to western Europe has already generated more than a hundredfold return both economically and politically for the United States. Conversely, failure to give sufficient priority to the concerns of the many contributed greatly to the downfall of such governments as that of Iran, even to the rallying of virtually all Third World countries to the OPEC cause in 1973 though rising oil costs bore most heavily upon the poorest countries.

Third, knowledge must be consciously mobilized for the benefit of progress, not only in the sense of mobilization of the natural sciences as with the Green Revolution, electronics, and aircraft, but equally with the mobilization of the social sciences, as with the creation of new institutions such as those spawned at Bretton Woods and the evolution of the three-tiered primary health care system in China with its barefoot doctors. Both often go hand-in-hand, as in the remarkable victory achieved in 1979 by the decade-long international cooperative effort to eradicate smallpox, which was made possible by the invention of freeze-dried vaccine and of new highly localized saturation inoculation techniques. The effort not only saves scores of thousands of lives every year but earns the United States a saving of some $100 million or more annually on its $50 million investment in the programs.

Will civilization—confronted with the predictable problems of an expanding system—abandon its vision of the future, set aside its creativity, and resign itself to a destiny of conflict, disparity, and deprivation? Some scholars already claim that the progress of the last generation was only a historical fluke. Not in a generation have expectations of world development—and the determination to continue progress through imagination and hard work—been at such a low ebb.

We are, hence, in a *crisis of civilization.*

That is a terrible tragedy. Our civilization has evolved through dark ages and wars, through unspeakable barbarity and uncounted persecutions, through untold deprivations and unrelenting calamities. For only a brief four decades has organized civilization—through governments of the world's nations—seriously attempted to establish basic principles of humanity as the birthright of all people. For only a brief four decades has hope been kindled that all of us might share in a decent life.

For the first time the world stands poised, possessed of the resources and of the knowledge, to mount, if it so chooses, a decisive push against mass hunger, ill health, and illiteracy, and in so doing to establish a base of productive and consumptive capacity to sustain economic progress for all countries and all people. It is not our capacity to achieve this goal which is in question; instead, it is our wisdom to understand that we must do the job, and our will to do so. I am optimistic that we will respond positively. My tempered optimism is rooted in recent history and example. In the short span since 1945 the economically poor nations of the world have doubled their average incomes and halved their rates of infant mortality. In the same period, they have increased their average literacy rate from under 30 percent to over 50 percent. Over the last two decades alone, through colossal effort and in the face of rapidly rising numbers, they have pushed the school enrollment rates for their six- to eleven-year-olds from 47 percent to 64 percent, and they have substantially increased their per capita food production.

By any historical standards, these are impressive achievements. And in the industrialized nations, where one sometimes detects a tendency to regard the Third World as a vacuum waiting to be filled with development from the outside, these nations of the South deserve fuller recognition. For example, in the twenty years between 1955 and 1975 the people of Africa, Asia, and Latin

America brought 150 million hectares of new land into production—more than the entire present crop land of the United States, Canada, Japan, and western Europe combined. In the ten-year period from the late 1960s to the late 1970s India increased its grain production by a greater percentage than was ever achieved by the United States, the U.S.S.R., or China. As a result of such efforts, and of a doubling of land under irrigation, only one-tenth as many people have died from famine in the third quarter of this century as in the last quarter of the previous century, when the world was far less populous. The People's Republic of China, South Korea, Taiwan, Hong Kong, Singapore, Sri Lanka, and Kerala in India have all demonstrated that it is possible—with enough political will sustained over two or three decades—for countries still at real income levels comparable to those in the United States and the United Kingdom at the time of the American Revolution in 1776 to overcome the worst consequences of absolute poverty and to reach levels of life expectancy, infant survival, and basic education not achieved in the industrial countries until the middle of this century.

An important message of these two decades is not that the challenge of sustained human progress has been met or is being met, but that it *can* be met.

Within these great achievements of recent decades reside great disparities in the benefits they have conferred. Aggregate statistics mask the fact that the actual number of people afflicted by hunger, ill health, and illiteracy has risen even as the percentage has fallen and, I should stress, continues to fall. The total of the malnourished in 1970, for example, stood at an estimated 400 million. Today that figure is probably 450 million. Similarly, the actual number of illiterate people was estimated at 700 million in 1960, 760 million in 1970, and has almost certainly passed the 800 million mark. Future illiterates—the six- to eleven-year-old boys and girls who today are not in school—total 128 million. By 1985, that figure is expected to increase to 137 million.

Percentages are not people. It is not by percentages that the scale of any problem must be gauged. The real test lies in the answer to the question, "how severely does it affect how many?" To that we find that overall, the number of men, women, and children now living out their lives in absolute poverty is estimated at 780 million out of a total world population of 4.4 thousand million.

As we take stock of the present position and future prospects of sustained progress for all, recent history is both inspiring and humbling, demonstrating both the possibility of a decisive push against numbing, draining poverty in the context of broader economic progress, and the elusiveness of the goal itself.

In sum, the picture that emerges from the achievements and failures of recent decades is of a world population divided into quarters. Roughly one-quarter of the world's people have seen their lives change from material well-being to unprecedented affluence; roughly one-quarter have made the transition from hardship to relative comfort; roughly one-quarter have seen the promising beginnings of an improvement in their lives; and roughly one-quarter have been left behind in wretchedness. And virtually all of us are now in difficulties together.

The plainest lessons the past brings to the future are, first, that progress is not automatically self-renewable—that institutions and policies need to be adjusted and revised constantly to accommodate new realities; and, second, that progress does not automatically benefit the poor, and that if absolute poverty is to be shed then it is the by-passed people of the earth who must now be placed first.

Progress Abandoned?

Will governments—and the societies they represent—now, having encountered the necessary growing pains of a civilization's coming of age, abandon the precious progress that has only so recently been achieved? To advocate the rapid acceleration of developmental progress for the world's poorest people in order to sustain the promise of a world for all is to invite the charge of naiveté. It is a "naiveté" which I—and I hope people all over—intend to pursue with the utmost vigor. Working to continue the progress we have made—to sustain the determination—is not only a matter of justice. It is also a most productive investment in the world's economic and social future. The realism or naiveté of any goal is almost always as much a question of priorities as of possibilities. And it is not the possibility of achieving continued progress in the well-being of hundreds of millions of disadvantaged children and mothers which is in question. It is its priority.

Such minimal goals as freedom from widespread hunger and malnutrition, access to primary health care, and the provision of primary education for the great majority of all children and mothers worldwide, for example, could be achieved for an additional cost *less* than the amount equivalent to that which people in the United States *alone* spend on alcoholic beverages each year, or which the world now devotes annually to tobacco, or every four weeks to the task of maintaining and increasing the world's military capacity. However uncomfortable such comparisons may make us, they are necessary to put into perspective the accusation that the goal of making significant improvements in the lives of the world's poor by the end of this century is "naive," and to put in its place a decision about priorities.

A War We Are Losing

Governments that are willing to spend some $600 million a year on the weapons of war ought to recognize the imperative of combating *now* the deadly war that gross underdevelopment *already* wages against so many hundreds of millions of the earth's inhabitants. That war costs the lives of more than 40,000 infants and small children *each day* on its front line, and millions more suffer impairment and disability from the insidious weapons of malnutrition, disease, ignorance, and inattention.

Devoting an additional amount equivalent to less than 10 percent of the expenditures on military arms to waging war for human decency—a war we are now losing in many countries—could not only save the lives of these millions but also give dignity and purpose to a billion more while sharply increasing the prospects for a return to prosperity in countries both rich and poor. It would also sharply decelerate today's unprecedented explosion of population as well. We are learning that acceptance of family planning is heavily dependent on such changes as improved health care, fewer child deaths, and more basic education, particularly among women. So the same steps necessary to save the lives of several million children annually would also result in 12 to 20 million fewer births a year by the end of this century.

Present and future needs cry out with one voice. And each decade into the future will see a magnification of either the successes or the failures of the world community's response to the needs of the present times.

Bringing about a significant improvement in the lives of the world's poor by the end of this century will certainly need a significant increase in the resources available for the task. Reality also requires an increase in the effectiveness with which resources are deployed. We must rethink social programs to reduce their per capita cost while expanding their coverage, as with barefoot doctors in China and midwives in New York City. We must help in the restructuring of the total set of social sector programs to establish priorities that take advantage of the linkages among them. In short, a vigorous new emphasis on efficiency is needed.

One of the greatest opportunities for increasing the efficiency with which resources are deployed, thereby lowering their per capita costs, is the synergistic relationship among the different elements of social development. Village water supply and health education, for example, catalyze each other's potential benefits. Devoting resources to either in the absence of the other therefore leads to a "leakage" of potential improvement. Within the health sector, an emphasis on primary health care can result in several times greater beneficial impact per health dollar than through conventional programs, with their emphasis on hospitals and relatively costly curative measures. In the United States we spend more health-care dollars per person in the last months of life than in the previous seventy-five years of life.

There is need for more thorough examination of how apparently diverse programs can work in synergism with each other. It is not generally recognized, for example, that if there were to be $10 thousand million additional spending on the world's poorest billion people, investing in their increased productivity and their increased health, three-quarters of this expenditure should be in local currency. It would mean providing dollars or other foreign exchange to buy local currency for use within the recipient country. This would give the countries much if not all of the additional amounts needed to meet their urgent balance-of-payments problem to import goods to maintain the functioning of the modern sector of their economies. There is much to be said for, in effect, relating their balance-of-payments needs to this kind of a structured program, which would have the popular support of the world's citizenry, rather than justifying such support simply on the grounds of having to bail out these countries to keep them functioning as viable economies.

But these are questions of *priorities*, not *possibilities*. These are matters of choice in which both reason and emotion argue for humane concern for a life worth living. And now is a crucial moment at which to decide. So many lives threatened by the darkness of today's economic climate will not stand still to await economic growth and balanced budgets.

An Appeal to Reason

Today, world financial resources are affected by the two factors of increasingly difficult economic conditions in all countries and an unabated—indeed, intensified—arms race between many countries. In many if not most countries, these factors together result in even greater constraints on the resources available to build the basic capacities of poor people, and frequently result in the requirement that those who are least able bear the greatest—and a disproportionate—share of the cost of both.

How will the world respond to this fifth major crisis of the modern era? How will the world respond to this crisis of our civilization? Will we, as in the 1920s and 1930s, allow ourselves to be carried along by the currents of short-run advantage, easy "solutions," and narrow definitions of the community for which we are responsible? Or will we take our future, as well as our conscience, into our own hands? Will we go forward convinced, as the late Barbara Ward has said, that hope is a risk we have to take? Will we go forth, recognizing, again as Barbara Ward has said, that "we are either going to become a community or we are going to die"?

Can we as individuals make a difference? Yes, we can. The actions required are required largely from governments, but it is people who can create the understanding, the awareness, and the pressures that require governments to act. Each of the great social achievements of recent decades—the end of colonialism, the rise of civil rights, the fight for women's equality, protection of the environment—has come about not because of government proclamations but because people organized, made demands, and made it good politics for governments to respond. It is the political will of people that makes and sustains the political will of governments. Between the vicious and the virtuous spiral, a choice must now be made, a choice in which, through informed action or by default, each of us will participate.

Lessons from the Past

Munir Benjenk

The current global recession, the second in less than ten years, is painful and discouraging. It is undermining confidence, with negative political and business consequences. It gives place to dangerous notions about the economic future, fundamental doubts about the viability of economic growth, a resurgence of economic isolationism, political resistance to the adjustments needed for economic recovery, and a disturbing hard-heartedness toward the poor.

None of the organizations concerned with development has done nearly enough to confront such notions, including definitely the World Bank and also SID. The World Bank has sometimes acted as if the virtues of development were so obvious that universal support could be taken for granted. International agencies are paying the penalty for that myth, and we should become more accountable for the mandate extended to us. Indeed, today's indifference and hostility to our cause on the part of so many can be overcome only by telling the story of development as it is, and not in terms of the romantic or even ideological theses some of us have sometimes indulged in. And there is a story to tell!

In summary, the four principal lessons we might draw from the last twenty-five years of development are: that considerable economic expansion has taken place and that it must continue; that the world economy has become interdependent and will become even more so; that adjustments to new situations must be made so that future economic development is sustainable; and that more attention should be paid to issues of justice.

Let me elaborate on these.

Development has been, and should continue to be, characterized by economic expansion. The world economy now produces twice as much per person as it did twenty-five years ago. This growth has been a remarkable achievement. It was not evenly shared, but neither was it concentrated entirely in the industrial countries. In fact, many middle-income countries outperformed both high-income and low-income countries. In particular, two groups of Third World economies, the oil-exporter and the newly industrializing countries, have consistently grown much faster than has the world economy as a whole. The largest low-income countries—China, India, and Pakistan—have also evidenced some dynamism in coping with their immense problems. These giant nations have achieved virtual self-sufficiency in food and have also become significant industrial powers. Though still very poor, they are now able to compete internationally as exporters of sophisticated manufactured goods. Whatever the views about North-South political relations, it is encouraging that parts of the South evidence such economic dynamism.

Over the last ten years an uncertain world economy has been buoyed up, to some extent, by continued expansion in these more dynamic parts of the developing world. We expect them to help lead the global economy out of the current recession. And their resilience bodes well for a steadier pattern of global growth in the future. The resilience is further strengthened by growing links among the developing countries. South-South trade is expanding. Large numbers of workers have migrated from East and South Asia to the Middle East. And East Asia is selling technology in South Asia and the Middle East. These links among the developing countries make them less vulnerable to shocks that originate in the high-income countries.

Unfortunately, most of the world's poorest countries have not participated much in these dynamics. Most low-income countries, particularly those in sub-Saharan Africa, have grown much more slowly than the high- and middle-income countries. We can be somewhat heartened, however, that economic expansion over the last generation allowed for widespread gains in human welfare also in the low-income countries. For example, the average literacy rate in the low-income countries went up from 23 percent in 1955 to 51 percent in 1980. Life expectancy in the low-income countries is now sixteen years longer, an increase in life expectancy for the low-income countries of fully one-third.

The pattern of economic expansion established over the last generation is a robust trend that will—and should—continue.

Another aspect of past development that can and should continue is increasing interdependence. Current economic problems are strengthening the temptations of economic nationalism. But international interdependence is already such an important reality that the costs of trade restrictions, for example, are increasingly obvious for all to see. The world economy, which used to depend primarily on engines of growth in North America and western Europe, is today powered from numerous poles of dynamism—Japan, of course, and also several groups of countries in the South. The resulting level of interdependence opens up new possibilities for interventions at the global level to make the international economy function better: Worldwide energy development is one obvious area for action; food is a second. Drought in the Soviet Union provoked famine in Ethiopia by raising the price of internationally traded grains. Timely rains in North America's grain belt affect prices in Bangladesh.

Capital markets represent a third area of increasing interdependence where "global macroeconomics" can be helpful. Many of the middle-income countries are rife with high pay-off investment opportunities. It makes good sense for them to attract international investment funds. Whatever can be done to assure a continued flow of investment to these countries also strengthens the international monetary system.

Finally, a fourth area for cooperation to maximize the benefits of interdependence is manufacturing. A number of developing countries are showing themselves to be more efficient than the "mature" industrial countries in producing certain types of manufactured goods. This success has been a major source of rapid growth for these countries. The resulting gains in the overall efficiency of the world economy benefit all countries. Consumers everywhere get more value for money. In order to take advantage of such opportunity, the mature industrial countries must continue to resist pressures for protectionism and develop their own areas of comparative advantage.

Expansion and interdependence—these favorable features of the past should continue. But two lessons from the past suggest changes we need to make.

Especially during this last decade, we have learned that past development patterns must be adjusted in order to achieve *sustainability*. It is now obvious, for example, that patterns of energy use that characterized most of the last twenty-five years cannot be sustained. Similarly, agriculture and the development of human resources can no longer be neglected without eventually affecting the whole economy adversely. In the past a number of countries directed relatively few resources to these sectors, sometimes financing instead expensive projects and programs with only marginal returns to the economy. Fortunately, the global economic difficulties of the last ten years have forced many countries to become more concerned about waste. Realistic pricing and prudent investment have become higher priorities. Such adjustment is often painful and politically difficult. It is also expensive, and one reason for the slow growth of the last decade is that efforts that might have contributed to expansion were instead devoted to transition to more sustainable patterns of development.

The rate of population growth, a key long-term issue, has also begun to decline in many countries over the last decade. There is now virtually no country in the world without some sort of population program—quite a change from the situation we confronted ten years ago. However, governments have not yet faced the population issue with the same urgency they now bring to the energy issue. And if we fail to bring population growth rates down to sustainable levels, we risk future strains on the world economy that might make the energy price shocks of this past decade seem as mild as hiccups.

Sustainability, then, should definitely be a third facet of our vision for the future.

Finally, we should emphasize one last and crucial aspect of the future of development—justice. Over the last twenty-five years of development the poorest people have, in general, been left behind. The low-income countries have lagged behind the middle- and high-income countries. And within national borders, poor groups of people have too often benefited less from general economic expansion than have the relatively well-off groups. This long-term trend is not desirable. Nor is it conducive to world stability.

Nearly a fifth of the world's population still suffers absolute poverty, without enough income to provide the basic necessities of life. Thus, drawing on the lessons of the past, we should make certain the future includes vigorous efforts to make lower-income people, especially the absolute poor, more productive; that is, they must be included in the process of development. On this point, present trends are against us.

Low-income countries have generally suffered most from the recent world-wide economic difficulties. Yet one of their few lines of assistance from the rest of the world—IDA, the World Bank's fund of concessional resources—was cut by 40 percent in 1981. Also, within countries many governments are cutting back on programs designed to bring poor people more fully into the process of development. Short-term budget and balance-of-payments problems tend to take precedence over long-term investments and human resources.

In response to these pressures, the World Bank recently completed two separate evaluations of its own efforts to bring poor countries and poor people more fully into the development process. The findings of an exhaustive study of IDA over the past twenty years indicate that IDA's effort for the poorest countries worked. The best evidence for IDA's success is that twenty-four countries —including such success stories as Korea, Thailand, and Ivory Coast—have now graduated from IDA to the World Bank's regular lending program, and many are also able to get access to financial markets for their needs. A task force review of the bank's overall attempt during the past ten years to invest more of its resources in increasing the productivity of the poor concludes that efforts in this direction have generally been effective.

The impact of the World Bank is extremely limited in comparison to the scale of change that is needed. But the fact that our poverty efforts have paid off confirms that equity can be achieved in development without sacrificing efficiency or growth. The question for the future, then, is whether political will can be mobilized to support such efforts on a much larger scale.

The four lessons from the past sketch out a vision of future development that is at once attractive, ethical, and possible. It is a future worth defending. We should be frank about the mistakes of the past twenty-five years of development. At the same time, we can also affirm that unprecedented progress has been achieved and that it is possible to help the peoples of the world dream workable dreams.

The Human and Cultural Dimensions of Development: Accomplishments and Failures

Soedjatmoko

A global village may emerge from increasingly complex interdependencies, but it also may *not* emerge, if we look at the growing asymmetry of those interdependencies and the rapid fragmentation, rediffusion of power, and explosions of raw violence in the world. But more particularly, what lessons do present conditions offer us about the first twenty-five years of development experience?

Perhaps the most sobering truth is that development, defined as the endeavor to manage the transformation of society, has been just one of many important factors determining the present state of the human condition. For we cannot in good conscience assess the accomplishments and failures of two and a half development decades without taking into account their overall historical setting of war, revolution, and social and political upheaval.

We should realize that in the Third World alone there have been more than one hundred wars since 1945. Apart from outright war, many Third World societies have been rent by serious domestic conflict, along, but also across class, ethnic, religious, or ideological lines, resulting both from the destabilizing impact of development and from the absence of development.

We have witnessed the complete polarization of societies and the mindless escalation of sometimes blind and sometimes calculated violence, the collapse of political institutions, of political systems, and even the wholesale destruction of the social fabric of a society. We have also seen the militarization of many societies. The rapid rise in arms purchases is only one manifestation. But in all cases the human, social, and cultural cost has been tremendous. Some of the turmoil has been the result of change, which governments may have played some role in initiating but which they subsequently have been unable to control. These almost autonomous processes have been affected by population and employment rates and by growing access to information through education, communication, and exposure, directly or vicariously, to other lifestyles. This has led to higher expectations, profound value changes, and higher levels of political consciousness.

In fact, one major feature of the period under consideration has been the growing self-assertiveness, in almost all parts of the developing world, of the traditionally powerless and of those marginalized by development and modernization. This time span also marked their political awakening. It is no exaggeration to state that in many different ways the little people are now on the move. In some cases they have simply moved up the economic development ladder; in others, their rise has been accompanied by conflict and met with violence. But their heightened expectations and their refusal to continue to accept their lot have also led to massive population movement—urbanization and migration within and across national boundaries and even between continents. We are now living in a world whose peoples are in an even more literal sense on the move—willingly or unwillingly—as a matter of government policy, on a scale unprecedented in time and scope. In Asia alone, if we accept only the more conservative estimates of internal and international migrants in recent years, some 50 million people are involved. We have among us a veritable "nation of migrants" with a population larger than all but six Asian countries. Around the world, upwards of 16 million refugees of war, oppression, and natural disaster are adrift. An additional 20 million workers, by some estimates, are in jobs outside their home countries.

In the face of the immense magnitude of these often violent social, political, and historical convulsions, and of the unbelievable scale of human suffering, despair, and rage but also of heightened religious intensity, the development planners and practitioners often stand powerless and speechless in the realization that the development effort to which they are committed is one, and only one, of the many interacting forces of change in their society. Gone are the early naive illusions of development as an endeavor in social engineering toward a brave new world. Multiple goals have replaced the initial single focus. There is now a greater understanding of the profound interaction between international and national factors in the development process and an increasing emphasis on human beings and the human potential as the basis, the means, and the ultimate purpose of the development effort. Nevertheless, it should also be recognized, despite all the glaring inadequacies of present more sophisticated strategies and methods and the general underestimation of the power of the forces at work, that international development still constitutes one of the most noble efforts of humankind in the second half of this century to create a more humane global community.

Accomplishments and Failures

Drawing up a balance sheet of accomplishments and failures of cultural development policies by using the conventional cultural and social indicators will not lead us to what I sense to be the central problems in this area.

To illustrate: the tremendous *increase in school enrollment* in the Third World should of course be entered in the ledger against the growth in absolute numbers of illiterates the world over. What is, however, equally significant—and here we move off the balance sheet—is that these figures of educational expansion tell us little about the long-term impact of the *kind* of educational experience provided on those millions of Third World children. The statistics do not tell us how well their education prepares them for their life situations, or the degree to which, because of its generally urban bias, modern education has contributed to cultural impoverishment, cultural discontinuities and alienation in the countryside, and to the present anomic behavior of so many of the young. In many places considerable proliferation of cultural facilities in the rural as well as the urban areas has apparently not significantly reduced the pressures toward urbanization.

Weighing the *larger number of women* in the registered labor force in urban areas against the loss of income for women in the countryside as a result of the modernization of agriculture does not indicate the degree and structures of exploitation, deprivation, and despair of those women.

Similarly, the *expansion of higher education* has not—with some notable exceptions—led to the significant scientific or technological innovations that could lead the way to a more autonomous trajectory of development and industrialization. This may in part have to do with the lack of interest of economic planners in the development of basic science capabilities in their countries. It may also have to do with a too instrumentalistic view of knowledge and culture. There is also a lack of interest, or even hostility, on the part of political leaders in providing political space—the essential precondition—for the flowering of science, experimentation, innovation, or simply for new ideas and synthesis: that is, academic freedom.

To give just one more illustration: in many countries that have chosen a national language rather than the one of the former colonizer, only very inadequate efforts have been made to make modern science more accessible and capable of taking root in the intellectual mainstream. Such efforts would include a massive translation program and endeavors to develop the national language into an effective vehicle for modern scientific communication. More surprising, but equally disturbing, has been the fact that neither the "basic needs" nor the "development from below" concepts have spelled out the implications for the use and development of minority languages as vehicles for development and for the expression of social and technological creativity. These neglected issues in turn open a Pandora's box of questions about the capacity of a society to keep adjusting the sensitive balance between the requirements for national unity and the fuller, more equitable involvement of minorities in national life so that they become active participants in the decision-making process as well as beneficiaries of development. Finally, in many languages the hierarchy of terms of address and other such factors have been used to perpetuate the inferior status of women; such important instruments of oppression should have received much greater attention in language development policies.

Changes in the position of women have been ambivalent at best for those in the middle class and definitely negative for those among the urban and rural poor. Changes in attitudes toward work and gainful employment, the impact of family planning on the family and on attitudes toward female babies born to already large families in some cultures, dietary habits and notions about health, all affect traditional concepts of family life. These should no longer be weighed in isolation but should be considered together with the traumatic impact of massive migration and urbanization on family life, on concepts of family, and on the large number of single heads of households coping with old as well as new problems.

The easy way to draw up a balance sheet on *human rights*—and many have taken that path—would be to list countries on a scale of so-called human rights performance. It is of course of the utmost importance to establish a floor below which violations of human rights invite international expressions of opprobrium or sanctions. Still, we should also realize that quite often violations of human rights are manifestations of the failure to manage both the drive for economic growth and the structural changes necessary to broaden the social base of the development process, as well as failure to come to grips with the causes of endemic poverty. And many among the countries who sit in self-righteous judgment cannot and should not avoid sharing the responsibility for these terrible conditions. They too should share the responsibility for not helping to develop more effective and comprehensive theories for the democratic management of structural transformation in development. In fact, many major institutions of higher learning in the industrialized world—the alma maters of many Third World leaders and developers—seem to have lost interest in the search for theories that reconcile the often conflicting requirements of freedom and those of governance. This lacuna, after the collapse of the first generation of political institutions patterned after the Western models of democratic government, has left many of us in the Third World with a keen sense of abandonment. For no balance sheet can in any way reflect the bitter fact that after the attainment of national independence, many of our countries have lost their freedom, leaving us with the gnawing suspicion that our patterns of "development" may have contributed to that loss.

And what, in addition to what has been said about human rights, is there to be said when governments, for ideological or other reasons of political or economic convenience, have gotten into the business of expelling minorities on a massive scale, or of exporting the labor force without assuming responsibility for their conditions of work in the recipient countries. At the same time, other governments, often signatories to the Helsinki agreements stating the right to leave one's country, are engaged in efforts to keep these unfortunate people bottled up in their own countries under untenable conditions. Such are some of the ironies and perplexities when one looks at the human and cultural dimensions of the development experience so far.

Notions of Power—Dynamics of Social Change

Twenty-five years of development experience seem to suggest, then, that beyond the conventional cultural policies and related cultural and social indicators there lies a host of insufficiently explored cultural factors. These affect a society's response to modernization, the often alternating choices between isolation and openness, a society's capacity to maintain national and social solidarity and cohesiveness in the face of major social, cultural, and structural changes that upset sensitive traditional, social, and political equilibria. It also affects a society's need to project its evolution and its capacity to incorporate innovation, science, and technology in ways that are consonant with its own sense of moral purpose.

Our concern with the human and social dimensions of development should therefore pay a great deal more attention to its interaction with the massive, powerful, and almost autonomous dynamics of social change at the national and at the international level. But that concern should also extend to the pervasive influence of traditional notions of power and the meaning of development, its institutions, as well as the concept of the state and its role and transformation in the development effort. Our basic failure to reach the poor, to come to grips with poverty and with the dualistic economy, provokes the following observation: The persistent low priority in development planning and implementation accorded to the countryside, the persistent bias in favor of the center and the urban areas—but also the way in which so-called modern political and developmental institutions often become simply new bottles for essentially the old wine of traditional power relations—is not only a function of the dominant interests of the elite but has also to do with the centrality and pervasiveness of the traditional political culture, traditional concepts of power, social order, and hierarchy.

These determine the perceived propriety of relations between the governing and the governed, between men and women, between state and society. They explain a great deal about the difficulties in turning an essentially law-and-order and tax-collecting colonial bureaucracy—paternalistic at best, exploitative at worst—into a developmental, public service, emancipatory type of bureaucracy. Modern training in development administration with its emphasis on efficiency and effectiveness has tended to strengthen deeply rooted colonial and precolonial patrimonial notions about the official's relationship to the public, and it has strengthened their inclination to disavow the legitimacy and importance of people's participation, self-management, and self-reliance as essential vehicles for development.

The simple question of assessing the accomplishments and failures of twenty-five years of development experience has led us far afield. Such an assessment makes sense only if conducted in the context of the major convulsions that have marked this period. It is obvious that simply drawing up a balance sheet of achievements and failures of cultural development policies may have only limited usefulness; it does not significantly add to our understanding of the dynamics of macro-social and cultural change and the formulation of more meaningful concepts of development. That will require a clearer understanding of the setting of the almost autonomous processes of sociocultural change within which the development effort, in the narrow sense, is made and with which it interacts. It requires also understanding of the interaction, complex and large scale, between the national development effort and a rapidly changing international environment. It further requires an appreciation of the impact of the strength and pervasiveness of cultural tradition on the institutions and processes of modernization.

This realization takes us far beyond the notion of development as an endeavor in social engineering. It steers us toward an inquiry into the dynamics of the historical processes of social transformation in different cultures and the alternating waves of self-chosen isolation and openness. It warns of the possibility of growing dysfunctionality and irrelevance of cultures, or their capacity to adjust while maintaining a sense of cultural continuity through a growing endogenous capacity for cultural reinterpretation, redefinition, and self-renewal.

This brings us to the ongoing global debate about the external tension and mutual interpenetration between modernity and tradition. The debate speaks to the "end of modernity" and "the return of the sacred," about secular and transcendental conceptions of life, and about the place of science and technology in these.

Against this background, the assessment in its broadest terms of the human and cultural dimensions of the development experience so far assumes an added significance in that it may provide pointers to the larger question. Out of the present turmoil, through different trajectories of development and industrialization dictated by an unprecedented combination of demographic pressures, poverty, and high energy costs, may there not arise eventually a variety of non-Western modern civilizations, side by side with that of the West? Would it not be conceivable that these may exist in a condition of rough parity with the West while rooted in Islamic, Confucian, Hindu, and other cultures? Is a culturally pluralistic, more equitable, and peaceful international order not possible?

Of Zoos and the Human Condition

Both the successes and failures of twenty-five years of development experience have shown that the organized pursuit of material improvement does not automatically bring in its wake freedom, human dignity, justice, and civility. These values have in fact often fallen victim to the development endeavor, even when the provision of basic services includes access to education and legal protection.

We should not forget that a zoo also is a place in which the basic needs of its inhabitants are met. Freedom, human rights, equity for women, respect for the rights of children, and the right freely to organize, for the rich and powerful as well as for the poor and the weak, must also be independent goals of the development effort. Unless these conditions exist, together with explicit strategies for democratic structural change that would enable people to liberate themselves from oppressive social structures that perpetuate their dependency and their powerlessness, there is little hope that the cultural goods and values that make up a humane society can grow. Only such societies have the resilience, the capacity for autonomous creativity and innovation. Only these have the capacity for continuous redefinition and self-renewal essential to their survival in a crowded, competitive, and rapidly changing world. From the pride, the sense of identity, and ultimate adherence to the sense of moral purpose and meaning embedded in the deep structure of their cultures will flow their unique strength.

It can be said that one of the major problems at the heart of the development process is how to resolve the disparities that inevitably arise within ethical or ideological bounds that prevail within a given culture. Failure to include these values as goals and guideposts equivalent, in the development effort, to economic growth would make these disparities unmanageable and would make it impossible to deal with the sense of powerlessness and moral outrage that fuel revolutions. The violent convulsions and the cultural and religious backlash of the power and intensity witnessed in the last twenty-five years are sufficient testimony to the importance of these values.

It is not enough to assess the effectiveness of cultural policies designed to "overcome" so-called cultural obstacles to development, nor is it enough to meet the requirements for economic growth. The flowering of those intangible but essential conditions referred to earlier in this section requires creation of the political space and the underlying social structures that together constitute the human and cultural context within which societal growth takes place. These conditions need constantly to be addressed and monitored; assessment of the conventional social and cultural indicators of the so-called quality of life is not sufficient.

The same holds true for international development. With growing interdependence it is no longer possible for any nation in isolation to safeguard its security, to ensure its national interests, and to pursue its developmental goals. Our common concern and responsibility now lie in the following areas: controlling the destructive capacity of nations that threatens us all; overcoming the persistent large-scale poverty that degrades the poor and the rich alike and denies the humanity of each individual; suppressing the random or systematic violence that brutalizes whole societies; denouncing the violation of human rights resulting from the incapacity to deal with poverty, equity, and justice.

The survival of humanity under decent and civil conditions will require unprecedented levels of mutual understanding and tolerance and much higher levels of international and people-to-people cooperation than ever before. We are still groping for the capabilities and instruments to achieve this, for we are still only learning to perceive and treat the human race, in all its diversity, as a single unit of civilized life of which we are all an indispensable part.

Assessing the Data for Human Development

Interdependence, however asymmetrical, forces us to see our own problems of survival and development also in global terms, and to search for mutually compatible local and global solutions to these problems. The first steps in this learning process have already been taken. The World Bank's annual report on international development, the reports on the state of the environment, on population, on the military balance, among others, do help us to monitor both progress and regression in these areas, to identify problems to be addressed, and to suggest ways of dealing with them. What is missing is a humanistic assessment of these data. We still lack an evaluation of their implications for the human and cultural dimensions of our societies and for humankind now and in its succeeding generations.

Such an assessment would help us to determine whether—and how far—we have traveled the road to self-destruction. Are we moving toward the peaceful, antlike society of 1984, or to a more viable humane, diverse, and dynamic global community? It would also help us to measure ourselves against our perceptions of ourselves as human beings, against the values by which we define our cultural identity in the value-configurations specific to each nation. It would further aid us in making the difficult choices and trade-offs in our responses to intractable old problems and in facing the new challenges of a world in a process of rapid but profound transformation. Such an assessment would also force each of us to ponder the implications of these data for the meaning of life individually and collectively.

Collectively, such periodic assessments would make explicit the different interpretations emerging from different schools of thought, and different cultural and ideological perspectives. This in turn could lead to the kind of communication on which mutual understanding on a global scale, human solidarity, and mutual tolerance could be built. Periodic reports would help us learn to treat the world and humankind in all its diversity as a single entity.

Finally, an ongoing assessment could help monitor our progress in preparing ourselves to live peacefully, civilly, and humanely in a world of eight thousand million people by developing the necessary social, artistic, cultural, and management arrangements. The United Nations University is at present exploring the desirability and feasibility of periodic, possibly annual, reports on the "State of the Human Condition."

Part 2

Workable Dreams—A How-To From Local To Global

Introduction: A New Development

Ponna Wignaraja

The problems raised by the rich getting richer—along with destabilization between and within countries, alienation in all cultures and ages, the arms race, the waste of resources and environmental concerns, concentration of power, and the like—cannot be approached, let alone solved, by means of the prescriptions of the past thirty-five years. The depth of the current development crisis in both industrialized and Third World countries—both capitalist and socialist—the failure of post-1945 patterns of development, and the emergence of new global problems leave us no choice but to look for new options.

As the crisis mounts and the world system becomes both unmanageable and manipulated in the interest of the few, the need for increased enlightened national and international action is paralleled by deep uncertainty and widespread disillusionment with the capacities of most governments or international agencies to act adequately. We need therefore an innovative and a progressive response. Anything else would be time-barred and counterproductive.

In looking for options we need also raise some basic questions about the whole intellectual framework for future development priorities and possibilities. The ideological rigidities, the confusion of concepts, the mishmash of theory, as well as the eclecticism and the kind of empiricism we see being touted in the name of practicality (and without any conceptual framework for thinking or approaching the problem) have complicated the rethinking process and themselves have to be reassessed. A new framework would be pluralistic and without the definitiveness of the past—which is also part of the challenge we have to face.

Finally, we cannot any longer keep throwing around words like "participation," "self-reliance," "decentralization," "rural development," "community development," "poverty-focused planning," and "basic needs" without clarifying exactly what we mean by these. There are too many contradictions arising from the abuse and mystification of these concepts. They begin to mean different things to different people. For example, a "new international economic order" by itself means little unless alternative development strategies are pursued in both industrialized and Third World countries—capitalist and socialist alike. These alternatives must themselves find legitimacy in activities in which the people themselves have participated. The intellectual underpinnings for this cannot, as in the past, be provided by a priori theorizing. We need to look again, and in depth, at the reality of the human experience and see whether there are examples of development in wider human terms with people's participation that provide a material basis from which we may attempt certain generalizations and that may bring about the structural changes necessary to reverse processes we clearly see are leading to a dead end.

Some Recent Approaches

The romantic and idealistic approaches taken by charitable institutions, religious organizations, and the small-is-beautiful groups have taught people to undertake good deeds, but experience shows these can also be tranquilizing and may not be getting at the real issues. We see evidence also of ideas introduced by radical political parties looking for a political constituency. They are able to mobilize people by arousing their anger at how the system works, but when this has led to the "big bang" type of revolution, we have seen that what people really want may be compromised. These groups have not succeeded in carrying through the desired changes.

There have also been the spontaneous people's movements and experiments. These may be in response to national or local issues in both industrialized or Third World countries. They may be weak and isolated, but they nevertheless constitute a social experience and need to be better understood, as they may well provide some genuine seeds of change. These experiments may not always have a clear-cut ideological orientation in conventional terms, but they may yet provide answers to questions we are now asking as we respond to the new compulsions for change.

Finally, there are initiatives taken by national governments and international organizations. Are these, in effect, attempts at welfarism within existing structures? Are they processes of co-option, or do they presage the transition to social change in different historical and cultural situations?

Lessons of Experience

Our experience with the types of approaches described points up certain features and raises certain issues. Are the only available options really "capitalism" or "socialism" in their cruder versions? Or are there other culturally conditioned options that permit people to enjoy a simpler, more satisfying life, that encourage their creative energy, that are nonexploitative and more egalitarian, more participatory and truly democratic? For industrialized countries, irrespective of whether the surplus is generated by the private sector or government, i.e., private capitalism or state capitalism, is there an alternative way of life away from consumerism, the arms race, and alienation, especially among young people? For poor countries, is there an alternative to dehumanizing poverty? Are there other paths to the satisfaction of the felt needs of the people other than through the imitative development pathways of the past one hundred years?

Our experience makes it clear that we have no choice but to go through a long revolution. The compulsions for change are such that there has to be a different kind of mobilization, "conscientization," and organization of people and a different man/nature/technology mix. No matter how we describe the processes, we cannot escape the issue of power. Were we better able to understand dominant power, to develop and exercise countervailing power, we might yet be in time to reverse present dead-end processes.

We examine in the next pages some workable dreams, experiments, proposals, and thoughts-in-progress aimed at reversing dead-end processes and generating a new development.

Relationships between Disarmament and Development: How Disarmament Would Promote Development and Security

Inga Thorsson

The Mayan people developed and expanded steadily over seventeen centuries in the lowlands of Guatemala in Central America. Doubling on the average every 408 years, the population had by A.D. 900 reached five million, with a density comparable to that of the most agriculturally intensive societies of today. At this peak, at the highest level of Mayan civilization, agriculturally, culturally, and architecturally, their world suddenly collapsed. Within decades the population fell to less than one-tenth of what it had been. Why? The apparent reason, Brown says, was soil erosion.[1] The Mayan people probably never grasped what curse of God brought their civilization to collapse and their natural environment to anarchy. As their inheritors of Earth, we can only speculate, or search for reasons. We know, of course, that however armed the Mayans may have been, their downfall could never have been stopped by armies or accumulation of weapons. But unlike the Mayans, we of today's world are constantly exposed to the ultimate threat of nuclear war. On that level, the equation may be simple: if there is a global nuclear war, there will be no development of any kind; in the absence of nuclear war, there can be some kind of development. Only with disarmament can we reasonably expect development to "achieve a life of dignity and well-being for all world citizens," to quote one important formulation of the fundamental aim of the world community.[2]

While too few have grasped the scale and the intensity of the contradiction between the arms race and development, quite a few have, judging from the low-key words of a man of clear vision, Philip Noel-Baker. He said at a conference in London in January 1977:

> There are more than a thousand million men and women in the world who cannot read or write or do the simplest sum. Their illiteracy helps all too powerfully to keep them poor. It prevents the rural proletariat from learning and applying the known agricultural techniques which would double their crops and change their lives. Illiteracy bars their path to social, cultural and political progress.
>
> Yet if UNESCO were given a fund of $200 million for a worldwide literacy campaign, it could free every nation from this evil handicap. Two

hundred million is approximately the price of two strategic bombers of the latest type.

The nations of the Third World suffer grievously from diseases which have disappeared from the "developed" West. Malaria still kills great numbers, and weakens millions more so that their productive output is reduced. Trachoma is very simple to cure, but if untreated, it makes the victim blind, his life a burden to himself, and him a burden to society. Leprosy makes its victims segregated social outcasts. Yaws, a diet deficiency disease, covers the body with running sores, makes a man unfit for work or play, and allows him no real rest.

These four diseases impose a heavy annual load of economic loss and human suffering in the Third World. Yet all of them are easily preventable. The World Health Organisation could eliminate them, wipe them out now and for the future, for an expenditure of $500 million—about the cost of an aircraft carrier.

And this is not all, for the world hungers. Twelve hundred million individuals who have to live on incomes of less than $150 a year remain hungry from the cradle to the grave. They never know what it is to have a solid meal. But, as Willy Brandt said in 1980 in introducing his report *North-South: A Programme For Survival,* "one-half of one percent of one year's world military expenditures would pay for all the farm equipment to increase food production and approach self-sufficiency in food-deficit low-income countries by 1990."[3]

This is sometimes called a conventional juxtaposition. But it is not. Rather, it focuses our attention on the historical fact that governments have, over the past thirty years, spent vast resources on armaments, resources which—on grounds of morality, on grounds of equal human justice, on grounds of enlightened self-interest—ought to have been directed to ending world poverty and building human and material development. This can never be called "conventional." Because this is how world armaments have become one of the main causes of poverty and underdevelopment.

There have been many attempts over the years to more concretely relate disarmament to development, to show how the most destructive possible use of scarce resources, namely, the arms race, negatively influences our possibilities to redirect these resources for better and more constructive use. These initiatives have come from experts in development. An expert body within the United Nations, the Committee for Development Planning, stated a few years ago that military expenditures constitute the single major obstacle to the transfer of appropriate resources from the rich to the poor countries. Military expenditures thus constitute, to express it in more positive terms, the great reserve for economic development in developing countries.

The Great Reserve

It may be said that common sense alone tells us that military preparations are an economic burden. But for most countries the "real problem" of defense is not its directly conceived costs, but how to finance a military machine, which the political and military leaders consider "necessary," without too great economic disruptions. The needed level of military preparations is measured against perceived foreign (and in some few unfortunate cases, domestic) military threats. Most would argue to their constituencies that the economic limits for defense are far beyond what has ever been contemplated. Hence, few governments have had any political interest in reducing the absolute levels of military spending over the past three decades. The case for or against increases in military spending has always been exclusively based on foreign policy and military factors. The military has brought a relatively cheap good, namely "security." Economics have played a very subsidiary role. But these notions are passé.

Over the past few decades, the concept of national security has been given an overwhelmingly military character. It is assumed that principal threats come from other countries, their weapons or armies. Therefore, national security has developed into an elusive goal, defined in geopolitical, strategic, or military terms, a goal in itself changing but always military. Clearly, national security cannot be a goal in itself, least of all to maximize military strength. The purpose of security must be to secure the independence and sovereignty of peoples, their freedom and their means to develop economically, socially, and culturally, which defines exactly what I would like to call "development." Yet, the threats to these ultimate goals of national security may arise less from one nation's relation to another—here I leave aside for the moment the ultimate threat of nuclear war—but more from the relationship of humanity to nature. These threats may be as fatal to us as soil erosion was to the Mayan world. It is meaningless to accumulate arms in protection of these threats. Existing and impending ecological stress, resource scarcities—notably in the field of energy and certain other nonrenewable raw materials—and a growing world population now threaten the security of countries everywhere. Today's stress and constraints may translate into tomorrow's economic stress and political conflict. To the militarist, this is an argument for more arms. But neither bloated military budgets nor sophisticated weapons systems can halt deforestation or solve the world food crises. That would be an attempt to solve one nation's security problems at the expense of others.

It is easy to argue, then, that the arms race itself has become a threat to the security of nations. Few countries have enough capital available to finance an arms race, and, at the same time, in view of the potential depletion of oil reserves, to transform their petroleum-based economies. By focusing on military factors threatening security, governments turn a blind eye to less obvious but more dangerous threats. It is said that U.S. President Carter had a list of sixty countries that potentially could "go nuclear" in the next twenty years or so. With narrowing energy options and increasing food deficits, some countries may indeed find nuclear weapons a handy and inexpensive shortcut to "security."

It is imperative that nonmilitary challenges to security are treated and met as nonmilitary. If this is not recognized, if states fail to accept and persevere in tackling these challenges through voluntary measures and cooperation, there is a grave risk that the situation will deteriorate to the point of crisis where, even with a low probability of success, the use of military force could be seen as a way to produce results sufficiently quickly. This is far from being a remote possibility. In recent time there has been a marked and increasing tendency in international relations actually to use or threaten to use military force in response to nonmilitary challenges, not only to attain "security," but also the secure supply of goods and to the well-being of the nations facing these challenges.

Against this background the U.N. Study on the Relationship between Development and Disarmament concludes that on grounds of morality, on grounds of equal human justice, on grounds of enlightened self-interest, the vast expenditures on armaments ought to be directed to ending poverty and building for long-term, sustainable human and material development.[4] The arms race and underdevelopment are not two problems: they are one. They must be solved together, or neither will ever be solved. The governmental experts from all parts of the world unanimously agreed that the world can either continue to indulge in an arms race with characteristic vigor, or it can take deliberate steps toward a more suitable international economic and political order. It cannot do both.

It is important to note that the study represents the most comprehensive research effort of the United Nations in the field of disarmament.

One of the tasks of the group was the establishment of a reliable data base on the present-day utilization of material and human resources for military purposes. This proved impossible, since reliable data are not available for a majority of countries. Most countries, among them some major participants in the arms race, provide very little information or analyses of resources devoted to their military effort. As a result, the estimates provided in the study are based largely on data available in Western countries.

Nevertheless, the study has documented—in accordance with a consistently conservative approach to data—that at least 50 million people are directly or indirectly engaged in military activities worldwide. This figure includes

○ about 25 million in the world's armed forces,
○ some 10 million worldwide in paramilitary forces,
○ approximately 4 million civilians employed in defense departments,
○ an estimated 500,000 qualified scientists and engineers engaged in research and development for military purposes, and
○ at least 5 million workers directly engaged in the production of weapons and other specialized military equipment.

There are some indications that the actual number of persons around the world—soldiers, sailors, airmen, bureaucrats, scientists, engineers, and general workers—directly or indirectly affected by the more than $600 thousand million devoted to military preparations in 1982 is greater, perhaps considerably greater, than 50 million.

Conservative estimates suggest that global industrial production for military purposes in 1980 amounted to more than $127 thousand million, 95 percent of which took place in the industrialized countries. We have also calculated, although statistics are sketchy, that anything from 3 to 11 percent of world output of a selected group of important nonenergy minerals is used for military purposes and that 5 to 6 percent of the world's petrol is consumed by the military.

Military research and development remains by far the largest single objective of scientific inquiry and technological development. Approximately 20 percent of the world's qualified scientists and engineers were engaged in military work at a cost of about $35 thousand million in 1980, or approximately one-quarter of all expenditure on research and development (R&D). Military R&D alone accounts for more financial and intellectual resources than are devoted to R&D on health, food production, energy, and environmental protection combined.[5] In the United States and Britain, for instance (no information is available for the Soviet Union), more public money is spent on the development of military technology than on all other government-supported R&D programs combined.

Military R&D has increased to about 10 to 15 percent of world military spending, compared with only 1 percent before the 1945 war. Here the crucial fact is that virtually all this R&D takes place in the industrialized countries, 85 percent in the U.S.A. and the U.S.S.R. alone. Adding France and Britain would push this share above 90 percent. In 1977 the "United Nations Study on the Economic and Social Consequences of the Arms Race and of Military Expenditures" stressed that "military technology is moving further and further away from any conceivable civilian use, and is anyway focusing on fields which are mostly irrelevant for the solution of the more important present and future problems of the world." That study also states a truly remarkable fact: "how little that is new, not how much, . . . has come to the civilian sector from military R&D effort."[6]

It stands to reason that even a modest reallocation to development objectives of the current capacity for military R&D could be expected to produce dramatic results in fields like resource conservation and the promotion of new patterns of development, better adapted to meeting the basic needs of ordinary people. This is, inter alia, evident from the fact, which is also among our findings, that on an average, a military product requires twenty times as much R&D resources as a civilian product.

A Deathly Trade

In purely financial terms, worldwide military expenditures by 1982 will exceed the astounding level of $600 thousand million, representing 6 percent of world output. Every government should realize that this amount is roughly equivalent to the value of all investable capital in all developing countries combined. Since the war in Korea, military expenditures in the most heavily militarized states remained on a high plateau. And because "peacetime" spending is so high, even fighting a hot war brings only a fractional increase in military budgets. In real spending, total or per capita, military budgets have not experienced any significant decline for thirty years.

The international trade in arms is rarely officially recorded. In spite of the lack of comprehensive data, it is estimated that more than $35 thousand million is annually traded in the international arms traffic. Of this figure, 75 percent represents imports by developing countries. In itself, this is hardly surprising. The capacity of the developing countries to manufacture modern weapons is extremely limited. Four countries—the United States, the Soviet Union, France, and the United Kingdom—dominate the international traffic in arms, accounting for 80 percent of the cumulative value of arms export in 1974–78. Another four countries—the Federal Republic of Germany, Czechoslovakia, Italy, and Poland—accounted for over 10 percent, so that just eight countries supply over 90 percent of the international arms trade.

A clarification and a word of warning seem necessary when discussing the recipient side of the international traffic of arms. It is not true, for instance, that the developing countries generally squander vast resources on armaments, although the overall trends are frightening. The share of world military expenditures carried by the developing countries has grown during the 1970s from 9 to 16 percent. Still, about 125 developing countries are responsible for 16 percent of world military expenditures while 35 industrial countries consume the remaining 84 percent. Military expenditures per person in the developing countries amount to $28 per person, the corresponding figure for the industrialized countries being around $300. One must also keep in mind that weapons imports are heavily concentrated in particular regions. For example, five countries in the Middle East accounted in 1977–80 for more than one-third of all major weapons imported by developing countries.

If we look ahead and assume a future rate of real increase of military expenditure by, say, 2 or 3 percent annually—which is a modest hypothesis by present-day standards—the value of the additional resources that will be denied the civilian sector over the next twenty years, that is, resources over and above the present annual amount of about $600 thousand million, would be equivalent to one-quarter and one-half respectively of current world production.

Fairy Tales and Ghost Stories

In the past it has been argued that military spending is beneficial to a country because it accomplishes three things simultaneously: it increases national security, it creates jobs, it has a generally stimulating effect on the civilian economy.

The general public believes this because it seemed to be so in the past. People saw that the war economies during 1939–45 produced more guns and more butter simultaneously. Yet it has been pointed out that such an inference is incorrect because we must consider the short-term and the long-term effects. Governments also generally shy away from informing the public on the real economic and social costs, particularly in longer terms, of military expenditure.

Military outlays fall by definition into the category of consumption and not investment. As a consequence, steadily high or increasing military outlays tend to depress economic growth. This effect may be direct through displacement of investment and indirect through constraints on productivity. The historical coexistence in industrialized countries of high levels of military spending and high growth rates during the 1939–45 war and during the 1950s and 1960s were unique phenomena, due to very particular circumstances, which cannot be repeated and which cannot be taken as evidence of a causal relationship between military outlays and growth.

The U.S. administration's military shopping list is impressive. More than $1.6 trillion are scheduled in defense spending between 1982 and 1987. More than 3,900 jet fighters, bombers, and transport aircraft are planned for, as well as 8,800 tanks and cannon-carrying vehicles and, during the next decade, about 14,000 strategic and tactical bombs and missiles for the U.S. nuclear arsenal. If these intentions are realized, they will amount to a 50 percent increase in military spending, as measured in constant dollars, within five years, out of which weapons procurement and military R&D receive the most concentrated attention. The American economic debate has already demonstrated the signs of the stress and disruption that such increase in military spending is causing the U.S. economy. It is argued that defense spending of this magnitude will create crippling bottlenecks at key choke points in private industry, reignite inflation, and thwart the productive surge that is essential for stable economic growth. Already, at the beginning of the program, such signs are present. Because the Pentagon can and will pay whatever is necessary to obtain a product or service, it forces up prices for civilian industries that compete for the same resources. And the greatest pressure is likely to fall on precisely those industries (aerospace, microelectronics, etc.) that are already running at nearly full capacity. Aggressive military demand will mean higher inflation. Available statistics show that the administration's assumptions on military inflation are already overtaken by reality. Jobs in the defense industry are concentrated in aircraft, communication equipment, and ordnance, industries that employ disproportionately large numbers of workers such as engineers from groups with low unemployment rates, and disproportionately few from groups with high unemployment such as the unskilled, the young, and Blacks. The military expansion may thus provide far fewer jobs than previous booms, above all for the unemployed.

Productivity is equally hit. Since 1950 productivity in America has actually been increasing at a slower rate, as compared with the most successful competitors —Japan and West Germany, the lag being 3 to 5 percent per annum. *The Economist* noted in 1981 that 115 million Japanese are investing every year considerably more in new equipment and capital goods than 220 million Americans, so that in Japan the average machine is six to seven years younger than the average machine in America.[7] Toyota manufactures nine motor cars per worker against Ford's two. Since 1974 labor productivity in the American economy has been increasing by a meager 0.25 percent per annum at the cost of inflation, which is twice as high as in West Germany and Japan. These trends are now reinforced and accelerated.

It is noted in the Disarmament/Development Report that most governments have shied away from any thorough public cost-accounting of military activities. Although the United States is extremely open, the dark sides of its defense buildup are generally downplayed. Presently it is admitted by the administration that the economic hazards do exist, but it is argued that careful planning, tight management, and accurate cost estimates could reduce their impact. Yet it is precisely those three qualities that have traditionally been most lacking in defense spending!

Ten Paces East, Ten Paces West

A worldwide race for arms would of course not exclude all economic growth and social development, but development would be relatively slow and highly uneven geographically. The arms race will not only further sharpen the contrast between developing and industrialized countries, but also between the two large military blocs.

Although the economies of the socialist countries, operating under a system of centralized planning, are usually satisfied with more modest growth rates, these rates have been clearly insufficient, in view of the retarded position of the centrally planned economies in terms of productivity and technological progress.

The conventional ways of estimating Soviet military expenditures are debatable,[8] ranging from the official U.S. exaggerated assertion that in 1980 the Soviets spent an equivalent of $175 thousand million (or over 50 percent more than the United States did) on defense, to the Soviet official global figure (about 17,000 million rubles) of its "defense budget." This latter figure on the other hand clearly does not cover and correspond in any way to the advanced Soviet military technology and the size of the military forces it has produced. Defense spending comparisons must of course also include the outlays of American and Soviet allies. Publicly available evidence in this area tells a very different tale. Studies by the International Institute for Strategic Studies in Lund, for example, show that the Soviet's Warsaw Pact allies spend about $20 to $30 thousand million dollars annually on defense. America's allies, by contrast, allocate three or four times that amount—more than $100 thousand million annually. Even if we allow for a wide margin of doubt, it seems obvious that the United States and its allies outspent the Soviet Union and its allies on defense by more than $300 thousand million in the past decade.

The stress placed on the Soviet economy by its defense efforts is obvious, not least to the ordinary Soviet citizen. The Soviet trade deficit with the West, widened by huge food imports and falling world petroleum prices, doubled in 1981. For the third consecutive year the Soviets' harvest in 1982 was far below consumption needs, resulting in sharper food deficits and pressing needs for imports. In presenting the draft eleventh five-year plan for 1981–85, Soviet leaders declared that priority was to be given to production for social and consumer-oriented demands. It seems, however, that since then these goals have had to be abandoned and the military share of the Soviet economy is increasing. "During the eleventh planning period an increase is planned for the capacity to produce consumption goods in the heavy industry and defence industry...," to quote the plan. It should here be noted that Soviet leaders frequently refer that change in economic policy to a more tense international climate. The message contained is unequivocal and clear: increases in personal standard of living must wait since resources must be reallocated to the defense of the state in a hardening international climate. Civilian and military production in the Soviet economy seem to become more and more integrated. Furthermore, reduced prospects of growth in the Soviet economy imply that production for civilian consumption has to be increasingly sacrificed to meet political goals in defense production. Historical examples indicate that the Soviet people are prepared to make considerable sacrifices in critical situations. The armed forces constitute a powerful buyer with direct links to the producer/purchaser, the state. Since no public political debate or discussion on these allocation choices is tolerated, one is forced to conclude, first, that despite the costs, Soviet leadership will certainly match any perceived or real increases in military threats; second, that the decision to do so will be increasingly more harmful to the civilian economy and to prospects for a better standard of living for the peoples of the Soviet Union and the eastern European countries.

Fairy Tales Revisited

On the basis of the U.N. report and the research commissioned for it, one can confidently conclude that military budgets are dead-end expenditures in all kinds of economies, be they market, centrally planned, or mixed.

Military expenditures do not foster growth. Through their inflationary effects —thoroughly analyzed in the study—and the general economic and political malaise to which they contribute, military expenditures inhibit the capital investment required for development. Through the drain on the most valuable research talents and funds, they restrain productivity gains and distort growth in science and technology. The military sector is not a great provider of jobs. On the contrary, it is shown that military outlays are among the least efficient kinds of public spending. They drain away funds that could relieve poverty and distress. The very nature of military spending heightens tensions, reduces security, and underpins the system, which makes even more arms necessary.

It is widely acknowledged that the true foundation of national security is a strong and healthy economy. The study presents overwhelming evidence that the contemporary military establishment significantly distorts and undermines the very basis of sustained economic and social development in all countries.

Two important studies forecast world economic performance at different levels of military spending.[9] The study draws on an econometric world input/output model developed for the United Nations by Nobel Prize laureate Wassily Leontief.[10] In this model the world is divided into fifteen economically homogeneous regions. Alternative economic trends are calculated for each region in six alternative hypothetical scenarios for military spending up to the year 2000. The base scenario is an extrapolation from data of the 1970s, implying unchanged trends of military spending, expressed in a constant share of GDP in the year 2000 as compared with 1970, the base year. The authors also develop two armament scenarios for even further unchecked arms competition and three scenarios for different levels of disarmament.

Generally speaking, in the input/output model, growth in consumption per capita between 1970 and 2000 varies greatly among the fifteen regions, but growth is projected to be faster in all three disarmament scenarios in all regions, except for one, namely, the oil-producing countries, where growth would remain unchanged. On the global level, macroeconomic indicators (e.g., investments, trade, production of manufactures, and food) increase if military outlays decrease, and decrease with higher outlays. Of primary commodities, only nickel and petroleum would be produced in lesser amounts in a disarmament situation.

An intensified worldwide arms race would drastically hamper economic and social development, particularly in the poorer regions, but also in the superpowers, especially in the Soviet Union.

One disarmament scenario calculates the effects of a hypothetical reduction by one-third of the 1970 level of military spending in the Soviet Union and the United States, followed by a further reduction by one-third in the year 2000. For the rest of the world, this scenario implies a reduction of 75 percent of the base level in 1990 and to 60 percent ten years later. It is further assumed that some of the "disarmament savings" made in the industrial countries would be transferred to the poorer regions. In this scenario there would be a substantial increase in consumption per capita, most noticeable in the developing countries, but also in the United States (+3.7 percent) and the Soviet Union (+6.3 percent). Leontief and Dutchin show that if, on the other hand, military expenditures would double their share of GDP, *all* regions would register reductions in consumption. These reduced levels would also hit the United States and Canada (-2.6 percent) as well as the Soviet Union and eastern Europe (-19.3 percent)!

There seems to be a clear common interest among states in effective disarmament. One must take into account, however, that strategies of "inflicting costs" to an adversary by deliberately engaging in an economically disruptive arms race are apparently gaining popularity among some. For example, U.S. Defense Secretary Weinberger has remarked that denying or reducing the Soviet Union's hard currency earnings would curtail its ability to buy computers, microelectronics, and other modern industrial goods from the West "to develop a military-industrial complex," or that attempts to delay Soviet natural gas deliveries to western Europe would force a reallocation of the Soviet five-year energy plan "with profound implications for the Soviet economy."

All states aspire to be independent in providing for their security. Maybe the key words "all states," "independent," and "security" indicate the reason why states do not disarm, as plain common sense would demand, and conversely free resources to develop the social and economic well-being of their people. Earlier we discussed the static approach to security. Here these inhibitions will be left aside, and focus will be placed on the technological feasibility and economic potential of converting resources from military to civilian purposes.

The main object, in economic terms, is to devise short- and long-term policies designed to consolidate the goal of disarmament with economic goals of growth, monetary stability, full employment, and foreign trade balance. While, as a matter of course, conversion itself will have to await some measure of disarmament, preparation and research for an economic policy cannot be deferred until such time.

The defense industry everywhere is characterized inter alia by a high degree of geographical concentration. It also involves a considerable degree of specialization of its work force. This apparent exclusiveness should not prove to be an insurmountable problem for two reasons. First, conversion and redeployment are not phenomena uniquely associated with disarmament. Any form of economic and social change represents a continuous process of conversion. Particularly in modern industrial economies, the factors of production must respond continuously to the development of new products and the phasing out of old ones and to the introduction of new production techniques. Second, conversion is feasible because a significant part of military demand is for goods and services essentially identical to civilian ones.

Primary responsibility for conversion, in an overall sense, inevitably falls on the central government, particularly as regards planning and initiation of preparations for such a process. If transition is to be as smooth as possible and to involve the minimum waste of finite resources, it is vital that every effort be made to anticipate the extent and the character of the conversion problems that will arise. It is therefore obvious that preparations for conversion should be among the first steps on the road to disarmament. This would include the creation, within each country with a significant military industrial establishment, of a core of people with knowledge and expertise on conversion issues; the development of contingency conversion plans by plants engaged in specialized military production; the broad involvement of all affected parties in conversion planning, including management, trade unions, national defense research institutes, and regional and local authorities.

As a potential asset for alternative, socially productive uses, the R&D component of military outlays is of utmost significance. Already the 1972 report on the subject identified more than seventy possible alternative uses for R&D. Present investigations suggest, in more elaborated and detailed ways, more than one hundred such alternatives. For instance, production workers in the military sector could quite easily transfer their skills to the development, production, and installation of solar energy devices. Environment, housing, and urban renewal are other areas likely to gain from the possible rechanneling of military R&D. New transport systems, particularly in urban areas, are sorely needed and have long been regarded as a major civilian alternative for the high-technology industries in the military sector.

Obviously, the achievement of disarmament measures that will release real resources will in the first instance most directly benefit those states that are affected by these measures. Practical ways by which disarmament may be effected in the developing countries could take many forms. It is widely recognized that besides changing economic relations to the benefit of developing countries, increasing the magnitude and predictability of flows of capital to developing countries as grants or on concessional terms, is of vital importance. One proposed way of fostering these flows would be to establish a special fund for development to be financed from budgetary savings obtained through the implementation of disarmament measures, as well as a levy on armaments, or voluntary contributions. The group of experts unanimously agreed that the approach to financing such a fund—from savings that are won by concrete disarmament measures or a portion thereof allocated to development needs would be the most feasible. It suggested that the administrative and technical modalities of such a fund be further investigated by the United Nations with due regard to the capabilities of the agencies and institutions presently responsible for the international transfer of resources.

As quoted earlier from the U.N. report: "The world can either continue to indulge in an arms race with characteristic vigour, or make deliberate steps toward a more sustainable international economic and political order."

Notes

1. Lester R. Brown, *Building a Sustainable Society* (Washington, D.C.: Worldwatch Institute, 1981).

2. Jan Tinbergen (coordinator), *Reshaping the International Order*, a report of the Club of Rome (New York, 1976), ch. 5.

3. *North-South: A Programme for Survival* (London: Pan Books, 1980).

4. U.N. Document A.36/356, 5 Oct. 1981 (Sales No. E.82IX.1).

5. Colin Norman, *The God that Limps: Science and Technology in the Eighties* (Washington, D.C.: Worldwatch Institute, 1981).

6. U.N. Document (Sales No. E.78.IX.1).

7. *The Economist* (London), 24–30 Jan. 1981.

8. Ruth Leger Sivard, *World Military and Social Expenditures*, 1981 (Leesburg, Va.: World Priorities, 1981). See also Arthur Macy Cox, "The CIA's Tragic Error," *New York Review of Books*, 6 Nov. 1980.

9. Wassily Leontief and Dutchin, "Worldwide Implications of a Limitation of Military Spending" and "Worldwide Implications of Hypothetical Changes in Military Spending," Institute for Economic Analyses, New York University, June and Aug. 1980.

10. Wassily Leontief, *The Future of the World Economy* (New York: Oxford University Press, 1977).

The Two Great Challenges of Our Time

The Barbara Ward Lecture*

Robert McNamara

How to Relate Poverty and International Interdependence

In analyzing poverty and interdependence Barbara Ward was almost too successful. Her writing about aid, about shelter, about environment was so lucid that she convinced many of us that we knew more than we really did. She turned heresies into fashions. For, once people have been persuaded to adopt a fashion, even a justified one, they can as readily be persuaded to abandon it unless they are very familiar with the evidence. Barbara Ward was saturated with that evidence: the evidence that hunger does kill the poor of Asia and Africa and that because small farmers are efficient, the world that frees their resources to cure hunger would be a more productive place as well as a more just one; the evidence that rich countries' income depends on trade with developing countries so that all suffer if some are forced into excessive contraction by rising protectionism or by insufficient financial assistance.

Barbara Ward applied to the Third World the central lesson she learned from her early work in the great depression—the lesson that the magic of the marketplace about which we hear so much these days, while necessary to alleviate poverty and while necessary to build economic health out of national interdependence, is not sufficient in itself. She learned that rich and poor states as well as individuals are "members one of another" and are not isles. She explained, expounded, expanded on this theme often in pain, often in illness until yesterday's heresy became today's conventional wisdom. But conventional wisdom is vulnerable. The academic who strives to be original or the politician who seeks to intellectualize and appeal to self-interest now tends to decry aid, to blame the poor for their poverty, to argue that the rich can safely ignore their interests. Such crimes seem grave because they attack the recent conventional wisdom. In fact, they are merely selfish. They are ignorant, and the conventional wisdom became conventional because it was wise. Certainly the fashions in international development during the 1970s—export stabilization, North-

---

*Barbara Ward who died in 1981 was chairman of SID. Known and revered for a lifetime of inspired writing and leadership in many areas of development, her many publications include *The Rich Nations and the Poor Nations* (1962), *Only One Earth* (1972), *The Home of Man* (1976), and *Progress for a Small Planet* (1978). In 1980 she received the Jawaharlal Nehru Award.

South dialogue, rural development—do have their irritations, their jargon of pretentious or ill-informed advocates, and it is easy for the populace of the 1980s to present these irritating incidentals as if they were the substance of the matter. By such tactics some people less knowledgeable than Barbara Ward have been persuaded to abandon the fashions she helped to create.

Yet it is justified intellectual fashions that are now under threat. They became fashions only through hard work. Because their advocates collected, analyzed, and communicated the evidence and the fashions, such trends have led to wise but fragile conventions of cooperation between rich and poor countries and have also seen both groups of countries adopting policies that take some account of poor people's needs. These recent conventions are now being undermined by a new, depressing go-it-alone skepticism. In the 1960s and the 1970s the world began to weave a complex skein of arrangements for trade liberalization, capital flows, and food security, and it is this skein which is in danger of being unraveled by a series of experiments—experiments in aid cutting, in fiscal management, in mercantilism, in drastic reallocation of functions between public and private sectors, and the like.

Unfortunately, many of the experiments have all too little intellectual content. They appeal to the short-run budgetary concerns of some governments and rich countries. But they are, taken together, appallingly perilous. In two areas in particular—the risks to the survival of the absolute poor, especially in Africa, and to the stability of the international economic system—these random experimenters could pick and pick at the skein until they unravel the entire world economy. We can prevent these dangers, but only by swift action. We shall have to explain the evidence and the analysis. We shall have to prove that it is not only possible but efficient to attack poverty and to live well and interdependently and that the alternative—blind reliance on growth via autarkic national planning or unassisted private markets—carries totally unacceptable risks. Never mind if this is yesterday's fashion. Never mind if it is the conventional wisdom. It is true. The evidence, some of which is presented below, supports this contention.

The Evidence

First, what is the evidence for claims that national economies do depend on each other? The failure in any major group does involve losses for all. The familiar arguments for expanded trade adequately supported by credit are sound the world over. Let us suppose that the developed market economies seek to safeguard jobs, even at the cost of their own consumers and even at the risk of higher inflation; that they do seek to safeguard jobs by protection against the manufactured and semimanufactured exports of the developing countries. In 1980 those exports amounted to $64 thousand million. But the imports into the developing countries from the developed countries were nearly two and one-half times as great—$154 thousand million. A trade war, with the Third World country victims retaliating by raising their own trade barriers, would lead, in the industrialized countries, to the loss of more jobs, as exports fell, than these countries would gain by keeping imports out. Even without retaliation, the loss of an efficient source of export earnings could compel Third World countries to curtail imports from the industrialized nations. The cumulative many-country, multilevel harm done by protectionism is complex and subtle. Popular pressure to protect this or that inefficient sector—and we have seen a lot of it in the United States in the last several months—often causes us to lose sight of the harm protectionism causes. The initial damage that the European Community does by protecting its agricultural products or its textile industries, or that the United States does by protecting its domestic sugar producers, may be quite undramatic. But the total effect of such measures involving secondary spin-offs and retaliatory moves is indeed vast. Because it is undramatic, protectionism is perhaps not the best example for convincing the public of the damage done by selfish, ad hoc bilateral responses among nations. Damage is not just to the country against which the action is directed, but to the system itself.

A better example, potentially all too dramatic, concerns the interdependent world system of financial flows. Financing short-term trade credits and long-term investments involves banks as well as governments, commercial as well as concessionary loans, and linking not just the Western industrialized OECD group and the oil-importing poor, but also the oil exporters and the socialist countries in the COMECON group. These capital flows illustrate the total interdependence not just of pairs of countries but of a world economic system that depends for steady growth upon safe but gradually expanding credit. Borrowing and lending transactions, each perfectly rational from the standpoint of the actors, can in their totality make it harder for the system to avoid cumulative recessions or to reverse them once they begin.

The oil-importing developing countries between 1974 and 1978 averaged about a $30 thousand million yearly deficit on current account. By the early 1980s that deficit had increased two and one-half times to $75 thousand million a year. Just over half of it is financed by private capital and almost all of this corresponds to money recycled via the banks by the developing world's creditors —firms or governments of OPEC, or the West. Each individual bank or syndicate has sought to place its own share of the surplus mostly in a few developing and COMECON oil-importing countries. No single bank knows the up-to-date total size and structure of the debt of each borrowing country, and no world central bank has prudential oversight of it. It is easy, therefore, for a country's debt to expand beyond its likely capacity to repay, as each bank overexpands its own lending in honest ignorance of the country's total position. Recently, such debts have become larger, more reliant upon hard nonconcessional private credits, and more heavily concentrated in a few Third World countries. However, contrary to the fears of some, I do not believe that this situation is likely to produce a financial crisis.

It is true that South Korea, Brazil, and Mexico owe the banking system more than the total capital and reserves of the nine largest U.S. banks, but they are very unlikely to declare defaults. The real risk is a risk of deflationary credit contraction. It comes not so much from default or even rescheduling, although twenty-six developing countries were in arrears at the end of 1981. The real risk comes from the steps that are taken to prevent the defaults and the reschedulings. Banks begin to lend to risky cases at shorter term at higher or variable interest—or not at all. Borrowing countries deflate or raise protective barriers to cut imports, and all this erodes the credit base just as surely as a default itself would. Thus, all these corrections, just like default and its repercussions, make it harder for the world economy to get out of a recession through a real trade-led recovery. At the end of 1981, oil-importing developing countries owed $400 thousand million for foreign credits. They were spending one-fifth of export earnings to service that debt—and all of these countries are vulnerable on the trade front to a fall in commodity prices, to recession in their markets, or to protection affecting their manufactured exports. In this environment an unexpected, uninsured, nonrepayment by any borrower—a poor country, a COMECON government (Poland), a domestic firm (Braniff), or another bank (Penn Square), all of which has occurred in the recent past—will be likely to cause other banks to reduce lending by a multiple of the nonrepayment. Who suffers directly? The answer is clear—the weakest borrowers, the customers believed by the bank's board to be risky, the domestic firms and the overseas governments judged to be near the edge of creditworthiness. These increasing risks have already restrained bank lending and will continue to restrain it in the future. Net private long-term capital flows to the oil-importing developing countries were $36 thousand million in 1978. They declined to $34 thousand million in 1981, even though the dollar price of traded goods in the intervening period had risen about 50 percent. Developing countries have had to respond to the reduced real inflows of capital by contracting imports. They have had to reduce the risks of rescheduling but at the cost of increasing other parties' risks and at the cost of deflating the world economy. What then can be done to reduce the risk that the interdependent world financial system—since 1945 a powerful engine for transmitting development among nations—may become an equally powerful engine for transmitting deflation, depression, and default?

Strengthening the World Financial System

Some of the answers have already been suggested by the description of the problem. The real value of concessional assistance must be restored, and it must be increased relative to the value of the more volatile nonconcessional credits. Both concessional and nonconcessional funds will contribute most to economic performance and thus to the safety of the debt as a whole if they are distributed among recipient countries according to development capacities and needs rather than according to the narrowly focused political objectives of particular donor governments or the justified requirements of private bankers for good returns from a few familiar low-risk borrowers. As private banks exercise greater caution and in light of the expected continuation of this practice, other sources of funds, better coordinated with domestic policy improvements, should be introduced to replace the developing country borrower's lost liquidity. The IMF's extended financing facility and the World Bank's structural adjustment lending program are such vehicles, and it is vital, therefore, to increase these forms of lending. But it may be that the world needs more than this. As desirable as higher IMF quotas and expanded World Bank's structural adjustment lending are, they may not be enough. Means should therefore be devised to ensure the continued expansion of sound private credit.

Within a country, the Central Bank is a lender of last resort to the banking system. It thereby limits the damage from default—the damage to depositors and to some extent, by preserving the system's capacity to lend, the damage to potential borrowers. With the vast growth in international banking credit and with the dependence of developing countries upon that expanding banking credit, does the system need some international lender of last resort? Of course, this cannot simply be a device to bail out banks that have made imprudent loans. A lender of last resort must be able to modify the behavior of banks that may otherwise make excessive claims upon it. But if defaults can echo through the system, bankrupting the prudent along with the imprudent, perhaps, in the management of international financial flows, the morality of insurance is a better guide than the morality of punishment. I shall not here examine in detail the several ways or the several agencies that could handle the simultaneous needs to expand, to render safe, and to insure the system against the risk of default on lending by private banks to developing countries. But it is certainly not too soon for the international community to begin consideration of how best to provide the services of a lender of last resort.

Assisting the Poor

It is the growing interdependence of nations, political as well as economic, that causes the poverty problem to be increasingly dangerous both politically and morally. Poverty is morally unacceptable—unacceptable to the sense of justice of a rising number of strong, articulate people. This implies that research, private investment, and concessional assistance to support production that involves work for the poorest is a top priority for the 1980s. Yet it is exactly this sort of activity that is most seriously threatened today. Concessional assistance, including assistance from the IDA, paid for one-fifth of the low-income countries' gross investment in 1979, and it helped many governments to give more attention to the needs of the poor.

What is happening to such flows? In real terms, aid to the low-income countries rose by 65 percent between the early and mid-1970s. Since then it has fallen by about 5 percent. Meanwhile, the real value of aid to the middle-income countries about doubled. Also during the 1970s the structure of aid improved in two respects: in 1970 only 16 percent of concessional assistance flowed through the multilateral institutions; by the end of the decade it had doubled to 32 percent and, after adjusting for price changes, assistance for food and agricultural production had more than doubled in real terms. What lies ahead in light of these moderately favorable trends of the 1970s? Recent disbursements and even more recent commitments reflect a grim political reality. Commitments of aid by all donors, OPEC and OECD together, fell by 8 percent in real terms between 1977 and 1980, and those to the 1.2 thousand million people in the low-income countries, excluding the least developed nations, fell by an appalling 28 percent. Meanwhile, among the OECD nations, the share of the multilateral agencies in aid disbursement declined. In 1981, in a single year, official development assistance from OECD donors fell by 8 percent in real terms. I have no doubt that we will see sharper declines in these same indicators.

The political roots of the weakness in support of multilateral development agencies are familiar. Although France, Germany, and Japan are seeking to increase aid, their search for bilateral impact has reduced their relative interest in the international agencies, and even more serious, the United States and OPEC, for different reasons and in different ways, are both reducing their aid efforts. As a matter of fact, in 1981 official development assistance from the U.S. government fell by 26 percent in a single year in real terms. Both the United States and OPEC are redirecting their development assistance toward bilateral objectives, particularly in middle-income countries. Of course, multilateral institutions should not monopolize aid, but the evidence is overwhelming that these agencies, being freer of pressures to support nationalistic foreign policy objectives, can channel their aid to where it is most needed and where it will be most productive. The low-income countries, poor rural people, and bilateral donors all stand to lose if the weakening of multilateral aid continues.

There have been a few hopeful signs recently. For example, the Versailles Communique by Heads of State of industrialized nations spoke out for further concentration of official development assistance on the poorest countries. It advocated special arrangements to overcome funding problems of the IDA and promised special encouragement for programs and arrangements designed to increase food and energy production in developing countries that have to import these essentials. We must try to mobilize support to follow up these brave words, but we should not deceive ourselves. Presently, the prospect for aid in the 1980s, especially for multilateral aid, is not good. If that prospect is realized, the poorest people in the poorest countries will be the losers. This is especially unfortunate in light of two important conclusions from recent research and one implicit challenge.

The first conclusion is that with respect to a high percentage of project investment, and in many areas of economic policy formulation, there is no conflict between investment and policies that contribute to efficient growth and those focused on the reduction of poverty. The second conclusion, however, is that despite a reduction in the percentage of absolute poor, the antipoverty programs—and here I would include the antipoverty program of the World Bank—have not been equally effective among all groups of the poor. The challenge of course arises logically from that second conclusion.

To attack the residual, the hard-core poverty, the poverty of the landless, the jobless, the unschooled, something more or something new is needed. Unfortunately, while we have learned a lot about efficient ways to increase income and productivity for the asset-owning poor, we have not learned how to increase the productivity of the asset-less poor, especially in slack seasons and in lean years. It remains, therefore, a major challenge to the governments of the major countries as well as to the aid agencies of bilateral donors and the international institutions alike to find productive, efficient ways to involve in the development process those people with few or no assets. In the developing countries with the lowest incomes such as Bangladesh, even a program for small farms and for the urban informal sector would leave out the poorest 25–35 percent of the population—those most at risk. Yet they, too, have not only rights and hopes, but also if they are adequately fed, fully functional brains and bodies. To leave them out of the development process has to be inefficient, quite apart from considerations of humanity. Shortages of saving, shortages of foreign exchange, shortages of aid provide no excuse for being inhumane and inefficient at the same time. These, then, are the two great challenges of our time: to substantially reduce absolute poverty and to construct relationships of interdependence, to build a world economy that stabilizes growth and distributes benefits widely. It can be done.

Facing the Challenges of Our Time

To whom are these challenges addressed? Who or what is supposed to attack absolute poverty or stabilize growth and the international flows of goods and money? Should we rely on the operations of firms and banks, strongly motivated by the search for private profit, or should we rely on governments and international institutions?

Firms, banks, governments, international institutions, all have special strengths and dangers. Dogmatic attempts to rule out one or the other only do harm. Nobody today believes that governments should decide what crops are to be grown on each plot of farmland, but neither should the elimination of malaria be left to market forces. Away from such extremes, the problems become much more complicated. The arguments about private, public, joint, or cooperative efforts become more serious and more important. My concern is not so much *who* is to meet the challenge, but *how* to meet it. How should we react to the lessons so far? The main lesson about poverty is that in an environment of growth, it can be effectively attacked. But then such attacks have failed to improve the income or productivity of some of the poorest of the poor, on whom absolute need and especially risk of caloric insufficiencies are concentrated. The main lesson about interdependence is that when trade is restricted and capital flows are constrained for whatever reason, the repayment capacity of Third World countries is in danger, and this threatens the capacity of lenders to support high and rising levels of economic activity worldwide. There are three ways to respond to these challenges: to do less of whatever seems dangerous or inadequate; to apply more of the medicine that has, after all, achieved a considerable advance over the past two decades; or to modify policies in ways that learn from both successes and failures. That last approach seems obvious but it is, in fact, very difficult and very unpopular. Change and learning are less attractive, radical, fundamental, than sudden lurches into do-nothing isolationism, or into do-everything expansionism. But the challenges of poverty and interdependence will not be met by naively setting to work axes among the institutions already available, nor will they be met by applying more of the same mixture as before.

How does this apply to our two problems? First, can the serious risk to the world economy implied in the size and structure of the Third World debt be simply met by lending less? Certainly not. Borrowers will find themselves forced to contract and therefore less and less able to repay the loans they already have. So, is the answer to lend more? Again, certainly not if in the last five years quick-maturing bank loans—many not directly linked to productive investment and concentrated on a few developing countries, thereby forming a growing proportion of the West's lending to Third World—are to serve as a pattern for the future. That path leaves most development requirements unmet, and it meets the rest in ways that expose the world's financial system to very great risks. Hence, only the hardest option is feasible in the medium term. What the developing countries need is a gradual expansion of private bank lending alongside dramatic improvement in the distribution and quality of that lending through the rapid buildup of supervision linked to lenders of last resort and with concessional and other lending—long-term lending—forming a growing proportion of total capital flows.

A similar undogmatic approach is needed in the attack on world poverty—an attack that has combined and enhanced economic efficiency but missed some of the very poorest of the poor. It is fashionable to argue that you cannot cure poverty by throwing money at it. Certainly handouts and well-meaning but badly planned projects will not help. However, more resources are a necessary condition for bringing the poorest into the development process. With poverty, as with interdependence, we can meet the problems, we can fill the gaps, we can cut the risk, but we cannot do so by drastic cutbacks. We cannot do so by a retreat into reliance upon pure self-interested profit seeking and niggardly private charity. Such reliance, after all, has given us hundreds of years during which the world has experienced no reduction in mass poverty and in which economic conditions, even in peacetime, were battered every dozen years or so by internationally transmitted waves of default and depression. On the other hand, the past forty years have seen, alongside decolonization and despite cold war and the oil shocks of the 1970s, an unprecedented and sustained sharing in growth, stability, and reduction of poverty. This has involved steady learning-by-doing as both public and private concessional and nonconcessional flows of capital have expanded and reinforced each other. The attacks on poverty and instability have thus achieved partial success. To apply exactly the same strategies to the newly revealed problems, to the persistent deprivation of the very poorest, to the new risks of default, to widespread economic stagnation, would be unwise. But to abandon the attack altogether, to retreat into a fantasy world where all marketplaces are magical, would be dangerous and self-defeating. Markets can work, and they can be trusted, but not unless public agencies —national and international—create the conditions under which such markets can operate in a stable manner and in which the poorest can reasonably hope to benefit from participation in those markets.

Avenues to Success

Of one thing we can be sure: the magnitude of the problems and the inability of any single nation to solve them by its own actions do require greater communication among nations. In 1981 the first summit meeting among leaders of rich and poor countries alike took place in Cancun, Mexico. More such meetings, institutionalized to take place on a regular schedule and with well-prepared agenda, are needed. They will not lead to instantaneous solutions, but they will expand understanding—understanding of common needs and of the potential for action that would perhaps benefit all.

In one of her last public appearances in the summer of 1980, Barbara Ward, speaking on the power of ideas and the need to be visionary, declared, "I would say we must dare to be headstrong, that we will be dedicated, and that we will not cease until the ideas that are represented here—ideas of world justice, of world community, of interdependence of our beautiful planet—will be realized." Should not that vision be our guide to action?

Development by the People: How to Approach Strategies for Survival

Andrew Young

Change movements in the United States really began with people. As Mahatma Gandhi said, "There go my people. I must catch them for I am their leader." I always remind myself that Martin Luther King did not go to Montgomery, Alabama, with the idea of starting a bus boycott. He went, essentially, to complete his Ph.D. dissertation and he was seeking a quiet place in Alabama where he would not be distracted as he might have been in Boston or Atlanta or New Orleans, where he also had job offers. And yet it was in Montgomery that a Rosa Parks decided to sit down on a bus—an action that began a people's movement around a particular grievance that everybody shared. But that proved the moment in which something should be done about it and in which Martin Luther King, as a leader, was thrust forward as he tried to articulate a response. I think that is the way the civil rights movement in the United States has proceeded, and the success of that movement through the 1960s was that it responded to people and their needs. It tried to create a nonviolent context for them to articulate their grievances and resolve them within the American system. The problems were always perceived and articulated by the people.

I would tend to disagree a little with those who say that the people out in the streets really are those who are struggling to survive and who have almost nothing to work with. In times of recession, it is not they who jump out of windows. The people in the streets are the ones who develop. They are the ones who develop the coping skills and the community mechanisms for survival and have done so in every country down through the ages. We see that happening in the United States. Our contribution as people who had been a product of these communities but who had achieved a bit more experience and education was somehow to help to nurture that along. We did it essentially by seeing to it that it fed into the mainstream of the media, of the economy, and of the politics. Insofar as the idea of drinking at a water fountain or voting became articulated, it had to become articulated in a way that it could communicate to the majority of people in these United States. That requires some relationship to the media. We understood the media in America, and I think the media on a worldwide basis have been a powerful education vehicle. Time on the Huntley-Brinkley television show was about $100,000 a minute, and we saw our two or three minutes a night coverage as articulating to the world, the court of world opinion, the grievances of the poor. We saw that as invaluable nights in educational TV.

The whole purpose of demonstrations was essentially to get a message about a problem across to the nation.

The other factor of power, in addition to the power of truth in the media, was power in the economy. Even before the politicians responded, this enormous capitalist system of ours responded at the local level. It responded essentially because it is more vulnerable. You have to get 50 percent of a politician's power in order to threaten it. But the profit margin of most businesses is 10 or 11 percent, and if you can shave off one or two percentage points of their profit margins, you get their attention very quickly. The ability to mobilize a withdrawal of economic cooperation, even among the poorest of the poor, had a powerful impact on getting the attention of the economic structure, which did not like this kind of organization of consumers, whoever they might be and whatever their reason. Finally, once the message began to come across and the power structure of the economy began to respond in some way, religious and social leadership would by then have taken up the cause and you were able then to create a coalition of what Dr. King used to call a "coalition of conscience" —the people of goodwill. Once that coalition was capable of generating a majority, then and only then did the political order respond. That, essentially, has been the history of grass-roots movements in the United States.

It has been a much more successful history than we can imagine, for we have seen, particularly among Black Americans, a generation of income from somewhere in the neighborhood of $40 thousand million annually in 1960 to approximately $125 thousand million annually in 1980. What that means is that the poorest segment of this enormously rich society now controls resources equivalent to all five Scandinavian nations combined and greater than the nation of Canada. What we see now is another kind of extension of that grass-roots movement—largely being led by the Reverend Jesse Jackson. It is beginning to challenge corporate America to share not only in the employment benefits of the economy, but to share in the contract and ownership benefits. But what the Reverend Jackson is saying is that we are no longer going to remain at the neocolonial stage in our relationship to the mainstream of the American economy. We are going to be genuine partners. We are not interested in aid from corporate America. We are essentially interested in trade. We are essentially interested in working out contract agreements whereby if we represent 20–25 percent of the market potential, we want to begin to talk about 20–25 percent of the ownership and contracts. We see now a new approach to the kind of domestic colonialism that the poor, particularly the Black poor, have been experiencing in the United States. That is still a movement which is coming from the bottom—from the plight of the unemployed, from the questions being raised by the hungry and homeless who find themselves not able to sustain the kind of support the federal government provided during the 1960s and the 1970s. What that situation does, however, is to redirect the attention of the minority in America from a federal budget for social programs of only about $300 thousand million, which though significant compares less favorably with the trillions of dollars that are available in the private sector. When we talk about sharing these resources, when we talk about full participation and the benefits there, we are talking about a significant grass-roots movement that has not yet received notable public attention but that is slowly but surely gaining contracts and concessions from some of the major but more vulnerable corporations in America. That is one stream of continuity from the grass-roots movements of the 1960s.

Another stream is what I think we are trying to do in the city of Atlanta. We are trying to return to that local base. We are trying to determine if those things that we as a group of citizens were not able to do nationally and internationally cannot be done locally. We want to find out if it is not possible to at least have a *city* with a sense of development. If we cannot get the federal government to be concerned about world hunger, perhaps we can get local government to be concerned about world hunger. Perhaps we can get the 430 of the Fortune 500 companies that have a local operation in the city of Atlanta to see what it is that they should and could be exporting in terms of personnel, in terms of capital, in terms of technology, in terms of resources—what it is that they can do to respond to the need of the world for development. This is not just a humanitarian rationale. It is because we are aware in the city of Atlanta that we are a part of an economy that is in a worldwide recession if not depression, and that recession in Atlanta means depression everywhere else. Somehow we must find a way to get ourselves out of that. We must be saying to the businesses in Atlanta and to the universities in Atlanta that they are not going to solve their local problems until they begin to think and act globally, that indeed it is only as we do become in reality an international city and that as we invite the rest of the world to share our university system will we begin to build the kind of cultural bridges that will lead to economic bridges which will help us to generate employment. The economic future of the city of Atlanta is dependent on the development of the world, even as the economic future of the United States in the 1960s derived from the Marshall Plan for Europe and Japan in the 1950s. Thinking along those lines at every level, but essentially responding to the people that gave us the power to *be* in decision-making positions, is some attempt to preserve the integrity of a grass-roots movement.

I received a contribution when I began to run for public office from a lady by the name of Miss Eva Davis. Miss Eva Davis went around to the grocery stores and to her neighbors and she borrowed eggs, flour, and she got sugar contributed, and then she took all of these ingredients and she made cakes, donuts, and cookies and sold them on street corners. She came to my headquarters one day with a dirty little handkerchief, and in that dirty little handkerchief she gave me $33 and she said, "Here, I want you to go to Congress to represent us." I've never forgotten that that's who I represent. One of the reasons why I always said things that got me in trouble at the United Nations was that it was not Jimmy Carter who sent me there—it was Miss Eva Davis.

And indeed, the very presence of Jimmy Carter, a southerner in the White House, was possible only because of a grass-roots Black movement that not only liberated the Black south, but liberated the White south as well. It not only created some little relief from poverty for Black people, but it made the south something of what we now call the "sunbelt," or the growth region of the United States. On a worldwide basis we can anticipate that kind of redemption of our total world economy if we would but listen to the least of these, to those who are the strongest, those who are struggling with the real problems. If we can but find ways to channel their movements in media, in religion, in the economic order, and in the political order.

I do not despair about where we are now. For just as we have seen enormous revolutions in the United States in civil rights over the past twenty years, in spite of the present-day despair and gloom, there exists a tremendous hope and power among the peoples of the earth. As a result we will probably find that the year 2000 will afford us more progress in the twenty years from the decade of the 1980s than we have seen from the 1960s to the present.

How to Storm the Last Refuge of the Pornographer

Tarzie Vittachi

Lateral Information: Communicating a Different Scale of Values

The debates on the New International Information Order aimed at correcting imbalances in the system of information as it operates between North and South have produced a false dichotomy. Soon after the debates began it became an issue between freedom and responsibility: freedom of the press and the responsibility of the press. It seemed as though the people from the South were talking about responsible journalism and that the people from the North were the defenders of the besieged bastions of press freedom. That was a false dichotomy because it is impossible to have one without the other. You cannot have freedom without responsibility, and you cannot be responsible unless you are a free person.

The reason for the sterility of that whole debate and the stridency that it produced was perhaps that discussions were not conducted among journalists. That is, it was not a debate among journalists about communication. It was a debate in which governments got involved, in which ministers of information got involved (and unfortunately many ministers of information are not in the business of providing information, but rather of keeping information from people), and in which a strange breed of persons called "professors of communication" played a role. Their discussions provided some useful language for a while until it became the same kind of stale language, the jargon, that seems invariably to plague debate on development issues.

The whole debate got derailed some years ago and now has come to a jangling halt because networks of information have grown up and the people involved are communicating because they *must* communicate with each other. They got tired of waiting for the debate to produce something new—new means of communication, new ideas about communication—and so the people who are concerned about and professionally active in efforts to redress poverty have simply gone ahead and created effective communication networks. The efforts taking place all over the world really constitute a kind of guerrilla journalism. What is most interesting: it produces real evidence of what people's needs are and how these needs are being met or not being met. An alternative journalism has begun to become a reality.

The networks around the world are extensive and, indeed, very impressive. They are particularly interesting because they suggest horizontal or lateral processes of communication—people-to-people communication—which is a new and positive step in the field of communication services. Historically, people have communicated from top to bottom. The introduction of the printing press revolutionized that, but later the printing press was used, indeed monopolized, by people who made a business out of communication. Messages under these circumstances always come from the top down. Now, however, people have begun to realize that the conventional media are no longer interested in people-to-people communication. They are interested in "readership" and "outreach" and things like that. The values that structure established prevail all over the world, both in the North and in the South—values based on the principle that we print and we broadcast what is saleable. That is the ultimate value. Journalists have tried to explain information and communication in other terms, with all kinds of language, like "freedom of the press" and the various slogans, but the fact is that ultimate values are market values. So information in today's world is sold like any other commodity. That is what international publisher Rupert Murdoch understands in New York, in London, and in Australia when he buys up newspapers—he will give the public what it wants, and of course, this is the last refuge of the pornographer, to give the public what it wants. Publishers like Murdoch and his team of editors would deny that they have any other function but to sell their newspaper. That is one end of that whole spectrum.

The other end of the scale is represented by the people-to-people communication described above. In the debate on a new information order, the ultimate in false solutions to a problem was, in my opinion, suggested by the call for training for Third World journalists. A fund, with limited resources at its disposal, was established to finance this in the hope that this would stop the outcry from the South for improvements in the balance and relationships prevailing in the present information order. Having spent the past twenty years as a journalist trying to train Third World journalists, I would say that while there is undeniable value in training, an even more important consideration is, what are those journalists doing with their training in the search for real global communication? That is, a system in which true *communication* takes place, fairly and humanely, and in which messages are not simply passed from top to bottom. That is what the debate should be about: those who are technically trained, what are they doing with that training?

H. G. Wells remarked in 1919 that man made the aeroplane and the ape got hold of it. He was reacting to the capacity of the aeroplane to drop bombs, poison gas, and other lethal weapons in the 1914 war. Here we are today with perhaps the most entrancing forms of journalism and means of communication, but what are people doing with this? The nearest we have come to doing anything humane is what is now being called in New York "infotainment." So while Third World journalists are being trained, perhaps we should simultaneously be educating the most powerful journalists in the world: an education which is far superior to that provided the rest of the world and which begins with dropping some of the scales from our eyes.

We have to work toward an alternative journalism, an alternative view of journalism and a practice of journalism with a different scale of values. An American journalist, we may recall, Henry M. Stanley went to Africa and found

Dr. Livingston, he presumed, in the jungles of that continent. He came to London, was welcomed as a great hero and explorer, and was invited to Manchester by the Manchester Chamber of Commerce. In a long speech to that body he said, "There beyond the gateways of Africa are 50 million naked blacks waiting for the textile mills of Lancashire to clothe their nakedness, and the iron foundaries of Birmingham are producing the red metal that will produce the trinkets that shall adorn those dusty bosoms and millions and millions of poor, benighted heathens are waiting for the Christian message to enfold them." That was how it was a hundred years ago, at the height of the imperial age, and perhaps that point of view, because it was a part of the thinking of that time, could even be defended. But this was the zoological view of other people. It was the pattern in Europe then to treat other people as savages and barbarians waiting for Euro-Christian messages to enfold them. However, the same zoological values found today in our journalism is cause for resentment. These persistent patterns lie at the core of that whole process called the debate on a new information order. The Japanese, for instance, are the Africans of yesteryear, still regarded in this kind of fashion: "the strange little yellow men do not even speak good English so how is it that their productivity is so high?" That is the general impression I get when I read about the Japanese. And the situation is worse for the poorer countries, because poverty is a sure sign of "undevelopment" or "undeveloped people."

For an Alternative Journalism

An enormous constituency has been growing for what might be termed lateral communication. There is evidence of this in the many conferences we hear on development. So many people are talking about similar things, similar values, similar ideas, people who are concerned with the urgency of doing something about growing destitution. All the discussions and conferences about disarmament, communication, economics, all this is about the problem of misconceptions through which we gain our image of the world—the scales through which we perceive the world.

We should not, in this alternative journalism, repeat the mistake that has been made in value terms by the conventional press—reporting only events. Ninety-five percent of the news issued in our newspapers or by the broadcast press is about who did or said what to whom last night. While those events are very important—people should know what took place last night—it is extremely important to report the processes that gave rise to those events. This is very difficult for journalists to do. They have been trained for the most part to report events, because events are saleable. There are noble exceptions to this around the world, reporters who try to report on the processes that create these events.

This huge process I see as a kind of cartoon in which the globe wears a very wide steel belt from tropic to tropic, with a few breathing holes here and there. This belt is worn by armed dictatorships from East to West across their bulging middles. The belt, the cartoon shows, is suppressing ordinary aspirations of a thousand million human beings. These people are trying to survive under that belt and this belt cannot be kept tight. It will burst. It is already bursting, though people do not connect the reasons why. It burst in Iran and it was a surprise to the conventional press. As I am a Third Worlder, it was no surprise to me or to many of my colleagues. We were reporting western Asia, as we called it, and we could see the process that was unfolding. We knew, for instance, that the Shah's famous land reforms were just a lot of hogwash. We knew that the first thing he would do, and we were right, was to reform the lands of the mullahs. It was an ancient process. From at least the time of Henry VIII this was the practice with the land of the Catholic church. We knew that the revolt would come from mullahs, though we knew nothing of the Ayatollah Khomeini. We are not prophets, but we knew that a revolt would start there, and it did happen that way.

There were more surprises. Liberia was a surprise. Nicaragua was a surprise. We shall have many, many more surprises from the people who live under this belt, and that is why it is important that journalists, and others concerned, urgently consider alternatives and explore ways to strengthen a lateral journalism.

How to Produce a Possible Balance of Equations in North-South Relations

Robert Moore

The history of the last four centuries has been one of penetration by Euro-America of what has come to be called the developing world through trade, religion, conquests, and by that very bloodless form of conquest known as the media. It is the media that have given to many Third World people as well as to their Western counterparts the peculiar image of the world and sometimes even the concepts of what constitutes development and underdevelopment. During this period and until quite recently, the developing world has been largely at the receiving end and the North has been at the contributing end. I once asked some Canadian children in a city called Guelph to define the world. One child who came originally from India told me that the world was a place on which the West was found. Now, there you have an example of that bloodless form of conquest in which a child whose parents emigrated from India actually defined the world as where the West was. The vocabulary of development has largely been the vocabulary of domination. Third World people have, more or less, seen their own development and sometimes discussed it in terms of the images and concepts that have been put out by Western experts in order to train their minds as to where they ought to go. So, what we are now beginning to find is the Third World liberating itself from the images and vocabulary of the North. It is the liberation from the thralldom of words—for Western civilization is fundamentally a civilization of words, and behind those words are metaphors, and behind those metaphors are a whole perception of reality which, in taking the mass media and its products, we of the developing world have absorbed. So, liberation in its fullest sense means liberation from imagery that was dictated to us. We now have to turn around and find a new and relevant imagery in which we can perceive the world untrammeled by Western vocabulary.

Faults in the Factors

Stalin once said that of all the instruments of power that the Soviet state used to enforce acquiescence of its people, none was more potent than the dictionary. In other words, Stalin's regime defined the meaning of words for the people. It therefore defined the meaning of reality because it dictated, through words, the way in which they would see reality. As a result, Stalin was able to achieve that peculiar querulous submission for which his regime is famous. We should perhaps apply not Stalin's examples, but Stalin's concepts to the whole business of the North-South equation. The North-South dialogue (different from the North-South equation) has done two things if it has done anything at all. The dialogue has established that the exchange was conducted so far in terms that are fundamentally those of the North, in other words, in terms of economic issues. Second, the dialogue has proved how inadequate those terms are for interpreting the world of the late twentieth century. For while the subject of economics and its preoccupations dominated the strategies of bargaining and dominated proposals and counterproposals, what really was now taking place was a conflict of perceptions of the world, which is perhaps the reason why the dialogue has not gotten anywhere. The two sides are talking about symptoms. They ought to dig deeper and start talking about perceptions.

The dialogue is basically one of looking at the world in the most fundamental and even, perhaps, primal sense. That is to say, looking at the world on one side in terms of its finiteness and on the other side in terms of what is supposed to be its projected infinitude. People who live in the consumer society think in terms of infinitude of satisfactions. People who live near the poverty line know something about the finiteness of their way of life and learn something about the finiteness of the globe's resources. There arises then a conflict of perceptions of what power is and what you do with it, whether you subject it to moral considerations or even considerations of self-interest, whether you subject it to the wielding of power by and domination of the few, or you subject it to distribution so that the many can share in it. In other words, the North-South dialogue should really be, in one of its aspects, about the management of global power rather than merely about the management of global economics. And certainly fundamental to this conflict of perceptions is the relationship between people and resources and people and expectations. The North-South dialogue is therefore the tip of the iceberg, with the obvious concessions being that we have to aim at people's perceptions rather than simply at people's interests.

Some Principles for Changing Perceptions

The Third World ought to begin a counterpenetration of the North, employing approaches aimed at altering people's perceptions right where they are. In other words, Third World people should do a turnabout, alone if necessary, or in tandem with like-minded international and/or Northern NGOs, to get to the people at the local level so as to begin tempering and changing their perception of the reality of twentieth-century Earth.

Some of the leaders at the Cancun Summit of world leaders indicated that they were willing to make structural changes in the world's economic system, but they feared what would happen to them when they went home and presented the meaning and significance of these changes to electorates who could later punish them at the ballot box. Clearly, if you run a democracy, you are not going to run a democracy of limiting expectations and deteriorating desires. You therefore present to your people all the things that escalate their desires, not limit them, for if you limit them, the opposition is always ready and willing to take over from you and to perform that job more ably than you can do. Leaders, therefore, may be prisoners in their own power and if they are, it is necessary for NGOs and Third World citizens who feel that we must go below (or above) the leaders to the people to start such educational programs.

One initial proposal in this connection would be to develop ways to more thoroughly use Third World diplomats in their postings in Northern societies. For instance, diplomats are people trained to be discreet, to act behind the scenes, to be judicious with their words, nuanced in their logistics, and usually maintain a low profile. Instead of discreet diplomacy we should perhaps try what might be called "expository diplomacy." In other words, Third World diplomats should now be trained to go out and speak to Canadians, Americans, West Germans, the French, Scandinavians, and the British at their own level, instead of being locked away in their embassies and missions attending only cocktail parties and receptions at which they claim they make ultimate communications and barter ultimate positions. They should be trained to go out and meet people, not their elected or appointed "representatives," and in particular talk to opinion-formers. This will certainly take a new orientation of diplomatic training. It will mean that sending beautiful little notes in which "His Excellency of So and So presents his compliments to His Excellency of So and So and wishes to inform him that..." ceases to be an important part of the diplomatic day. Instead, going out to talk to reporters and other media people, church people, trade unionists, and farming cooperatives would become a part of the Third World diplomatic routine. Ambassadors and their staff cost a lot of money to any country that has them. To be able to use them more efficiently than they are presently used will at least be an exercise in cost-effectiveness.

Second, it seems to me that the Third World should work with those agencies in the North that themselves desire change at the local level. Competent and lucid communicators from the Third World could be brought for short periods to the Northern countries, under the auspices of groups such as the NGOs, to talk to people, introduce them to what it means to live in the Third World, and give them the alternative lexicon. Not only should the NGOs be involved in this sort of thing but so, too, should those great repositories of stored up but often uncommunicated wisdom, the universities of the industrialized countries. If the Group of 77 or the nonaligned movement could set aside fellowships to send learned and lucid Third World academics to Northern universities for even short sabbaticals, they could act as excellent agents to bring the academic community in the North nearer to an understanding of what it is the Third World is saying about the nature of the world's environment and the distribution of the globe's resources. These people should also not lock themselves away in faculty seminars but should be encouraged to talk to students as well. Universities have a way of creating generations of opinion. Talking to students and faculty becomes important, therefore, since in these groups are the people who will eventually either get into government positions, head up NGOs, or advise governments. Academics are often put on boards to advise members of cabinets, provincial and state governments, and therefore Third World academics' being on equable terms with North American and European academics will in fact prove beneficial to both groups and for the new sense of perception that is required for change. The nonaligned movement can assist this process through a secretariat to fund precisely this sort of sensitizer, dispatched to the North on a regular basis to interact with people who are concerned or have yet to be concerned or whom they will *make* concerned with the perception of the world as seen from the South.

Another essential feature in sensitization will be the movement of women from the Third World who come to the Northern countries to interact with their women and to talk with them about those very things that concern women most: how, for example, if a New International Economic Order is realized, do you market wisely for your family, do you resist your mate's attempt to have three cars in the family instead of one, do you learn the practice of creative eating instead of overwhelming eating, and, in fact, how do you change the ethos of a civilization from overconsumption to intelligent acquisition? Women can do this much more potently than men, and since the women's liberation movement in the North is becoming more and more a power to be recognized and an actuality with which to negotiate, the relationship between women from the Third World and women from the North would be a highly explosive mechanism.

Finally, the conscience of the North is still largely located (where it is not agnostic) in the religious bodies. Some churches take an extremely paternalistic view of the Third World, but the liberal churches and the radical church leaders would seem to meet the Third World halfway. To ignore the churches in any attempt to change the perception of the world would be to deny an excellent opportunity. Churches operate not only as organs of worship, they also operate as sensitizing organs. Churches not only preach, they also hold study groups and have women's groups, women's institutes, and so on. Churches prove very powerful media. The Third World would therefore benefit greatly by interacting and interfacing with the churches.

Balancing the Equation

Interdependence refers, among other things, to the mechanism of mutual intercommunication. One penetrates with images and with words. If Third World people learn, first of all, the dictionary of the North and then learn the alternative lexicon, not by introducing new words but by giving the old words—like "survival," "economy," "finiteness," "justice"—new and broader meanings, this would suggest one action that lends real meaning to "interdependence."

Both the North and the South share a condition of underdevelopment from which neither will emerge without the recognition that twentieth-century Earth guards a bonanza revealed only through the fair distribution of resources between man and man, woman and woman, and through respect for an environment that is constantly shrinking and, as Barbara Ward has said, "infinitely finite."

How to Keep Man at the Center of Development: Public Management and a Woman's Response

Ulla Olin

There is now general agreement that women's contribution to societal well-being is undervalued and that something needs to be done to change the present state of affairs. A number of changes have, in fact, already been instituted. Nevertheless, there is less than full agreement both on what the nature of the problem is and on desirable remedies.

Beginning with the nature of the problem, one may discern a number of basic characteristics, all related to development. A major purpose of development is to increase the output of society's resources, human and nonhuman. This may be achieved through the introduction of new or modified methods of production, which in turn require changes in economic and social organization. In deciding on development strategies, we typically assign much greater weight to perceived economic advantages than to social implications, even when the latter are substantial.

Development tends to carry with it an intensification of the competition for scarce resources. The competitive aspect of population growth, one feature of the development process, is intensified by the inevitable tendency to polarize resources: "Unto everyone that hath shall be given, and he shall have abundance: but from him that hath not shall be taken away even that which he hath," as the evangelist Matthew puts it (25:29). Life has always been easier for the haves than for the have-nots, but the differences become extreme in periods of rapid change, as we are experiencing at present.

These problems have now become so intensive that they constitute a major topic of international and national political debate. Their relevance for the relationship between the sexes is less clearly understood. Obviously both men and women are being squeezed by polarization. One may even say that it is of more direct concern to men since they are the main actors in the struggle for power and influence that determines government policy. However, for this very reason, as part of the political game, men tend to push women—who already are in a subordinate position—even farther down the social ladder, privately and publicly. It is in this respect that women everywhere are faced with special problems, which go beyond the social structuring that in varying degrees is a feature of all societies. The situation has in many instances become acute.

What is the remedy? Programmatic declarations of the women's movement often urge as the panacea equal rights in the sense of equal sharing by men and women of all duties and responsibilities. Change is occurring but, typically, in a piecemeal fashion, and it shows little sign of seriously upsetting the traditional division of labor between the sexes. Both men and women take up new occupations but they do not mix much. At the same time there is the rather disquieting feeling that we may be at some kind of watershed in sexual relations. There *is* a need for change but there is at the same time a lack of agreement on just what should be changed and what is the underlying rationale.

The Family as a Model of Social Organization

A serious problem in industrialized and Third World countries alike is that large numbers of women are forced to carry a double work load, i.e., they work long hours outside the home and retain chief responsibility for child care and the management of the household. Since the family is the basic unit of social organization everywhere, it has become a common target for criticism by the women's movement, particularly in the industrialized countries. The socialization of children which takes place in the home and is continued at school is blamed for the different patterns of behavior in boys and girls. If parents and teachers could only be made to treat boys and girls the same way, it is argued, women would no longer suffer the discriminatory treatment that is their current lot. Underlying these prescriptions is the belief that, except for differences imposed through training, male and female behavior is identical. While these ideas are generally not shared by women's leaders in the Third World, they are nevertheless of considerable impact everywhere in that they form the conceptual basis for the attitudes of confrontation that are found the world over.

Without suggesting that training is not an important factor in human behavior or that there should be no battle of the sexes, I believe it is possible to approach the problem of family behavior from a different angle. Male and female differentials in behavior, while to a significant extent dependent on learning, have their genetic basis in sexual reproduction, which is the dominant pattern in nature and which to a very large extent determines the infinite variation in our behavior. As such it has its roots far back in the evolution of life, the laws of which are now quite well understood. To suggest that human training and conditioning can do away with these matters is sheer folly. Nevertheless, human arrogance does not hesitate to do so. Moreover, our folly is so deep-seated that many people are unable or unwilling to see that by aiming at complete control of our behavior they deprive themselves of the measure of control that can be had by listening to the voice of nature.

Seen in this perspective, male and female behavior is in significant respects a matter of complementarity. Not only that, but I believe a case can be made for viewing the roles we play as family members as the paradigms for all human behavior, whether in the actual biological family of which we are members or in the larger social units that are assuming an ever-increasing importance in the human pattern of survival. Differently put, male and female complementarity can be argued to have an important role to play in private as well as public management, and the family, in the extended or tribal sense, may be seen as the ultimate model for all human social organization.

By this I do not suggest that past, outmoded family patterns constitute a model for the future. Family behavior can be modified to suit changing conditions, but we always have needed and always will need families. It should be added that components of the complete public family, the nation-state, need not themselves consist of full-fledged families but may be limited to one sex or certain age groups, reflecting similar subgroupings in the private family.

As already noted, the basis for this hypothesis is the theory of evolution, which states that life is its own purpose. As life proceeds via destruction and renewal, reproduction becomes the major concern of all species, including homo sapiens. To survive and reproduce, we must produce our sustenance in interaction with the environment that surrounds us. In doing so, we are highly dependent on our brain, which enables us to engage in abstract thinking and symbolic representation. This is the basis for the scientific and technological advances that support and structure our economic systems. Based on ever-increasing specialization, they have forced us into social units that of necessity become larger and larger. Conceptually, these too are products of our ability to view the world in abstract terms, and the nation-state, which derives its name from the Latin verb *nasci*, to be born (into the same family, race, or stock), may with justification be called a symbolic family.

The support of the symbolic families, into which the modern world is divided, requires the creation and maintenance of cultural and physical infrastructures of many different kinds. Without these—religious and educational institutions, public services, roads, harbors, airports, etc.—our societies would disintegrate. It is therefore not farfetched to suggest that the support of public facilities represents acts of symbolic reproduction or extension of the self into the future. In other words, regardless of whether we are biological parents, we are all involved in reproductive behavior.

A serious problem with the large-scale social organizations within which we are forced to operate in the modern world is that they tend to dehumanize the social relationships among individuals or groups of individuals. While we are becoming increasingly interdependent, the scale and methods of interaction are such that our contacts with each other become increasingly impersonal. This has been recognized as a serious problem ever since the beginning of the machine age, now succeeded by the computer age. What has received less attention is the effect of this development on the complementary relationship between men and women.

Men, Machines, and Women

While men have always been the dominant sex in public affairs, indirectly women have usually made a significant contribution to public management as long as the scale of interaction was small or modest. Without being seen, women were quite active in determining societal affairs. However, as modern technology increasingly invades all areas of life and, as a result, transfers more and more activities from the private to the public arena, men have become a dominant force in most spheres of life. Women, with their continuing responsibility for child care, feeding, and housekeeping, have become relegated to the home and to occupations that are of no or little interest to men, either because the pay is very low or because the work requires a high degree of manual dexterity or patience, qualities that women possess to a greater extent than do men. Particularly among the poor, this situation is forcing women to carry the double burden of the work of mother and housekeeper and of income-generating activities outside the home. Men, on their part, do their productive work away from the home and take little interest in housekeeping activites, in which they no longer play an active role.

The genetic basis of these differences in behavior is in part quite obvious. Men's involvement in the physiology of reproduction is very limited while for women it is a commitment of years. In more or less obvious ways these differences extend into other areas of behavior. Thus, in practically all cultures, women are not only responsible for the nursing of babies but also for the feeding of the family and for much of the socialization of children, while men have traditionally been responsible for intercommunity affairs, including public safety. In general, women tend to be tied to the home and its vicinity whereas men are quite mobile. In the course of cultural evolution and economic specialization, the links between male and female functions and reproduction have become less obvious and in many instances have disappeared. A closer scrutiny of the situation will, however, reveal a greater degree of continuity than is usually assumed.

Without any attempt to be exhaustive, I would like to refer to some of the findings of recent studies concerning the biological basis of male and female behavior. Intellectually, men and women are on a par but they tend to excel in different areas. Men are better than women in tasks requiring spatial perception and thinking. They are also more exploratory, a feature that may be presumed to be linked to their interest in spatial concepts. Women, on the other hand, tend to have greater verbal skills than men. They also display greater manual dexterity than men, who, however, do better than women in mechanical tasks that require skill in handling spatial concepts. The intellectual interests of women tend to focus on more immediate problems, while those of men, because of their relative preoccupation with space, lead them toward longer-term undertakings.

Of no less interest are male and female differentials in social behavior. As is commonly believed, careful tests have revealed that boys are, indeed, more aggressive than girls. Girls are generally more protective, solicitous, dependable, and nurturing than boys. If we combine intellectual and behavioral propensities, it is fair to suggest that men are more object-oriented and women more people-oriented in their pursuits. Occupationally, these tendencies are, among other things, reflected in a heavy concentration of working women in the service industries. To conclude, it should be noted that findings like these are of course a matter of statistical differences and probabilities. Men and women both have traits of male and female behavior; it is the intensity that varies. Moreover, because of the complexity of the underlying neuroendocrine systems, there always will be considerable individual variations, including exceptions.

To sum up, if one accepts the idea that men and women may to a significant extent have different inputs to make to the management of human affairs, then the relationship between the sexes is not so much one of equality in the sense of sameness but of restoring a measure of balance in the role of men and women in society.

As the public family assumes an ever-increasing role in our lives, it cannot be left to the exclusive, or near-exclusive, management of men. Both sexes need to consider their complementary responsibility for the survival and well-being of our societies. It is obviously not only women who suffer from the impersonal nature of modern society in everyday life; men also experience their share of the pain. Given present arrangements, increased participation by women may further the chances for improvement of our life conditions.

These observations are not a statement against equal rights. Equal rights are needed and have a crucial role to play, for example, to obtain equal pay for equal work and to admit women to traditionally male occupations. The point is that the problem we are dealing with is more complex than these issues would suggest. We also need public recognition of women's values and viewpoint, which, to a much larger extent than men's, focus on social well-being. We need governments and administrations with female as well as male inputs. Such a world may turn out to be at least a *little* different from the one we have now.

Women's Approach to Development: Some Examples

As their problems accumulate, women are becoming impatient with the lack of interest and concern of the male establishment and are beginning to take initiatives of their own in the development process.

With the limited resources and opportunities available to them, it is not surprising that women's projects are often on a small scale. Moreover, with little or no say in government, many women's projects are undertaken without official sanction and support. As such, they offer an opportunity to consider whether women have their own approach to development or whether they go about their problems the same way as men.

A study of some twenty women's projects, the majority of which represent voluntary efforts, seems to indicate that women's approach to development is quite different from that of men. The difference applies to objectives as well as methods of work.

While periods of rapid economic and social change present all classes with problems of adaptation, it is for obvious reasons the poor who encounter the most serious problems. The discussion will therefore focus on development activities involving poor women. Because of their poverty, income-generation is usually a priority need and, directly or indirectly, this is often women's entry point to any attempt to improve their situation.

Project Objectives. In view of the many and diverse demands on women—
they must look after and educate the children; collect, or arrange for the collection of, fuel and water; buy or fetch food; prepare the food; clean the house;
wash the family's clothing; etc.—it is seldom possible for them to concentrate
on income-generating activities without also making special arrangements at
least for child care. As a result, women cannot, like men, concentrate on one
thing at the time. They need to put together a package of activities if their
development projects are to succeed. High on the list for supporting services is
the need to arrange for child-care facilities. This is, however, only the beginning.

Women's basic motivation in engaging in new or improved ways and means of
earning or preserving money is to be able to improve the opportunities of their
children. This requires access to services of various kinds as well as resources for
the procurement of more or better food, clothing, and other consumer goods.
In addition, without improved basic services for themselves—water, sanitation,
fuel, health care, education, and training—women will not have the capabilities, time, and energy they need in order to be able to engage in economically
remunerative work. Women's projects therefore typically consist of an extensive
package of activities, the basic purpose of which is to improve the quality of life
for the entire family. It is not by accident that such packages often are referred to
as "better family living" projects.

For the poor, regardless of sex, a basic method for self-improvement is collective action, that is, organization. The incentive and leadership for such action
typically come from middle- and upper-class women who, either because of
their work or out of private concern for the plight of the poor, take special
initiatives to help a group of women help themselves. The dedication of the
leaders and the resourcefulness and self-reliance of these organizations, once
they have become functional, are often astounding. Important in the organizing
effort is securing the collaboration of the more influential women of the community. In most instances it is no less important to inform the men of the
purpose of the scheme and obtain their consent. If this is not done, the men
will do whatever they can to put obstacles on the road for fear of encroachment
upon their authority or loss of status in the family.

Project Modalities. Again, the entry point for women's development projects is
income generation, usually on the basis of self-employment. The means of
improving the capacity for earning an income include access to credit facilities.
The Self-Employed Women's Association (SEWA) in Ahmedabad in India found
that credit constituted such a basic need for any assistance to the women workers that it started its own bank. Other organizations have managed to provide
credit facilities for their members through special arrangements with existing
banks. Given the relatively high cost of small-scale lending, a more common
procedure is probably to raise capital through collective savings schemes. At
times, women manage to create revolving funds.

Combined with the efforts to raise money are various training programs, including literacy programs, vocational training of various kinds, training in management, accounting, and marketing, and the formation of cooperative enterprises. Reference may again be made to SEWA, which represents some twenty different trades and offers various kinds of technical assistance to all of them. In addition to vocational training and literacy programs, the members get assistance in purchasing raw materials and in the design and production of improved tools. Cooperatives are organized for the production and sale of certain products. As SEWA is formally a trade union, a great deal of effort also is devoted to negotiations with employers for better pay. Another important service provided by the organization is the provision of legal aid, without which these poor women workers are unable to defend themselves against harassment by the police and other public officials, who are in the habit of extracting bribes or other illegal payments from them. While SEWA has become a relatively large organization, with 4,500 active members, other smaller women's organizations reviewed operate in similar ways.

Project Results. While engaged in multipurpose programs, women often work harder than they did before they organized to improve their lot. An indirect benefit of their work is that social problems often resolve themselves without any specific action: the husband develops respect for his wife, stops beating her, may even help her with her work, and no longer takes to excessive drinking. Where this is not the case, the women often find time and energy also to attack these problems more directly. They may, for example, organize to force illegal drinking places out of business, promote the abolition of outmoded social customs and traditions that create major economic problems, such as costly wedding arrangements, and actively work for intercaste collaboration and association.

While women, with a minimum of outside stimulus and assistance, are quite adept at taking up new or improved methods of income generation, their primary interest in doing so is to better satisfy family needs and aspirations through the provision of basic services without which the family cannot thrive. While activities may expand to include interaction with larger units of administration, the local community remains the focus of the development program. Viewed from the perspective of family behavior, one may suggest that the women operate through the extension of traits of family behavior to society at large, viewed as an extended or public family.

From Conception, Through Delivery and Development: Women and Planning

The emphasis of this trait in women's behavior is not to suggest that men do not work for their families. They obviously do. But men's basic interests are different from those of women. Men thrive, for example, on long-term planning of monumental schemes, that is, on exploration of space in all its ramifications. The purpose of these schemes is above all to extract more support for human life from the environment. However, if this approach to our survival becomes dominant, there is, as we all know, a very real danger that the competitive urge to excel will get out of hand and we will end up destroying ourselves.

My proposal is that viewing the family as a valid model for social organization may give us a tool to counteract these tendencies. I also believe scientifically valid arguments lend support to such a hypothesis. Men and women are equally interested in the future but approach it from different perspectives. The male preoccupation with spatial concepts—to be able to see into the future and control it as much as possible—needs to be balanced by the female concern for human well-being. In view of the dominance of the basically male-controlled public family—the state, the corporation—over the basically female-controlled private family, there is an urgent need to include women in public management and to consciously strive to attain a mutual respect for the complementary roles of men and women in the conduct of human affairs. Equality is not only a matter of equal rights but also of respect for and appreciation of differences. The field is wide open for initiatives by both sexes but in particular by women, who remain most conspicuous by their absence from the public arena.

Sources

Judith M. Bardwick, *Psychology of Women: A Study of Biocultural Conflict* (New York: Harper and Row, 1970).

ESCAP/FAO Inter-Country Project for the Promotion and Training of Rural Women in Income-Raising Group Activities, "Transfer of Knowledge and Skills among Peer Groups" (Bangkok, 1979).

Rose Giallombardi, *Society of Women: A Study of Women's Prison* (New York: John Wiley, 1966).

Beatrix A. Hamburg, "The Biological Bases of Sex Differences," in S. L. Washburn and P. Dolhinow, eds., *Perspective on Human Evolution*, vol. 3 (New York: Holt, Rinehart and Winston, 1975).

Corinne Hutt, *Males and Females* (Harmondsworth, England: Penguin, 1972).

International Women's Tribune Centre, Inc., Project Data Bank (New York).

Ulla Olin, "A Case for Women as Co-Managers: The Family as a General Model of Human Social Organisation," pp. 105–28 in Irene Tinker and Michele Bo Bramsen, eds., *Women and World Development* (Washington, D.C.: Overseas Development Council, 1976).

Self-Employed Women's Association (SEWA), "National Workshop on Organising Self-Employed Women in India" (Ahmedabad, 17–18 March 1981).

Kuo-Heng Shih, *China Enters the Machine Age* (Cambridge, Mass.: Harvard University Press, 1944); and a study by Ju K'ang T'ien, "Female Labour in a Cotton Mill," included in the same volume.

How to Take the Law into Your Own Hands

Clarence Dias

Generally, most groups of the poor have a largely justified negative perception of law and, to the extent possible, have nothing to do with state law. But that is a luxury and an option available more to the rich and powerful than to the poor. Particularly if they adopt a mobilizing-organizing strategy, groups of the poor cannot afford to leave state law alone because state law does not in fact leave them alone. So the issue becomes one of mobilizing and organizing to deal with inevitable contacts with law.

What do we mean by the concept of people's law? It is an elusive, evolving concept and one that is hard to define, except negatively. That is, by sketching the pathologies that exist within law in Third World countries at the moment, we can negatively define people's law as an attempt to achieve a system of law administration and of justice that rids itself of the pathologies that one finds in present state law in these countries. Law, like technology, can be a good servant but is inevitably a bad master. Again like technology, and especially in most developing countries, law has escaped social control. While you have concern about the pollution of the environment because of the escape from social control of technology, you also have in many developing countries a similar legal pollution—a pollution of over-legalization and over-criminalization. In fact, the glorious concept behind the philosophy of law, the concept of the rule of law, has more often than not degenerated into the law of the ruler. In developing countries, state law is becoming in many instances an instrument for perpetuating particular kinds of dependency relationships and power relationships. Therefore, a quick run through the most glaring pathologies in state law in developing countries is perhaps necessary in order to try and make somewhat more explicit what is the approach behind this kind of movement by small nations toward people's law. The pathologies are very simple, commonplace, and are very well known. And yet, nothing gets done about them.

Pathologies in State Law

In the first place, state law is antiparticipatory, and in the context of a development ideology that emphasizes self-reliance and participation, state law and its institutions are antiparticipatory particularly when it comes to the poor and the impoverished and those who most need to be the beneficiaries of development. Within the law-making processes you find legislations and you find parliaments. But can people, groups of the poor, ever initiate measures of legal change? Very rarely. Can they even participate in measures of legal change that are vitally affecting them? For example, a particular country might pass legislation relating to city zoning that is going to affect slum communities and squatter communities. Or, for another example, a state in India is currently passing a wide-sweeping forest bill that will deal with forest resources in a manner dramatically affecting tribal and other rural communities dependent on forest resources. But the whole process of law making is not amenable to the participation of impoverished groups in the enactment of law even when it is going to affect them. Nor do they have a voice in the interpretation, administration, and application of the law. It is very difficult, in fact, to try to structure mechanisms to permit this participation of such excluded groups in these processes.

Other major pathologies include the carefully held monopoly over legal knowledge and information about changes in law. Access to the whole law reform process is usually monopolized by a very small and elitist legal profession, usually working very closely and carefully with the political executives. Access to a variety of legal institutions is extremely restricted. Take, for example, the courts. Access is possible only through intermediaries, the intermediaries being lawyers, the lawyers usually, in essence, buying and selling their services in a marketplace to the highest bidder. Similarly, access to remedies is often illusory. Court remedies are an illusion to those who do not have the financial strength to fight a court case for the ten or fifteen years it might take to go through the whole appellate process and to those who quite simply do not have the staying power. Similarly, access to the executive and to the legislature is equally restricted.

Another pathology that arises from state law stems from the fact that the delivery of legal services is professionalized, and the profession itself therefore stands as an intermediary, a barrier to access to the institutions and to legal services. This model of professional delivery of services perpetuates dependence upon the lawyer. The lawyer-client relationship is inevitably lopsided, with the lawyer making decisions all the way through—the lawyer decides what kind of a problem the client has, what kind of solution is to be pursued —but the client being stuck with the consequences of the decision that the lawyer has made. Basically, the professional is unaccountable except within very broad, general ethical channels of professional responsibility. This professionalized delivery of legal services results in very highly skewed laws relating to development. The laws relating to taxation, joint enterprises, corporations, and fiscal policies become increasingly functional to suit client needs. Laws relating to rural poverty, rural credit, and bonded labor are largely suffering from lawyers' benign neglect because essentially professional services are directed on the basis of someone's ability to pay for them.

In most developing countries laws suffer from another pathology: they are nonendogenous. They are essentially inherited and alien—drawn usually from the colonial experience, which not only displaces endogenous, easily understandable preexisting customary rules of law, but replaces them essentially with law that is alien and unintelligible, both in language and in conceptualization. Another major pathology with existing state laws is that they essentially facilitate the functioning of an international capitalist system. In most developing countries, areas of law that are of interest to actors in the large corporate sector together with the ruling national elite tend to get developed without aspects of that same law relating to, for instance, the harmful effects of the spread of agribusiness. Organized plantations—the banana and pineapple fields, for example—remain neglected and undeveloped.

People vs. Pathologies

Thus, in many respects, state laws produce and reproduce exclusion, dependence, impoverishment, and evasion of accountability by the wielders of power. Whether they be in the private sector or in the public sector. People's law would attempt to rid the system of some of these pathologies, and people's law would therefore emphasize a sharing of legal knowledge, to realize equal access to the legal process and legal institutions. People's law would also emphasize the concepts of legal self-reliance and, if need be, deprofessionalization. People's law would emphasize endogenous values and institutions. Therefore, people's law would be law relevant for a society whose vision reaffirms self-reliance, participation, redistribution of power and resources, and development as a human-centered concept.

From where will this elusive, perhaps romantic concept of people's law emerge? Experience working at grass-roots level gives hope that it will emerge from the struggles of people—the impoverished and the other victims of maldevelopment—to mobilize and organize themselves.

The Essence of People's Law

What is here under discussion is not legal aid and not legal services. What we are talking about is basically and fundamentally different. Legal aid merely guarantees access to law and access to courts but does not necessarily guarantee access to justice through law. Where the law is, in fact, skewed, having your day in court may still leave you a loser. Legal aid is based upon a culture of dependence. Inevitably it will foster a dependency relationship with the lawyer and inevitably it is nonparticipatory in the sense that the lawyer is making decisions for the client all the way through. Further, legal aid is based mostly upon a notion of charity.

People's law as discussed here suggests the notion of law as a resource. It is a resource used repeatedly as such on the part of the exploiters, on the part of those who perpetuate current situations of impoverishment. The operative question is, can it be turned around and made a resource for the impoverished?

Second, law is a source of power. It is a source of right. Can law be utilized by groups who are mobilizing themselves for self-help as one of the various tools in the process of empowerment?

Third, when it comes down to it, lawyers, by their very trade, stripped of all of the glamor, are essentially manipulators. They manipulate language in legal arguments and legal reasoning. They manipulate process—plea bargaining and how that evolved in the United States, or Perry Mason and his wildest manipulation of a jury are slightly exaggerated but fairly true versions of the extent to which legal skills have to do with manipulating institutions. Lawyers are manipulators of facts. Anybody who is familiar with the concept of legal fiction or with the notion of "beyond a reasonable doubt" is sufficiently aware of the extent to which facts that are on paper, facts that represent a reality, when they come into the courtroom, through permissible rules of evidence, end up not speaking for themselves but speaking quite differently. Lawyers are manipulators of interpretations of the various provisions of the law, inevitably looking for loopholes within the law. If that is the case and as legal skills are largely dependent on and based upon the ability to manipulate, can some of this manipulation be turned around in favor of the impoverished? Can lawyers manipulate, for example, existing social welfare legislation that exists on books but which remains unenforced? Can lawyers manipulate human rights covenants that governments in many Third World countries have signed, or covenants and conventions arising from the work of some of the international organizations?

However, the approach being suggested to accomplish this is not one of delivery of law through a lawyer, but of building up legal self-reliance. Information and knowledge about law should reside within the community; paraprofessional skills should be developed within the community to deal with routinized, ordinary day-to-day matters; the ability to decide when and how to use a lawyer should be developed within the community so that even when a lawyer is engaged as an advocate to press certain claims and demands, it will essentially be the community or the organization that controls the lawyer, rather than vice versa.

How to Bring the World into the Classroom

S. N. Leela

The world, as we have known it through much of this century, is rapidly changing. We can either work to shape this world in a wise and effective manner or become paralysed by its kaleidoscopic changes. To be our own masters we must understand our global environment for what it really is: a world in more rapid flux, a world in which neither the United States nor any other nation holds a preponderance of power or a monopoly of wisdom, a world in which events can no longer be ordered by those nations which had the bulk of economic, political, and military power. Since our schools and universities are the fundamental institutions through which we gain an understanding of the world, it must be upon them that we rely to illuminate our perceptions of the world as it really is.[1]

The geographic boundaries of the world since 1945 have shrunk, making it more interdependent. Faced with a scarcity of major resources required for production and consumption activities, with massive population movements, environmental concerns, and political instabilities, the world finds it increasingly difficult to separate domestic from global issues. Transnational corporations scanning the globe determine the global economic and business frontiers. The transcontinental jet age has brought citizens of the world closer, and the plethora of media has brought global issues to the doorsteps of today's citizens. Artificial isolation and intellectual compartmentalization hardly fit in today's world, nor can events be ordered to the choosing of American or European imagination or priorities.

Despite these cataclysmic changes, global issues are continually being categorized as pertaining to East or to West, to less-developed or to more-developed countries, to free market or to socialistic or communist societies. These divisions hardly bear any significance when a vast majority of the so-called educated elite in the Western industrialized nations barely can understand the present-day connotation of mass poverty, famine, world hunger, or population pressure, to cite a few of the major issues while, for all practical purposes, the world has become technologically a global village. The natural tendency for policymakers, and even a majority in academic disciplines, to focus mainly on internal, national problems and policies has resulted in a persistent underattention to global issues. "Global issues" for purposes of this paper are identified as global population dynamics, global food issues, global poverty, and global developmental issues of an economic construct.

Inadequacies in Curricula

The existing curricula in many American schools and colleges do not reflect the urgencies of modern international awareness, and a kind of vocationalism seems to have pervaded on a massive scale. Consequently, there is a lack of expertise to steer members of the future generation, who will face a world that will be even more interdependent. Equally serious will be the lack of understanding of world issues required for political decisions or even in considering economic trade-offs. The present courses in world cultures or various area studies do not impart an understanding of global issues. Most of the existing courses tend to deal with unique cultural components of individual areas without getting at the interdependent nature of the world. International economic, geographic, and political problems are not studied; the cooperative interactions of people on a global scale are overlooked. Yet these are the key issues and concerns for survival in an interdependent world. A new approach is imperative.

A similar conclusion was reached by the Council on Learning based upon the findings of a survey conducted by the Educational Testing Service (ETS) of college students regarding their global understanding. The survey was conducted among 3,000 students in 185 campuses around the country in the spring of 1980 and included a test of global knowledge, students' background and interests, their proficiencies in foreign languages, and, above all, their attitude toward global issues. The results of the survey, according to the ETS, were disappointing. College seniors answered an average of one-half of the knowledge questions correctly, with freshmen and second-year college students achieving 40 percent. Fewer than 15 percent of all seniors and fewer than 10 percent of all freshmen and second-year students tested answered more than two-thirds of the questions correctly. A dishearteningly small proportion of students had the knowledge necessary for an adequate understanding of global situations and processes. Although there are some academic institutions that possess excellent international learning programs, the vast majority of this country's undergraduates have only slight exposure to global issues during their college years.[2]

The Council on Learning and the National Task Force of Educators, public officials, and business leaders have come to the conclusion that "while many college programmes make substantive contributions to basic global understanding, much more needs to be done for most American students. Efforts to enhance the campus' traditional domestic concentration will require comprehensive reviews of the total curriculum and the learning experiences of each academic institution. To merely add international references to what has been largely treated as domestic concerns does not reflect a world in which these two dimensions have long existed as an integral mix."[3]

Further, the task force emphasizes that in order to prepare the college undergraduates and the elementary and secondary students for the twenty-first century, an all-out effort to internationalize the syllabi in all disciplines and to improve teaching preparations at all levels is essential. If this effort is not made, according to the task force, the students are likely to be unprepared for world changes and their further educational goals will be impeded. Hence, the Council on Learning recommended that in order to meet the challenges in the years to come a broad public discussion and understanding of key questions of policy, ranging from global ecology to food and hunger and other major issues, be integrated into educational processes so that Americans enter the twenty-first century with a view as wide as the world.

Experiments

The integration of global issues in an established curriculum requires a thorough investigation and recording of priorities for students seeking to find an understanding of the world in which survival and quality of life are the objective. Such an approach calls for an interdisciplinary effort, as against the regional studies presently offered in most educational institutions.

An experimental project, focused mainly on a thematic scheme, was conducted at Millersville State College in Pennsylvania from the spring semester of 1973 to the fall semester of 1977. The General Education Program for freshmen concentrated on major world issues such as population pressure, food security, and the environmental maze. Student evaluations indicated that the students felt the program made them aware of global issues; they said that they were more curious and more interested in learning further. The response from the participating faculty members was very favorable, and a continuation and follow-up to the program seemed desirable.

As a result of that experiment, a number of courses offered in the economics and geography departments at Millersville State College in the past five years have been largely thematic, focusing on global issues. The results, as evidenced by the students' opinions and evaluations, have been very encouraging. Themes reflect contemporary global issues, and the syllabus is augmented by varied reading materials and audio-visual presentations. Further, under the sponsorship of the Pennsylvania Council on Economic Education, a graduate course on global issues was offered at Millersville State College in the spring semester of 1982. The participants in this course were social studies teachers. An evaluation of the course reflected its innate value and the imperative need for a course of this nature. The teachers mentioned that the knowledge gained in the course assisted them in their classrooms and above all gave them an insight into many areas in which they were previously deficient. All of them categorically expressed that a follow-up to this course should be offered so that they could be better informed.

Many other institutions are involved in education on global issues. For instance, on 28 April 1982 at the University of Pennsylvania in Philadelphia, the World Bank conducted for social studies teachers a workshop on the theme

"Toward a Better World." The Institute for World Order in New York is focusing on "Peace and World Order Studies" and grants fellowships for educators to develop curricula and design world order courses. Many specialized workshops and seminars on specific topics on various global issues are conducted by universities and research institutions; for instance, Cornell University in Ithaca, New York, conducts workshops for educators on the topic "World Food Prospects."

All these programs, workshops, and courses emphasize the need for the development of a curriculum on global awareness, which calls not only for rearranging priorities in the contents of courses but also for changing their nature. Courses on global issues, complex and varied as these issues are, require an interdisciplinary framework.

Some of these issues are reaching a phase of global crisis for which a total understanding on the part of educational institutions is absolutely necessary. The suggested themes constitute only a "crash course" on some of the crucial elements of global problems.[4] A fuller comprehension of the necessary restructuring of curricula in educational institutions is required if we are to keep pace with the changes in this world. Global knowledge and realities cannot be compartmentalized into neatly structured courses. We must become immersed in these issues if we are to survive in a global setting.

Notes

1. Cyrus Vance, *Education and the World View* (New York: Change Magazine Press, 1980), p. 2.
2. *Task Force Statement on Education and the World View: Findings of "What College Students Know and Believe About Their World"* (New York: Council on Learning, 1 June 1981).
3. *Task Force Statement on Education and The World View: Recommendations* (New York: Council on Learning, 1 June 1981).
4. Topics to be covered under different themes on Global Awareness could include (*a*) Population pressure and its impact on resources—a simple lesson on demography; the carrying capacity of the earth; the dimension and consequences of population growth—on resources, on health and nutrition, on habitation, on employment, others; future prospects. (*b*) Understanding the problem of world hunger and global poverty—analysis of world hunger and statistical presentation of global poverty; food availability: production, distribution, and consumption patterns; food prices; the poor consequences of international food aid and patterns of food trade; future prospects. (*c*) Dimensions of global developmental issues—economic concepts; a macro-micro perspective of North-South relations; problems of trade, finance technology, uneven distribution of natural resources, employment; dialogues so far and the new international economic order; future prospects.

If You Can't Beat Them, Join Them; Or, How to Operate Your Own Financial Institution

Muhammad Yunus

Identifying the Problem

That development means improving the quality of the lives of the poor, both urban and rural, no longer seems to need any debating. But what often suffers from confusion is the proper identification of the poor and strategies to ensure change in the quality of their lives.

In a country like Bangladesh where 90 percent of the people live in the rural areas, concern about the urban poor is not expressed as frequently, or as vocally, as it is about the rural poor. A poor person in the rural area has no special claim over a poor person in the urban area within the general policy framework for development, but the overwhelming number of the rural poor does bias the attention of the policymakers in their favor.

We could gain conceptual clarity if we paid attention to the urban poor as well. The reason is simple. Social scientists, policymakers, and administrators, being for the most part urban people, understand the urban problems more clearly than they do the rural situations. In the absence of this clarity about the rural scene, generally, we, the urban intellectuals, tend to compensate for the lack of clarity with rich imaginations. Soon we become fully convinced by our own stories. Then, to make it worse, we go and collect the right type of evidence to justify and reinforce our stories. We find also that conventional methodology for social science research displays its true state of affairs when it is applied in unfamiliar territory. The situation can best be described as an unbreakable vicious circle that takes the researcher more and more away from the reality at every spin of the wheel.

In social science literature on Bangladesh one would never miss an axiomatic assertion that 80 percent of the people are involved in farming. If one leaves out the 10 percent urban population, this implies that the remaining 10 percent are rural people involved in nonagricultural pursuits. This has allowed everybody to treat the terms "rural" and "agricultural" as synonymous without ever questioning this equation. But even a simple computation would reveal that "rural" and "agricultural" are far from being identical. For the entire agricultural operation for one year in Bangladesh the total labor requirement comes to hardly 14 million work-years out of a total rural population of 81 million!

In a purely agricultural economy the poor person can be thought of as a poor farmer. But one can rarely find a purely agricultural economy. The objective of development is to bring about change for all poor people, not just poor farmers. By focusing attention on a particular occupation of the poor we only get ourselves confused. For example, in the development jargon of the international agencies the "small farmer" has somehow been built up as typical of the "poor" and the neglected. However, "smallness" of the "small farmer" has been allowed to vary from 2.5 acres to 25 acres to accommodate the variation from country to country. At no point is it questioned whether a person can be poor without being a small farmer, or whether a small farmer is really a poor person. In Bangladesh, for instance, a farmer of 2.5 acres occupies a fairly respectable position in the income hierarchy in comparison with the bottom half of the population. At times, to avoid this embarrassment in Bangladesh, "small farmer" is either substituted by "marginal farmer" (1 acre) or soft-pitched as "small and marginal farmer." The more conscientious scholars prefer to refer to the poor as "landless and marginal" farmers, but even in this expression there is a strong implication of farming as an occupation of the poor, including the landless poor. We are so obsessed with the "farmer" image of all rural people that we refuse to admit that there exists a class of people called "landless people" who are not landless farmers or landless peasants.

Many international agencies have a "Small-Farmer Development Program" but very rarely would one see any "Development Program for the Poor"—not because these organizations are apathetic to the development of the poor, but only because they have gotten their identification of the target group confused. The purpose of development will thus be better served if we avoid identifying the target group with respect to any particular occupation, such as farming, and simply use "poor people" or the "bottom half," or "quarter," or whatever the case may be. Serious conceptual damage is also done by categorizing the poor as "farmers." A "farmer," in all cultures, has an unmistakable *male* image. As soon as we identify a section of the people as farmers, our thinking gets drawn to exclusively male issues. One blissfully forgets about the existence of the other half of the population, the women. If they are remembered at all, it is always done in their capacities as minor helpers of the all-important male members of the household. It would be useful to remember that in poor families women are far more economically active than the women at higher levels of income. More heads of households are women among the poor than among the nonpoor.

The Basic Strategy: Financial Resources for the Poor

The days of "Big Bang" theorists of development are gone now (I hope). Nobody believes that prefabricated development can be installed by expatriate experts on a turn-key contract. Big-Bang theories, by their very nature, are heroic, larger-than-life, romantic, and of course attractive to anyone who has the responsibility of running a government. The theory assures the leader of solutions to all problems without anyone's lifting a finger.

But development is not going to happen that way.

Of the total labor-time at the disposal of Bangladesh, perhaps only half of it is gainfully employed. This dismal picture is no secret to anyone. Attempts have been made to eliminate this cause of poverty by intensifying farming activities. But there are limits to what agriculture can provide in a country that ranks among the highest in terms of population density. In fact, the vast manpower resources available in the country are largely considered useless because people are illiterate and lack skills. Illiterate they are, but certainly they are not without useful skills. The very fact that they are still alive, despite severe adverse circumstances all their lives, demonstrates beyond doubt that they are endowed with a very useful skill, the *survival skill*. This skill has passed the test of the centuries. This skill and training can provide an excellent time-tested foundation for the start of a development program and would mean making people the architects of their own fate, rather than imposing prepackaged scenarios of development for execution by them. The planner's job would then be to watch carefully how things happen around the poor, how they keep themselves afloat, which constraints restrict their upward movement, and to then design a program that will eliminate these constraints, help the poor use their full potential at their own initiative, and then gradually let them go beyond their initial capacity.

If we check the list of such constraints we soon identify one of the most formidable—the lack of financial resources. Under adverse, at times outright hostile, socioeconomic circumstances, individuals have either been forced away from their traditional trade or are unable to pursue their trade because of a lack of financial resources. It would be futile to argue that all able and willing people are kept away from pursuing their chosen lines of work only because they lack financial capital. There are many formidable constraints indeed. But what is being argued here is that nonavailability of financial resources at a reasonable "price" (monetary and nonmonetary, expressed and hidden) constitutes the single overwhelming constraint in allowing people to realize their chosen and feasible pursuits. If these financial resources can be made available to them at terms and conditions that are appropriate and reasonable, millions of "small" people with their millions of "small" pursuits can add up to create an overwhelming development success. With the appropriate credit support, millions can find self-employment, without any external assistance, by involving themselves in their familiar processing and manufacturing trades, providing transport services, storage of agricultural produce, marketing agricultural and nonagricultural inputs, outputs, and supplies, maintenance services to all equipment, and the like.

Availability of financial resources to the bottom half of the population will solve the first layer of economic problems, but, in its turn it will create, or bring into sharper focus, a new generation of problems: redesigning input delivery systems, linkages across the board, and so on. The precise nature of these problems will emerge out of the economic activities undertaken by the self-employed poor. Some of these problems will be resolved by the people them-selves as they learn by doing, employing their indigenous wisdom. National efforts need to be mobilized to solve the remaining problems.

Paradoxically, the vast reservoir of the unemployed landless in Bangladesh can be viewed as an asset. Indeed, their most attractive feature is that they are not tied to land. A life tied to land, as is the case for peasants, tends to make people conservative, narrow in outlook, and inward-looking. Landless people, having no ties to the land, are likely to be enterprising, mobile, and receptive to new ideas. Their existing condition makes them fighters.

In a tradition-bound society like that in Bangladesh, women end up receiving and absorbing all the woes generated by the economy and the society—especially the women of poor families. They have all the obligations in the world, but no rights, no security. They perform all the family chores, including raising chil-dren, but have no access to any activity that brings economic reward. They live at the mercy of their men. They are considered as liabilities both by their own family and the family of in-laws. Since birth they have been told in so many ways by so many people that they are a liability to the family that they learn to believe it themselves. They put in hard work, suffer through all the indignities, poor health, and diseases without complaints. Men abandon their wives at will, often leaving them with several children. It is extremely difficult for an abandoned woman to find another home for herself and her children. She lives the life of a condemned person, often resorting to begging for survival.

However, she usually has more household skills than are recognized. Her skill can be translated into producing things for the market. She can be an earning member of the family. Once a woman can become an earning member, her status in the family undergoes a positive change. If she can find support and strength from other women in the village to enter into the market economy, she can much more easily overcome initial resistance. An earning mother certainly becomes a better parent for her children than an earning father would. When a poor father begins making extra income, he starts to dream about himself. When a poor mother begins earning an income, her dreams invariably center on her children. The single most powerful influence on the state of women will definitely be the action that helps them become earning members of the family. Bringing financial services to their doorsteps may help them become so.

Existing Credit Institutions

Like many other institutions in Bangladesh, banking is primarily urban-oriented and geared to the needs of the economically fortunate. Its structure, character, and mode of operation are not amenable to providing efficient service in the rural areas, to say nothing of efficiency in service to the rural poor. As the inadequacy of the present banking institution in handling rural credit needs became transparent, more and more branches of major banks were opened in the rural areas. But this did not improve the situation. Rural branches turned out to be instruments for siphoning off deposits from rural to urban areas. The banking community tried to adapt its services to the rural reality by introducing special programs. These, however, remained token efforts that made no substantive change in the basic mode of operation.

Rural disadvantaged groups, such as the landless and women, remain totally outside the orbit of the banking system, although they constitute the largest societal group and are the ones who are desperately in need of credit for mere physical survival.

Money-lending at usurious rates of interest is an age-old institution in Bangladesh. The process of ever-increasing landlessness and impoverishment finds a very effective vehicle in the operation of the money-lender. The institution operates in a variety of ways and situations. Some operations have become so standardized and socially accepted that hardly anyone, neither the lender nor the borrower, seems to notice the highly oppressive nature of the contract. As an example: 10 percent-per-month interest rates are considered normal across the country. Interest rates can even go as high as 10 percent per day! Then, consider the range of types of loans. A maund of paddy borrowed at the beginning of the planting season has to be repaid with two-and-a-half to three maunds of paddy at harvest time. And there are many other such arrangements.

A wide variety of securities are offered for loans from the money-lender, including land, jewelry, household assets, labor, and agricultural produce. However, transfer of the use of land is the most common form of land security. For the borrowed amount of money a parcel of land is placed at the disposal of the creditor, who enjoys ownership rights over the piece of land until the total amount is repaid. In many cases formal documents are made to establish the right of the creditor. To render the repayment of the loan difficult, the creditor often refuses to accept any part payment of the loan. At the expiration of a certain period, the creditor has a right to buy the land at a predetermined price. Equally common is the phenomenon of obligatory labor on the creditor's land as another form of security. Under one system, traders advance loans against crops for obligatory sale of the crops to the creditor at a predetermined price, which is obviously lower than the market rate.

Around four-fifths of rural credit still comes from village money-lenders and, whether the borrowing is made for investment purposes or consumption purposes (such as, for physical survival, to marry off daughters, for medical needs, to meet some emergency situation, to bribe someone, for social occasions, to fight court cases), it becomes extremely difficult for the borrower to extricate himself from the burden of the loan. Most likely he will continue to borrow just to repay the preceding loan, ultimately to find his final salvation in death. Unless the poor can be liberated from the bondage of the money-lender, no economic program will be able to arrest the steady process of alienation of the poor.

The Grameen Bank Project

The Grameen (Rural) Bank Project (GBP) was launched in December 1976 out of the realization that present institutional arrangements in the field of banking bypass the rural poor in more ways than one. In the very conceptualization of these arrangements the real poor simply drop out of the sight. To help the "poor" the policy planners wish to help the rural people. To help the rural people, they wish to extend agricultural credit. Then they specify rules and procedures in such a manner that the real poor are excluded.

The GBP was initiated with the following objectives in mind:

○ To extend banking facilities to poor men and women.
○ To eliminate exploitation of the poor by the money-lenders.
○ To create opportunities for self-employment for the vastly unutilized and underutilized people in Bangladesh.
○ To bring the disadvantaged people within some organizational structure that they can understand, one in which they can operate and find sociopolitical and economic strength through mutual support.
○ To reverse the age-old vicious circle of "low income, low savings, low investment, low income" into an expanding system of "low income, credit, investment, more income, more credit, more investment, more income."

Operations were launched initially in Jobra, a village adjacent to Chittagong University campus. Local arrangements were made with the Janata Bank to extend loans to the landless. The entire operational responsibility was assumed by the Rural Economics Programme of the Department of Economics, Chittagong University. Later, in March 1978, the Bangladesh Krishi Bank (BKB) opened, upon request, an experimental Grameen Bank branch in Jobra. It was agreed with the Bangladesh Krishi Bank that all operational policies of the branch would be determined by the Rural Economics Programme (REP) of Chittagong University and the project would be managed by the REP.

REP was successfully operating the GBP in Jobra and two other villages when the managing director of the Sonali Bank expressed his willingness to start similar operations in the neighboring village. A Sonali Bank branch was launched in January 1978.

Gradually the GBP attracted the attention of the banking community at large. Managing directors of several branches along with the deputy governor of the Bangladesh central bank visited Jobra to see if the experience of Jobra could be given more formal support from the banking system. Out of these visits and consultations a proposal was prepared to extend GBP operations in the district of Tangail with the sponsorship of the central bank and the support of all nationalized commercial banks and the Bangladesh Krishi Bank. This project was launched in June 1979, and field operations in Tangail began in November 1979. However, as the bankers began feeling hesitant about going ahead with the project because of costs and with no prospect of earning a profit in the near future, IFAD came forward in 1980 to offer an interest-free loan of $3.4 million to the project. Funds were provided to the central bank on a 50:50 matching basis to be used for 100 percent refinancing of GBP loans at a composite interest rate of 4.5 percent (instead of the 10.5 percent, central bank rate). This resulted in profitable GBP operations, and the effect was to remove the initial cause of reluctance on the part of the banks.

When IFAD came in to help out the project, it was working through twenty-five branches in Tangail and Chittagong districts and was expected to conclude by mid-1981. With the IFAD support an expansion program was undertaken in four districts of four regions of the country, with a total of one hundred new GBP outlets expected by the end of 1984.

Organization and Operations

The Bangladesh Bank (Bangladesh central bank) has set up and is funding the cost of the project office. The project director has the responsibility of planning and implementation of the project. General guidelines and working procedures have been proposed by the project director and approved by all the banks. Within this general framework, all participating banks are required to hire a number of staff for each branch under the GBP, provide office space within the existing branch or rent separate space near the branch for the GBP unit, provide GBP unit staff with work aids such as bicycles, umbrellas, torches, boots, cash carry-bags. Further, they should sanction loans to the borrowers selected by the GBP unit under terms and conditions worked out by the project director.

Seven additional persons are recruited for each GBP unit. Selection of the persons is done by the project office in collaboration with the banks. Appointment letters are issued by the banks, which also pay their salaries. The jobs are temporary and the persons have no legal claim on the bank for jobs if and when the project is discontinued. Persons recruited are required to live in the villages to which they are assigned and are responsible for finding their own accommodations. Recruitment is as follows: One person is sought for the position of field manager; a master's degree is required for this position, which offers a salary of Tk. 1,250 per month. Five bank workers are needed, three males and two females; two years of college are required and the monthly salary is Tk. 500. One assistant bank worker is hired, usually a high school graduate or drop-out; this position pays Tk. 400 per month. The same salary is paid the one person who is hired as peon-cum-guard.

Each group elects its own chairman and secretary and must hold weekly meetings. Several groups in the same village find a convenient day and time to hold their weekly meetings jointly. This congregation is known as a "centre." All the group chairmen in a centre elect a centre-chief and a deputy centre-chief from among themselves. The centre-chief conducts the weekly meeting and is responsible for the observance of all rules prescribed by the bank. Further, all the male groups formed in a village together constitute the Village Landless Association. Similarly, all the female groups formed in a village together constitute the Village Women Association.

When a new group is formed it is kept under observation for a month to see if the members are conforming to the discipline of the GBP. They are taught to write their signatures, and obligations of the members are repeated to them to make sure that these have been clearly understood. At the end of the observation period only two members in a group are selected for loans, repayable in weekly installments. These first two borrowers are observed for their use and repayment behavior. Usually the weekly installment is 2 percent of the amount of the loan. In the meantime, other members have been told that if the first borrowers do not behave properly, the remaining members will not receive loans. This brings peer pressure to bear on the initial borrowers for good performance.

Following that, the next two persons in the group will get loans after a month or two of good performance of the first two. The same applies for the fifth member in the group, who gets the loan when all four previous borrowers have performed well. While loans are given to the individuals or to the group and although there is much informal interlocking distribution of responsibility, only the borrower is in fact responsible for the loan.

Every group member deposits one taka every week as personal savings. This is accumulated in a group fund account operated by the group. A group tax at the rate of 5 percent of the loan is deducted for financial services provided to the borrower through the group, and to build up a reserve for the group itself. Collection from the group tax is also deposited in the group fund account. The group tax is explained to the members as being like *Mushti-chaal* (a handful of rice which is separated from the bowl of rice when getting ready to cook the day's rice meal); you don't miss it, but soon you accumulate a sizable amount that becomes important economic support.

Individuals have no specific claim to the proceeds of the group tax, which belongs to all group members. Any group member can borrow from the group fund for any purpose, investment or consumption, with the consent of the remaining members at terms and conditions decided by the group. The group fund is explained to the members as being their own "little bank" to protect them from going to the money-lender when they need immediate cash for sickness, to avoid starvation, to meet social demands, and to pay maintenance expenses for themselves and their equipment, even to make a quick supplementary investment. So far over 5.5 million taka ($275,000) have been accumulated in the group fund.

Besides the group fund, group members have created another fund, called the emergency fund, basically an insurance fund for insurance against default, death, disability, and other accidents. This fund will be used to give life and accident insurance coverage to all group members, to repay bad debts, and to undertake activities that will improve the health, skill, education, and investment opportunities of the group members. The poor, at death, often leave dependents with no assets, but probably with some liabilities. Out of the emergency fund a life insurance program will be built up so that after the death of a member the family receives a reasonable amount of money to get started anew.

Similarly, livestock, poultry, and crops can be insured using the emergency fund.

No definite insurance package has yet been worked out. An attractive possibility seems to be the creation of an insurance trust that would be responsible for managing the fund and the program. This would be more profitable and more relevant than the emergency fund. As it presently functions, payment to the emergency fund amounts to an equivalent of 50 percent of the interest on the loan, which to the borrower appears as a 50 percent higher interest rate. Actually, what the borrower is doing is making a "forced" payment of insurance premiums against a whole package of emergency situations.

The basic principle of the GBP is that the people will not come to the bank but that the bank will go to the people instead. All GBP transactions are done with the group members at their weekly meetings. A bank worker attends the weekly meeting to collect installments and receive group fund deposits. All loan proposals are discussed with the bank at the meeting. All discussions are public so that the amount of exaggeration, misinformation, and willful suppression of truth can be minimized.

Criticisms of the GBP

Admirers and skeptics alike voice a number of reservations with respect to the GBP, including the following:

- ○ The GBP is too personality-based. The whole thing is dependent on one individual and therefore is not replicable.
- ○ It is too costly for the banks to make it worthwhile as a business proposition.
- ○ GBP clients will quickly exhaust their opportunities to market their products (as producers or traders). There will be too many sellers/producers around and too few buyers.
- ○ Massive GBP operations will be massively inflationary.
- ○ There will be constraints of funds for a nationwide GBP operation.
- ○ Limited GBP operation is of no consequence. It should be viewed as a freak phenomenon.
- ○ Loans to individuals encourage individualism and selfishness and destroy the prospect of collectivism and strength.
- ○ Credit to the poor kills the revolutionary spirit in the have-nots.
- ○ Credit alone is useless, even at times counterproductive. One must proceed in the integrated manner where credit will be one of many other variables such as education, training, family planning, marketing, technology, infrastructural development.
- ○ The GBP is bound to fail because the rural power structure will ensure its failure.
- ○ The GBP is apathetic to agriculture. Its loans to agriculture are only a very small part of its total disbursement. The GBP is a program that turns poor people into petty traders. Trading is unproductive. Therefore, the GBP is unwelcome.

○ Because of GBP operations, agricultural wage rates are increasing in the GBP areas. This will have sizable negative impact on the economy, outweighing the positive impact from the GBP operations.

○ Cooperatives can accomplish more efficiently the objectives set for the GBP.

○ The GBP is just one new name to be added to an already long list for carrying out exactly the same function.

○ Why can't we stop experimenting with so many models and settle down with one model? People are getting fed up with the thousands of experiments in the country.

Without going into a point-by-point rebuttal of these criticisms, we may however note that all these reservations arise from a lack of proper understanding of the GBP operations.

Impact of GBP

Over one-fourth of the total GBP loan amount went to agricultural production. However, the impact of GBP operations on agriculture should not be judged merely by the number and amount of loans going directly to agriculture. Almost all GBP loans have direct or indirect impact on the agricultural section.

Agricultural wage rates reportedly rise with the introduction of GBP operations in an area. A rise of 25 to 30 percent has been reported in some areas.

Given the credit support, landless people find it easier to own agricultural equipment such as irrigation pumps.

Dives in post-harvest prices for agricultural produce have been one of the most serious problems in ensuring fair returns to the farmer. At harvest time, monopoly traders are known to manipulate the rural market to force the price to the floor. By creating innumerable petty stockists and traders among the landless through the GBP, we can substantially reduce the leverage of the monopolists in manipulating the market. Price falls can be effectively defended by encouraging the entry of many buyers with ready cash.

If wage rates do go up with the introduction of GBP operations, inefficient farm operators will have to look for improvements in their operation. If not, they will either have to sell off land or opt for share-cropping. With many more landowners seeking share-croppers, share-cropping terms may change to the advantage of the share-cropper.

Landless groups may find it economically advantageous to negotiate and manage share-cropped land collectively.

In addition to marketing, landless people may enter into the processing of agricultural produce.

No matter how desirable the GBP may be in terms of social profitability, it must demonstrate that it is a good banking proposition. If the society at large benefits from the GBP operation and if the banking system cannot recover the full costs of its operation, then the society must take the responsibility of sharing the cost. Fortunately, the GBP has demonstrated that it is a very good banking proposition. At the concessional refinancing rate of 4.5 percent, more than half the GBP units are making profits. The remaining branches are close to break-even point in the two years of their operation.

The GBP so far has exploded several myths and dispelled many fears. The usual beliefs—that poor people are not "bankable," that they cannot find something from which to earn an income, that they cannot save, that they will run out of ideas and profit, that the rural power structure will make sure that the GBP fails, that rural society will not allow women to borrow from the bank —have all been demonstrated to be mere myths. GBP group members have accumulated over 6 million taka in their bank accounts. The GBP has not faced any opposition in any of the areas in which it operates. From the experience of individual loans, group members have gained confidence in themselves and are now entering into collective activities. For example, women's groups are now taking loans to own and operate rice mills collectively. They have borrowed from the group fund to sink hand tubewells for drinking water. They have even organized themselves to resist husbands who beat their wives.

The Problems

Performance of the GBP has been quite satisfactory. Despite an unusual flood in Tangail in 1980, repayment never faltered, showing how eagerly and seriously the landless group members have accepted this opportunity. Benefits derived from the GBP operation—in terms of asset accumulation, savings generation, utilization of idle work-hours, generation of self-confidence, improvement of the status of women in the family and in the immediate society—have been far more than what one could measure in terms of expenditure in taka units.

However, problems do exist, including two in particular. One is the lack of job security. Boys and girls working in the GBP units still maintain high morale, despite their frustrations about the lack of job security. Many of them very reluctantly leave GBP jobs after they have secured government jobs. Continually finding replacements for them creates administrative problems. The project office cannot maintain a reservoir of trained GBP workers to make them available wherever necessary at short notice. To get a bank to recognize a vacancy and appoint a replacement takes a long time because of bank bureaucracy. The GBP thus faces a double-edged problem of keeping trained people and finding quick replacements to avoid breakdown in contact with the group members.

A second problem is the general lack of enthusiasm from the banks. At the branch level there is a perceptibly cold, at times unfriendly, relationship between the regular branch employees and the GBP employees of the banks. This may be due partly to the administrative control exercised by the project office over the GBP employees of the banks (this the regular employees find annoying), and partly to the unorthodox ways in which GBP operates. It may also be because the GBP imposes an extra work load on them without any monetary compensation. Needless to say, there are exceptions to this general pattern in some banks and some branches.

Future of the GBP

Within the present project period—December 1984—the GBP is expected to develop a system whereby a project will make itself redundant and the banks will be able to manage this special credit program as a part of their regular business. But as things look now, one may be justifiably apprehensive about whether any bank left to itself will adopt GBP-type landless credit programs as an integral part of its business operation. On the other hand, officials from many of the participating banks advise us to set up a specialized bank to do this type of work rather than trying to make them do something they are not prepared to do.

They may be right. The GBP of the future is more likely to be a specialized bank than a special window in all banks. This bank may be set up in any one of the following ways. The options listed below are not mutually exclusive.

○ A government-sponsored specialized bank.
○ A government corporation, like a Small Investors Development Corporation.
○ A private specialized bank.
○ A nonprofit NGO specialized bank.
○ A private specialized bank owned by the landless group members themselves. GBP group members have already saved over 6 million taka in their group fund and emergency fund accounts. If the government permits (which I think they should), these group members might as well become the owners of their own bank. They can conceivably also create their own insurance company!
○ A combination of the two preceding options, i.e., a joint-venture specialized bank operated by a nonprofit NGO and the landless group members. This would avoid the management problem that would be posed under the preceding option.

What the GBP has already done for the lives of a small number of poor people certainly cannot be ignored. Men and women who were once a burden to the society at large, and their families in particular, became productive and earning members contributing to the economic well-being of the nation. They have learned to live with dignity and to cooperate with each other. They understand the advantage of forming organizations for their own good. People who became frustrated, seeing themselves up against a solid wall, now see a door opened before them, revealing endless possibilities. They can now afford to dream about their future.

How to Assist the Smallest Scale Economic Activities of the Urban Poor: Some Recommendations

Jeffrey Ashe

Among the more striking features of urban economies in the Third World are the hawkers who shout their wares in the streets and the "microentrepreneurs" who repair shoes, make brooms, and sew clothing in the back alleys and shantytowns. Depending on the country, from 20 to 50 percent of the urban labor force works in these smallest economic enterprises, where startup capital ranges from a few dollars to a few hundred dollars. In the poorest neighborhoods, more families own businesses than not, and these families make up a substantial part of the city's poor. Net business income often averages that of an unskilled laborer. The man pedaling a bicycle heavily laden with cargo for ten hours a day might earn twice that much on a good day. The woman selling cigarettes and candy and gum may earn considerably less. In many countries, the percentage employed in these small enterprises is increasing as larger businesses and other sectors have proved incapable of expanding rapidly enough to meet the employment requirements of growing populations.

Despite their importance, the continued growth and profitability of these microenterprises are hindered by several factors. Lack of small amounts of capital is the problem most frequently mentioned by business owners. In the Philippines, for example, 83 percent of the microentrepreneurs interviewed felt credit was their most important need and the most important service that could be rendered by direct assistance programs.[1]

Other problems include lack of adequate markets, especially in areas where population growth and economic development have stagnated or are declining, lack of reliable sources of raw materials and supplies, lack of business skills, and harassment by local authorities.

Since so many people depend on these tiny businesses, some development experts suggest they should be assisted directly. But direct assistance to the smallest economic enterprises of the urban poor is controversial. Some suggest that scarce development funds would be better spent investing in the rural areas or in larger enterprises with the expectation that benefits would trickle down to the urban poor. Others worry that a program that assists some businesses at this smallest level would necessarily worsen the position of others, if overall demand does not increase. Many feel that even if it were desirable to assist these small businesses, ranging from hawkers and vendors to tiny artisan shops with two or three employees, administrative costs would be excessive and the risks of default too high.

While the issues of the best allocation of scarce development resources and static demand for the products manufactured and sold by microbusinesses are extremely important, they are beyond the scope of this discussion. What we show here, however, is that the smallest economic activities of the urban poor *can* be assisted effectively and at reasonable cost. Examples are cited of programs that reach up to 3,000 businesses in less than two years with initial loans ranging from $10 to $300. Our research also showed it was possible to train poor youths in higher paying skills and help them start new businesses and, where people working together were able to pool resources and equipment, produce and sell collectively.

Direct Assistance Programs

The programs studied in PISCES, Phase I, fall into two general categories: (*a*) enterprise development programs, which provide credit and sometimes organizational and rudimentary management assistance to already existing businesses; and (*b*) integrated programs, which, in addition to providing credit and management assistance, often create new individual and collective enterprises and offer vocational training, generally within the context of a community improvement effort.

Enterprise Development Programs. Enterprise development programs, which assist existing businesses, effectively rely on the ability of the owner of the business to produce more and/or sell more. Existing businesses are assisted because the very process of translating an idea into an enterprise, even if that enterprise consists of little more than a few baskets filled with produce, demonstrates that the owner has the required skills and that the business is viable. If properly designed and administered, these projects are an improvement over the money-lender, generally the only alternative source of credit for business at the smallest levels. They provide money at lower interest rates, in larger amounts, and for longer periods. Often with two or three small loans, the entrepreneur can "think big" and see the potential for progress.

There are two types of programs reaching existing businesses: group programs that tend to reach the smallest enterprises and individual programs that tend to reach slightly larger enterprises.

Credit or Solidarity Group Programs. Of the programs studied, the ones achieving the largest degree of success in reaching higher levels of business understanding were the Working Women's Forum in Madras (a small NGO) and the PRIDECO/FEDECCREDITO program in San Salvador.[2] These programs each provided loans to nearly three thousand business owners in less than two years. Loans averaged $10 to $36 in Madras, and $80 to $200 in San Salvador. Repayment in both programs was close to 99 percent. Since administrative costs for this type of program are only 5 percent to 8 percent of the total amount lent, this type of program may be able to cover its costs and further capitalize its loan fund, assuming a very low default rate and an adequate interest rate.

Directors of a new program in the Dominican Republic, directed by the Dominican Development Foundation, adapted the methodologies used in both these programs to local conditions.[3] In its first eight months, this program has enrolled 1,600 hawkers and vendors. Loans have been approved for 450 business owners. Repayment is near 100 percent.

The established programs in Madras and San Salvador and the new one in Santo Domingo use essentially the same mechanisms to extend credit—the solidarity or credit group. These self-formed groups are made up of from five to ten owners of very small businesses who accept collective responsibility to repay the loan made to the group. Each group member uses his or her portion of the loan to invest in his or her individual business. Group members pay their quota to the group leader daily. Depending on the program, a collector/promoter from the program collects the loans for the group from the group leader, or the group leader pays the bank or lending institution directly. The solidarity group commitment is the only guarantee required in these programs.

This simple mechanism avoids the major problems of extending credit to borrowers at this level, that is, poor repayment history and high administrative costs. Promotion, group formation, and selection are largely in the hands of the small business owners. The experiences in Madras, San Salvador, and Santo Domingo demonstrate that after the first few groups are funded, members will take it upon themselves to enroll their friends and neighbors and will do so in a way that conveys an understanding of the requisite sense of responsibility upon which such programs depend. Furthermore, these experiences show that neighborhood residents depend on their networks of friendship and kinship in order to decide who is trustworthy and with whom to associate. It has proved extremely difficult for field staff to understand these networks well enough to form viable groups.

Individual Groups. Slightly larger microenterprises are often reached by innovative projects of commercial banks. Experiences in these programs were also very encouraging. Banks can often cover their costs or even make a profit delivering these loans. Once their loans are made, subsequent more formal credit arrangements between banks and microbusiness owners often ensue.

The Bank of Baroda, Multi-Service Center in Calcutta, administers its portfolio of four thousand loans to microenterprises with only ten loan officers. Each loan officer is responsible for administering 400 loans and for securing new clients. Interestingly, as in the credit group programs described earlier, bank officials group their clients by communities and depend on recommendations from other clients to involve new business owners. Administrative costs average less than 10 percent of the loan since lending requirements necessitate a minimum of processing and supervision. Loan repayment in this program has been about 90 percent.

The Philippine Commercial and Industrial Bank (PCIB), through its seventy so-called money shops scattered throughout the country, provides credit to established commercial stall holders in public and private markets. To qualify for a minimum loan of $125, the stall holder must have average daily sales of at least $7.50 and net profits of at least 25 percent. Loan installments are paid daily. Each money shop operates from a stall in a public or private market where there is a concentration of 400–800 sellers. A money shop has four employees, of which at least one is drawn from the leadership of the local market, thus ensuring that the bank will know that it is lending to good credit risks. By aggressively expanding into this market, the PCIB gains loyal clients, a significant expansion of its portfolio, and an important source of profits.

The money shops were expected to lend $3 million in 1980 in amounts ranging from $125 to $1,250. No figures were available from the bank on administrative costs per loan. It is clear, however, that the bank is making a profit on these loans, since seven other financial institutions are now competing for this lucrative and expanding market.

The Banco del Pacifico in Ecuador makes small loans to established artisan manufacturers with good credit history and cosigners. In contrast to the other projects, this program requires the completion of a credit proposal for each business and the development in detail of a plan for utilizing the loan funds. These steps raise administrative costs to 10 percent of the value of the loan. All field work is completed by part-time university students with no business training. The Banco del Pacifico has a portfolio of 900 loans to small artisan manufacturers. Nearly 400 new jobs have been created in these businesses, monthly sales have doubled, and income to business owners has increased significantly. Loan repayment is well over 90 percent.

Although the projects directly administered by banks span three continents, they share three important characteristics: (*a*) a separate unit in the bank with specially oriented, highly dedicated personnel for this type of lending activity; (*b*) very simple methodologies for processing and administering loans; (*c*) formal contractual relationships, but with formalities held to a minimum.

The projects demonstrate that at this level business owners often have realistic plans for business expansion. They also demonstrate that these businesses can expand sales and cut costs without written records or more formal management skills. Credit is frequently the principal constraint, not entrepreneurial skill. By keeping loans small (generally from $200 to $1,000), having frequent loan repayments, and stressing tight supervision, these projects avoid the high default rates that plague so many credit programs.

Some of those who received credit may eventually want to make more substantial investments in equipment and inventories. The adoption of formal record-keeping and other formal management practices was considered to be a prerequisite for larger loans; without this prerequisite, the borrower had trouble making repayments and businesses often failed.

Integrated Programs. Several of the projects studied created new individual and collective businesses and provided marketing outlets outside the local community and/or job skills training. Most of these efforts are part of comprehensive development programs. Their concern is not only enterprise development per se and the increase in income and employment that this might bring; equal emphasis is given to improving the overall socioeconomic conditions of those assisted. Consequently, these projects focus on needs ranging from health and housing to community improvement. Four of the most innovative of these projects are described here.

Located in one of the poorest communities in Bangalore, India, Bangalur Layout, a project of a local NGO, moved into enterprise development after five successful years of integrated community development. The project works intensively with 120 families that have a strong interest in "improving themselves." With the assistance of a local bank, the project has facilitated the financing of new businesses, with average loans of $61.25. These small commercial operations are like those commonly found in the community, so no additional skills or management training are necessary. Business ideas are presented to the staff by those who are soliciting the loan, so that there is from the outset a commitment to the business to be started. Administrative costs are nominal for this program because it is largely run by community volunteers. Loan repayment is close to 100 percent.

The National Christian Council of Kenya (NCCK), also an NGO, works in primary and secondary cities throughout the country. The vast majority of the participants in their programs are extremely poor women. Most have incomes of approximately $15 per month and have on the average approximately six dependents. They are essentially traditional people in transition toward more formal economic activities; they have very little business experience and very low skill levels.

The NCCK program both assists existing enterprises and helps in the establishment of new cooperative enterprises in conjunction with other community improvement efforts. These simple cooperative ventures—promoted by NCCK social workers with no special expertise in enterprise development—use the skills people already have as the starting point. The groups that are formed market their goods collectively, sometimes through shops run by the NCCK, and arrange for collective purchase of raw materials. Sometimes group members work in the same shop together. When these groups are successful, participants who were often previously only marginally engaged in the economic system have greatly increased their income. Administrative costs of this program are moderate.

The Village Polytechnic Programme in Kenya, which began as a nongovernmental initiative and is now administered by the Kenyan government, provides training for youth at a low cost compared with traditional vocational educational projects. It does so by involving the community in an assessment that determines the skills needed in the local community and utilizes local skilled artisans as trainers. Early in their training the youths sell part of their products collectively to defray some of the training costs. Part of the sales income is deposited in a fund that will establish a cooperative enterprise for the group after the training program has been completed. This fund is also used to purchase tools for helping V. P. leavers to set up new group and individual businesses.

Village Polytechnics are set up at the initiative of the local community with little staff intervention. After two years of successful operation, the polytechnic is eligible for government assistance to expand the program but the program is structured so that the initiative remains with the local community.

In Cameroon, two organizations engaged in community development activities began in the late 1970s to integrate artisan assistance activities into their respective programs in two major cities. The initial artisan assistance efforts of the Centre d'Éducation à la Promotion Collective (CEPAC) centered on a poor community of 50,000 people in Yaounde. Although not primarily a small business assistance organization, CEPAC effectively integrated artisan development activities into its community organizing and training, placing emphasis on the formation of an organization of artisans, the creation of a cooperative for the purchase by artisans of raw materials, and the guarantee of broad-based community control through the coordination of all activities by representative community-action committees. In addition, CEPAC assisted in local marketing analyses for the identification of viable product lines.

Similarly, in an extremely poor but well-organized settlement of 100,000 people in Douala, the Institut Panafricain pour le Développment (IPD) has been building up a local artisans' association and credit union as a basis for activities designed to enhance community self-reliance. It has also assisted in organizing production groups to form credit guarantee mechanisms and for the bulk purchase of raw materials. Further, it has delivered managerial and accounting assistance to local artisans and helped identify and introduce new product lines.

Characteristics of Effective Projects

Every project is a product of an extended process of project design as well as a continuous process of evolution. Most important seems to have been the daily interaction with program participants.

Field staff of these programs are frequently not trained in business. Their most important skills are the ability to relate to people in poor communities and to facilitate grass-roots organizations. Staff must see project participants as capable and able to improve their situation through their own economic activities. Paternalistic staff who see clients as incapable of making major decisions on their own or who see a need to tightly control the enterprises they assist were rarely successful.

No program we studied simply opened a microenterprise office in a central location and started to provide services. It is doubtful that such an effort could be successful, even if tried. To reach the poorest community residents, project staff first have to promote the idea directly in the community. Once the program and the staff are accepted in the community and community residents can see positive results, word of the program generally spreads rapidly.

The most important criterion for selection seems to be the individual's reputation among other community residents and local business owners.

Assuming that the program has selected a good client, the following generalizations about granting and repayment of very small loans can be drawn from the programs studied: (*a*) The first loan should be very small. It tests the individual's ability to repay and avoids overburdening the business with more money that can be invested. (*b*) A first loan to existing businesses should be for no more than three to six months. A series of small loans in increasingly larger amounts paid back quickly represents a manageable risk to both the business and the program. (*c*) If interest rates do not cover costs, financial institutions will have little incentive to lend. While those who receive loans at concessionary rates have an important advantage, many others, equally well-qualified, will not receive loans because of lack of funds. (*d*) The loan repayment period should reflect the cash flow cycle of the economic activity in question, and the time frame in which the *client* is used to thinking. Hawkers and vendors generally pay their group leaders daily, since they purchase and sell their stock daily. In other programs, loan repayment is geared to monthly income. (*e*) Programs should be very businesslike about loan repayment if they are to maintain good relations with financial institutions, encourage good habits among beneficiaries, and avoid the depletion of the loan fund.

Programs should combine job skills training with business training and intensive follow-up, if the job skills are to be put into practice.

Perhaps the most effective approach to dealing with marketing problems is to identify carefully the demand for skills and products within local communities and then match the areas of training and enterprise promotion to these needs. Another effective approach involves the direct intervention of the assistance organization in the identification or establishment of marketing channels for client enterprises in the country or internationally.

Implications for Donors

The number of projects studied is small; the numbers served, miniscule. Yet these experimental efforts show that the smallest economic activities of the urban poor *can* be assisted, often very effectively. Assistance is delivered through a variety of programs, with objectives appropriate to the strikingly different needs of the various levels of participants. Despite their diversity, organizations involved shared characteristics of strong, highly respected leaders who have a commitment to assisting the poor; an extremely dedicated and hard-working field staff who want to be involved in a program they believe in; decentralized organizational structures that extend decision-making responsibility to field staff and a high degree of autonomy that allows field staff the flexibility to adopt strategies they feel are appropriate; and simple, easily understood, cost-effective methodologies that are immediately relevant to people's needs.

If donors want to assist the small enterprises sector, they will have to find ways to work with these organizations and support their projects. They will have to find ways to accommodate and support decentralized and flexible small-scale projects.

There are four levels at which donors can facilitate the projects that reach the bottom of the economic scale. They can

○ strengthen small ongoing local nongovernmental business development efforts, or enable small local NGOs with strong community programs to begin PISCES-level business development efforts;

○ enable larger national NGOs, larger cooperatives, national development foundations, and government agencies with a history of efficient delivery of services and interest in assisting this sector to set up special units and programs to reach PISCES-level enterprises;

○ strengthen and expand ongoing PISCES-level programs of NGOs, banks, and government agencies and organizations; and

○ establish "umbrella organizations" that can service the needs of a number of small local organizations.

Given the characteristics of these organizations, donors will need to spend a good deal more time just to locate appropriate intermediaries and develop much simpler mechanisms for arranging loans. Also, they will have to restrict the amount of money they try to move and help organizations with complicated paperwork. Many excellent programs can be facilitated initially with small amounts of additional funds. But, when additional funds are needed, they should be readily available so services can expand with improved organizational capacity. In projects that assist the smallest of existing microenterprises, a $25,000 revolving loan fund can serve approximately three hundred clients organized into forty credit groups. As the organization develops, the loan fund can be increased gradually. With $800,000, the program can serve from twenty-five hundred to five thousand microbusinessess, depending on the average size of the loans.

The PISCES research clearly shows that microbusiness owners are reliable and can use small loans and other assistance productively. The research also shows there are effective mechanisms for delivering assistance. The challenge is to identify and fund enough programs to reach a significant number of people living in the poorest communities of the Third World.

Notes

1. PISCES case studies. This chapter summarizes the findings of three years of research and program development on direct assistance to the smallest economic activities of the urban poor carried out in Africa, Asia, and Latin America. The effort, known as the PISCES Project (Programme for Investment in the Small Capital Enterprise Sector), was financed by the Agency for International Development, Office of Urban Development, Bureau of Science and Technology, contract number DS-otr-C-0013, Small Enterprise Approaches to Employment, PISCES, Phase I. A second phase of this project (PISCES, Phase II, contract number AID-otr-C-1823) is now underway, and demonstration projects that reach the smallest enterprises in six countries are being set up

and evaluated. The final report on PISCES, Phase I, is available from the AID Project Manager, Michael Farbman, Office of Urban Development, Bureau of Science and Technology, Agency for International Development, Washington, D.C. 20523.

2. PRIDECO is a governmental community development agency; FEDECCREDITO is the nation's largest cooperative bank.

3. A nongovernmental national development organization with many years of experience in extending credit.

How to Create a Partnership between the Poor and the Powerful: International Business in Development

Lee Bloom

International business has an important contribution to make to the future development of the Third World, but we can do it only with the understanding and support of both governments and people. Leaders of the business community are as frustrated as others in the international community are with the meager results of the first decades of development and the progress so far in the 1980s. We are anxious to get on with the job.

Certainly all of us know by now that wishing for development is highly commendable, but wishing won't make it so. It would be tempting if development could be magically brought about by mandate. But development cannot be mandated. Talking about it in U.N. bodies, in the Brandt Commission, in nongovernmental forums, may stimulate understanding and encourage action, but talking won't make it so. Aid, whether from official government sources or private voluntary organizations, can bring about tremendous good. But unless it is put together in projects that become self-sustaining and self-generating, aid will not bring about development. Indeed, even private business investment, soundly based and well managed, cannot of itself make development a reality. The only way to make these wishes come true is to bring together people of a variety of disciplines and origins and to put all of their diverse resources —financial, material, and, most important, resources of human minds and hearts—to meet all of their diverse needs so everyone benefits in the end. The trouble is that, even among people who are committed to the concept of space-ship earth, the tendency is to deprecate each other's efforts. Business sometimes questions whether governments and private voluntary organizations really accomplish anything at all. Governments and private voluntary organizations question business motives. In political forums, it is fashionable to attack business, though privately the same speakers express different views. We in international business accept responsibility for these misconceptions. We have done a wholly inadequate job of communicating with the Third World or even with the people in our home countries. Some of us still hesitate to speak out at all and many are reluctant to risk investment in the Third World with no expectation of any short-term returns. But there are a number who think otherwise, and our number is growing. We know that if we are to prosper over the long haul, all of the peoples of this earth must have a decent standard of living. We are willing to invest without return for a sustained period if there is evidence of stability and an expectation of a reasonable return at the end of the day.

We are frustrated by the endless repetition of political positions in international bodies that has pushed constructive action into the uncertain future. The Brandt Commission strove to overcome this by working outside of the United Nations, yet it too had to struggle to escape the same pattern and, though the final document represents a cry for action from sincere and dedicated people, we are troubled that it gave almost no attention to the role that the business community can play. We had great hopes for the Vienna U.N. conference on Science and Technology for Development, but it too became politicized and lost its force. Out of these many failures, the business community developed a firm resolve to seek some credible mechanism by which we can provide Third World governments and people the kind of basic business and management knowledge and understanding that is needed to initiate the process of internal generation of economic resources and to tailor this help to the needs of individual countries as their governments and people see them.

To that end, at the 1980 Abidjan meeting of the International Chamber of Commerce, the ICC Development Board was established, headed by Daniel Parker, the former administrator of USAID. That board has been trying to work with a selected group of countries to develop such programs, but the board is still being viewed with suspicion. To try to establish credibility with the Third World, we feel it urgent that we establish credibility with private voluntary organizations who themselves have credibility in the Third World and with governments which have credibility in the Third World.

The United States Council for International Business, an affiliate of ICC, has established a task force on the contribution of international business to growth and development. Our task force is to disseminate to business people as well as to private voluntary organizations, government people, and others, a monthly newsletter called "Private Enterprise," which informs people about what the private sector is doing toward international development, what the critics are saying, and how business people can become more involved.

We want to help. We know we can do it. We want to work with other actors in the field, including private voluntary organizations. We invite contact with the U.S. Council for International Business, 1212 Avenue of the Americas, New York, New York 10036.

Dialogue: Go South into the Future: Palaver on South-South Cooperation

Kenneth Dadzie
Mahdi El-Manjra
Donald Mills
Alister McIntyre
Dragoslav Avramovic

Kenneth Dadzie

What is known as the New International Economic Order is aimed at the progressive removal of historical distortions in the pattern of international economic relations and in the structure of the world economy. These distortions are of two types, but both are caused by the uneven pattern of the international economic development that has transformed the developing world principally into suppliers of raw materials and that has brought their natural resources largely under external control. The first distortion is that the relations of developing countries with developed countries have been marked by a vertical division of labor and by imbalances in bargaining power. The other distortion is that economic relations among developing countries themselves have been insufficient and the evolution of their productive structures has been marked by a lack of complementarity. But both sets of distortions have constricted the development possibilities of the developing countries and therefore of the world economy as a whole; they have also reduced the weight of the developing world in the international economy. One can conclude, therefore, that a broadening and a deepening of economic relations and cooperation among developing countries are major objectives of the New International Economic Order, on the same footing as the restructuring of international economic relations.

The two objectives are distinct but also related. To strengthen the material basis of the power of developing countries requires an expansion of their productive capacity and of their scientific and technological capabilities. The other task is to put the material basis of this power to use by developing common policies and common actions, for instance, and by widening their options. The timing and directness of the impact of ECDC vary according to the type of economic cooperation. For instance, producers' associations may have an immediate impact. On the other hand, regional integration, including monetary cooperation and the common treatment of transnational corporations, will result in greater leverage only in the medium to long term. The enhancement of leverage does not, however, need to be direct in order to be positive. In fact, any widening of the options available to developing countries, whether in terms of new outlets for goods and services or in terms of new sources of capital, would tend to strengthen their bargaining position.

One can conclude from this brief sketch that economic cooperation among developing countries, besides being a major objective of the New International Economic Order, is at once a strategy for development and a strategy with respect to the establishment of equitable relationships with industrialized countries. Finally, it is also a tactic in the process of negotiation with the North.

Mahdi El-Manjra

South-South cooperation does not exist. The only South-South cooperation that exists is in documents of international organizations and of international institutions that make their living from such tales. There is no South-South cooperation because the existing international system cannot allow the existence of South-South cooperation. The existence of South-South cooperation would imply a change in the existing international system. But the change in that system can come about only if there are changes in models of development.

Stephane Hessel, chief adviser to the French minister of cooperation, writing in the French daily *Le Monde*, analyzes more than twenty years of development programs and concludes that all of them have failed. They have not contributed to the building of nations. They have not contributed to the guarantees or to the maintenance of human rights. On the contrary, they have reinforced existing structures and have delayed the possibility for the development of these countries. Why? Because of the model of development. In the 1980s people still believe that the problem of development is financial flow. A French government study concludes that each franc in Official Development Aid (ODA) provided by France stimulates six francs of trade for that country. In such a case who aids whom? Who is helping whom when we listen to the cries of resentment from those countries represented in the various international bodies—the IMF, World Bank, etc.—that provide the few millions of dollars in assistance to poorer countries? The money, our analyses tell us, either goes to experts or equipment, generally from the donor country. The recipient country then becomes a prisoner of that equipment, buying more and more of it.

People are trained, but where are they trained? In the country that gives the equipment and gives the fellowship. What happens to those trainees in terms of brain drain? They become the best people contributing to the development of the others. All this has to do with the models of development. The models of development that are in the Third World are totally useless. There isn't a single country that has the courage to stand up and say it works.

The latter statement is not made in a demagogic spirit. A group of thirty Africans, of which I was a part, met in Monrovia in 1979 in a purely informal capacity. The group was convened by the secretary general of the Organization for African Unity (OAU) to talk about Africa in the year 2000. Our assessment was that all the African experiments in development were a total failure. If those models were maintained, the situation in Africa in the year 2000 would be catastrophic. Within three months of our meeting fifty heads of state, members of the OAU, met in Monrovia and approved the Declaration of Monrovia for Endogenous Development and for Collective Self-Reliance. The declaration agreed that the existing models would not do. Unfortunately, the declaration proved an empty document. None of its recommendations have been applied, even though one year later we proposed a plan of action based on "endogenous development" for the first economic summit of African leaders in Lagos. However, the minute we put forward the notion of economic integration, all of the people there became frightened. Doubts arose about the African common market: "Should we have it in 1990, 1995, or 2000?" Or no, "Let's start gradually." "Let's do it by sectors." "Let's do it by subregions." The political will is not there because many of the regimes in the Third World can survive only in the existing international system. They like to *talk* about integration and cooperation, just as much as do the international organizations.

We may even go so far as to say that not only is the willpower not there, but today there are stronger obstacles blocking a change in the international system than there were ten or fifteen years ago. In Africa, trade among African countries is less than 4 percent of their international trade. In the region representing 50 million people which is the Maghreb, the inter-Maghrebian trade is 1 percent of the total international trade of these countries. In the Arab world, internal trade is less than 8 percent. International structures are in fact obstructing the growth of interregional trade.

In Dakar you can drink Moroccan wine, but that wine is bottled in Marseilles, in France. Peanuts consumed in Morocco from neighboring Dakar have also been packaged in Marseilles. What are the solutions?

Recent studies have shown that no economic grouping of less than 100 million people will be able to survive in the twenty-first century. Why? We are moving through the civilization of production from the so-called civilization of the industrial revolution, in which everything is based on capital and production, and entering the civilization of knowledge. In fact, we have already entered that era. Today in the United States two out of three people who collect a salary at the end of the month are people working in the communication and knowledge field. The projection for the year 2000 is that this figure will reach 85 percent. In France reports on the "informatization" of society show that 45 percent of the jobs in France are in the area of information. We begin to see that money is totally useless; money is not the solution. The flow of money is not the solution since the wealth is already there. The Third World is extremely rich. The wealth is in the minds of people. The wealth to develop effective solutions lies in the way knowledge is acquired, developed, and given, in how it is of social relevance.

We have seen countries with a lot of money, and where have they gone? Indeed, where are they going if they still have that money? Look for a moment at aid. Aid is today the greatest obstacle to development. In that connection I am encouraged by the efforts of present conservative leaders to limit aid to development programs. Indeed, I would even venture that we should encourage these leaders in their action since, in so doing, perhaps we would put a moratorium on this illusionary aid and instead strive for models of development that are endogenous and that urge greater self-reliance. They might, among other things, rid us of a few more international bureaucrats.

Donald Mills

There is no such thing as existing South-South cooperation? Maybe. Or maybe we have to find another way of describing what has in fact been happening in the South. Whether you go back a few hundred years or you look back at the last ten, fifteen, or twenty years, there has been interaction in the South. One might find another way to describe it, but we should take account of the fact that there has been interaction of some sort: There has been trade, though rather limited; there have been some investments; there have been regional initiatives and regional organizations of one sort or another. And one might say that these are really elaborations of the theme under an existing system. That is, these arrangements are not really predicated on what is seen as the need to make a drastic, radical change.

We now have a network, a complex of relationships in the South that express themselves in bilateral contacts, in regional contacts, and in regional organizations. In the Caribbean/Latin American region there are quite a few of these: the Caribbean Community, the Andean Group, the Central American Common Market. Whether they are worthwhile or not is another matter, and we note that some of them are in disarray. There are those who wonder, without saying that such arrangements should be disposed of or dispensed with, whether this movement for greater integration has really justified the tremendous amount of effort that has gone into it around the world, including the development of regional economic commissions of the U.N. system—Latin America, Africa, and Asia. These involve greater elements of what might be called South-South cooperation, but again express the notions, by and large, of the existing global system. Third World countries have created their own institutions, both at the regional level—institutions such as the OAU, the ASEAN group, SELA in the Latin American region—and at the global level, associations like the Group of 77 and the nonaligned movement, which may be seen as forms of interaction if not cooperation in the fullest sense of the term.

Recent times have seen an attempt to produce a philosophy, a program, and a global effort. It is interesting that the global effort has centered on the U.N. system, the nonaligned movement, and the Group of 77, and we may well wonder whether this represents an adequate approach. There have been many discussions (in the view of some people, too many discussions), and the discussions have tended to remain in the U.N. system. A look at the nonaligned movement reveals that there are certain operational recommendations that have been followed through—as in the areas of information and producer associations. These spring from notions at the global level, riotous within the non-aligned, about self-reliance and the coming together of producers into associations. The International Bauxite Association and others are an expression of this attempt at self-reliance. My own feeling is that South-South cooperative activities have tended to remain at the global level and have not really sufficiently involved, at the operational level, people in general. If the business of South-South cooperation is realistically to get moving, the public must be involved at all levels. We have not really found the key to involving and informing the public about major South-South initiatives. We must learn to move away from deliberations and the great work being done in conceptualization, planning, and to devise workable schemes for cooperation toward the creation of a constituency. This constituency does not need to know all the details of how you create a Third World bank, but it must be made aware that there is a movement—a movement of considerable implications for the Third World, one that could change quite drastically the relationships between the developing countries and the rest of the world.

The political leadership in our countries is involved to some extent in this movement from the top down, but I would venture to suggest that South-South cooperation may not have become a part of their personal commitment. How many prime ministers or presidents in the Third World could speak for more than two or two and one-half minutes on the subject of South-South cooperation? Do they even know anything about it? If they do not, that tells you that all the work that is being done is not going to get very far. Unless these people understand the political significance of this great movement and are prepared to take it on board as a part of their personal commitment, the efforts are doomed.

The media are also important. It should be a relatively simple matter to ensure that the media get information to pass on to the public. But we run into problems in the absence of the machinery and institutions. We still have not learned how to create the institutional machinery in the South that is necessary for these kinds of undertakings. The point cannot be overemphasized that in order to make fundamental changes in relationships in international affairs, we must be able to create the required machinery and fill that void in institutions.

Further, we should not see South-South cooperation purely in terms of economic interaction. In this, as in the North-South relationship, the fundamental factor is the cultural one. I believe that there are opportunities that can be created in this area. There is already some contact; the African Festival of Arts is just one example of expression of the culture of a continent that attracts people from all over, particularly the Third World. The strength of the Third World lies now more in what it can say and what it can demonstrate culturally than what it may be able to do economically. We must promote this very vital activity while at the same time creating institutions and cooperation in the economic sphere. Another area that needs to be explored is the nongovernmental sector—the Third System. We must engage the energies of persons who do not happen to work in the governments of the Third World. They are waiting for the opportunity to join forces with the people working in the official system to help establish really effective South-South cooperation.

The business people, the private sector, and other people in the productive and commercial sectors of the countries of the South must also be engaged. How much do they know? Have they heard about South-South cooperation? Has the term reached them, and is it a part of the parlance in their world? Some of them are actually engaged in trade, in investment, and in other communications with countries of the South, but they may not have heard that there is this major movement underway to better link up the countries and activities of the South.

If one were to invite the central bankers or the commercial bankers from a number of Third World countries to a two-day meeting with no agenda and just lock them in a room, they would find something to talk about and they would find the word "cooperative." We have to find the means of bringing the actors together so that they themselves will see opportunities. We should not make the mistake of trying to work out all the possibilities from the top and pass them on to other people. That may be one of the weaknesses in the North-South dialogue; we should not repeat that error in South-South cooperation.

There still exists too wide a gap between the preoccupations of people at the national level and the general public. Some of the things that those in the U.N. speak of as priority issues are of little or no interest to people. These defects in the North-South dialogue must not become patterns for efforts to strengthen South-South links. If nothing else, let us at least learn from the failings of the North-South process. We should also not forget that, while we try to develop a major program, small but very important matters can be tackled to the advantage of South-South cooperation in the interests of all people.

Alister McIntyre

Steps in cooperation among nations of the South are being taken, whether as specially organized efforts or as de facto arrangements. Available statistics on South-South trade are very sparse; indeed, the most recent details available are from 1976. However, we do have some overall data for 1980 showing that the value of South-South trade in that year was $92 thousand million, which accounted for 25 percent of the total exports of developing countries to all destinations. This compares with the figure of $9 thousand million, or 18 percent of all exports by developing countries, in 1970. So there is evidence that South-South trade has become increasingly important, both in absolute and in relative terms. Africa is the only region where the trade share among developing countries has not grown, remaining roughly at 10 percent of the total. In other regions, trade shares have increased significantly: in Latin America, from 16 percent to 19 percent; in South and Southeast Asia, from 26 percent to 31 percent; and in West Asia, from 14 percent to 23 percent. Commodity competition in trade is showing a growing concentration away from food and toward petroleum and manufactured goods. In the mid-1960s, food accounted for more than 40 percent of total exports, but its share today is probably slightly below 20 percent—in other words, just about half of what it was two decades or so ago.

Today, petroleum accounts for just over 50 percent of the total, and manufactures for about 30 percent.

These statistics identify three of the major problems facing an expansion of South-South trade and, indeed, facing any global system of trade preferences. First, how are the interests of the African region and, more generally, of the less advanced countries in the Third World to be accommodated? Second, how are we to give the petroleum-exporting countries a major stake in South-South cooperation? And third, how are we to fit regional and subregional groupings within a global scheme of Third World cooperation?

In 1970 trade between Africa and the rest of the South was roughly in balance, with exports and imports both being equivalent to just about $2.3 thousand million. In 1980, however, there was a negative trade balance of nearly $6 thousand million, with African exports to the South being equivalent in value to only about one-third of its imports from the rest of the South. It is not necessary to argue the case in any detail, for it is obvious that if Africa is to be encouraged to participate in further expansion of South-South trade, then special efforts will have to be made to promote African exports to the rest of the South and to facilitate the financing of any continuing trade imbalances. In the end, this will probably require a collective effort by developing countries to support the industrialization of Africa, including mechanisms such as joint ventures and the financing of trade through export credits, clearing arrangements, and so on.

Much the same is true for the least developed countries taken as a group. In 1970 developing countries exported $398 million to the least developed countries, while the least developed exported to them $307 million. Today, the respective figures are $3.3 thousand million of developing country exports to the least developed, and merely $570 million back from the least developed to the rest of the South. So the same negative trade balance that characterizes the African performance is very much part of the situation, if one looks at the least developed countries taken as a special category.

Turning now to the second issue, namely, a larger involvement for oil-exporting countries: It is commonly acknowledged that there are at least three ways in which South-South trade can facilitate the development of the oil-exporting countries. First, the South is an important market for petroleum, accounting in 1980 for 22 percent of total exports by the petroleum-exporting countries to all destinations. The oil exporters have, therefore, an interest in securing and expanding this trade through increases in their imports from the South, which would therefore strengthen the capacity of the latter to import from them. Since many oil-exporting countries maintained open import regimes, direct trade measures may be called for to promote an expansion in imports from other developing countries. Further, the oil-exporting countries are all trying to diversify and to develop a manufacturing sector. Access to markets in the rest of the South may be particularly useful to them for product categories such as petrochemicals, where there is already a worldwide tendency toward underutilized capacity and an intensification of competition for existing markets. Moreover, some of the more industrialized countries of the South are already supporting the industrial development of the oil-exporting countries through technical cooperation involving management contracts and licensing arrangements.

Direct investments in other parts of the South can increase the security of supplies of imported raw materials, especially of food, quite apart from the scope that such investments could offer for improving real returns. A convergence of interests among the oil-exporting countries and the oil-importing countries may be found in a cooperative package that includes not only trade but direct investments in trade financing.

I now wish to touch on the question of regional groupings, which are essentially the foundations upon which a global scheme for trade expansion has to be constructed. Despite the problems many regional groupings face, trade has generally continued to expand, in most instances because of formal or informal cooperation among central banks in the short-term financing of trade deficits. There is a tendency in certain quarters to write off these integration schemes, which may be short-sighted. Integration is a tender plant that needs to be nurtured over a long period of time. Countries tend to be too impatient with the maturing of the process, expecting major and instant results. Indeed it is a marvel that these schemes have survived at all with very little technical or financial support from the international donor community, either by way of assistance with regional production programs and projects or by way of back-stopping, clearing, and credit arrangements among partner countries. Skepticism and impatience have been so profound that some donors have deliberately encouraged individual partner states to proceed with national projects at the expense of regional projects critical to the cooperative effort. We need to summon again the vision and the foresight that went into the establishment of the regional and subregional development banks in the early 1960s and to encourage and broaden initiatives such as those taken by the European Community to set aside a part of the European Development Fund for regional projects. If South-South trade and economic cooperation are to succeed, the entire international community must make a concerted effort to underpin and support these programs.

A global scheme of trade preferences would require at least the following elements: it must go beyond the conventional measures of trade liberalization, involving the preferential exchange of tariff and nontariff concessions, to embody such direct measures for expanding trade as multilateral contracts—a technique that might be quite important in food trade. It must include joint investment schemes for taking advantage of the potential of the global Third World market as well as credit and payments arrangements. Second, it must embody differential treatment to the least developed countries, and perhaps for even a wider category of less advanced countries, in order to make the scheme sufficiently attractive to the different national interests involved. Third, it must include measures and actions to strengthen the regional and subregional integration movement, including concerted efforts to attract support from the entire international community. This is not to say that these elements can all be introduced at once. The realities probably require the phasing in of different components. But from the outset they should be conceptually part of the entire scheme if we are to succeed in building the collective efforts of the South for cooperation.

Dragoslav Avramovic

Finance is another area besides trade where we have seen some efforts at cooperation in the South. Financial cooperation among developing countries has moved into three tracks. One track has been provided by the surplus, oil-exporting countries, OPEC: assistance, both for balance of payments as well as long-term development finance lending. The most notable efforts here have been made through the institution of the OPEC Fund for International Development.

The second track for financial cooperation has been in the area of payments arrangements among developing countries and regional reserve schemes. Payments arrangements can be fairly modest. Perhaps one of the main problems is that these arrangements do not include payments for oil, which means that a key element in the trade relationships among developing countries, as Alister McIntyre discussed, the increasing role played by oil exports, is not really addressed. In addition, the general stringency in foreign exchange, a factor slowing down regional and subregional integration, has affected the scope, particularly in terms of extension of credit, of these payments arrangements. The other regional/subregional schemes have been somewhat more promising —the reserve schemes. These in effect suggest mutual help arrangements among central banks. We have seen this as a form of emergency assistance in the ASEAN group, in Central America, and the Caribbean as well as within the Latin American group as a whole. Efforts so far have been modest but promising for the future if external help can be obtained. In effect, these reserve schemes suggest a mini-IMF emergency scheme on a regional scale.

The third track, which was until recently a vague notion in a preliminary planning phase, is now an ambitious scheme of financial cooperation among developing countries that could lead to a relatively ambitious interregional Third World financial institution extending across the globe. Since 1974 the idea of recycling surpluses directly to the rest of the developing countries has been in the forefront of our thinking, but to date it has not materialized for various reasons. The idea, however, has been kept alive, and further impetus was given to the idea at the 1981 meeting of developing countries in Caracas. That meeting represented a major step forward in the organizational arrangements and the timetable for ECDC activities in general. The issue of finance was prominent in Caracas, and some six or seven expert groups were set up to work on different aspects of the question—joint ventures, investment opportunities, etc. The two most ambitious expert groups—and therefore perhaps most difficult to negotiate—would examine the feasibility of establishing a development finance institution of developing countries and the feasibility of establishing a balance-of-payments assistance facility of developing countries. Both things were given, in effect, to one expert group; after some serious preparatory work, this group did meet in Jamaica in late March 1982. It was quite a sophisticated meeting in many different ways because the entire problem was very seriously approached. Agreement was reached to carry out a technical study on the feasibility of a Third World financing institution on two broad levels: an institution limited to financing joint ventures, development projects, and export credit, including commodity finance and assistance to subregional and regional reserve schemes. Since joint ventures are included, and these resemble very much the operations of the World Bank's International Finance Corporation—although in this proposal the idea would be to stay with the project rather than move in and then move out, as the IFC would—a comprehensive scheme of that kind would witness something of an arrangement in which the entire structure of organized international finance is covered in an integrated manner. Of course, lines were sharply drawn between those who would operate the "big South bank" and those who would operate a limited South bank. Only the future will tell how this will work out. Behind efforts of this kind is of course the need to close the gaps we know exist in the present structure of international finance: joint ventures problems between oil-exporting and oil-importing countries; export credit which does not exist in sufficient measure; commodity finance, an issue that is not yet fully resolved; finance for energy and minerals, particularly after the unsuccessful efforts to mount an energy finance institution; and systematic assistance to regional/subregional financial groupings of developing countries. The existence of these gaps, which were identified in the Brandt Commission report, has led to attempts to reform and restructure the existing system and to set up a South-South institution.

The Jamaica meeting further explicitly requested that the study try to show that the resources that might be available would be new, and not just a shifting around of what is already available through the World Bank, regional development banks, and IMF. That is, it would tap the regional sources for funds. Further, the uses would be additive and not duplicate what has already been done. Finally, it was suggested that the use of agent banks for the operation of institutions of this kind ought to be explored, using, for particular operations, existing institutions rather than duplicating the entire machinery. The reason for this last suggestion is a concern for a truly cooperative and nonconfrontational atmosphere for the activities. It is too early to say what will result from all these efforts. Very serious matters are involved—matters that have implications for the future of the international financial system.

New Forms of International Financial Cooperation

Ricardo Palma-Valderrama

In many different ways an important change has been brought about in the world economy by OPEC. It is widely acknowledged that the OPEC countries have had a significant effect on the balance of international economic relations, urging a new conception based on the rational use of resources. In so doing they have been able to secure appropriate funds that are allocated both for their own development and to contribute to that of other countries. However, there is no doubt that the OPEC surplus is given an exaggerated importance that at the same time minimizes other, more dramatic changes in the world economic order—the abolition of the gold standard, the introduction of floating currencies, and, more recently, the conversion of a good part of the industrialized world to monetarism.

Assuredly, the largest amount of the new funds is handled through commercial banking, which has been operating with those resources it obtains under conditions that facilitate their use for international financing. This initial pipeline has been augmented by a system of financial agreements and agencies addressed to the search for investment opportunities and the financing of development in different regions of the world. The agreements and financing institutions have taken shape gradually, and their action in the service of development and in support of horizontal cooperation has emerged with increasing clarity.

The new financial resources also reach the developing countries directly: as loans that are granted to petroleum-importing countries with financial shortcomings, as funding for projects, or as investments aimed at diversification.

From the moment such funds were produced in growing amounts, they have been routed to the world economy and to the financing of development. They have contributed to the reinforcement of the Eurodollar market, strengthened the system of international banking, and brought into being financial institutions of a different nature. The efficiency of their action is essentially connected with those routing agents that receive the greatest volume. Nevertheless, the situation today and the experience gained may lead to changes. Whether these changes are brought about by the international banking system or by the system of horizontal cooperation of the development banks, they should be carefully but urgently considered, as there are policies that may require revision and deserve special attention.

Finally, it is essential to encourage financial cooperation both among countries of the same region and with those of other areas, by devising attractive plans for securing internal resources and directing them to the financing of development projects and progams that are parts of horizontal cooperative efforts.

New Kinds of Investment

The volume of foreign investment in developing countries has steadily increased since World War II. During the 1950s and 1960s, the dominant form was direct private investment, practiced mainly by multinational enterprises that set up affiliates with 100 percent or majority equity participation. The principal new forms of investment, all of which involved increased host-country equity ownership, include the following: project financing; joint ventures; licensing and technical assistance, including franchising; management contracts; turn-key and "product-in-hand" operations; international subcontracting; co-financing and parallel financing schemes; and trilateral cooperation.

The Eurocurrency Markets

It has to be stressed that not the OPEC surplus but the U.S. monetary policies of the 1960s (particularly the interest equilization tax, restrictions on foreign lending, and the setting of a ceiling on U.S. domestic interest rates) led to the creation of the Eurocurrency market. However, the conditions of the Euromarkets clearly suited the demands of managers of the OPEC surpluses for liquid dollar placements.

During the 1970s the Eurocurrency market undoubtedly eased the recycling of OPEC funds. National banking structures would have proved too regulated to assimilate the volume of funds without the formations of bottlenecks. But since the modest beginnings of the Eurocurrency markets in the 1960s, there has been little recapitalization of the banks operating within it. As a result of the inflationary effect of Western governments' helpless responses to oil price adjustments, there has been a market erosion of many banks' assets-to-capital ratio. Since 1979 Arab banks, whether government or privately owned, have become more actively involved in the continuing growth of the Eurocurrency markets. They have added considerably to their capital base, attracting a large volume of funds deposited in these markets. And if, as seems likely, liquidity in the international market declines over the coming years, Arab banks that have effected an increase in their capital base will be in a better position than many to attract deposits because their capital structure will look far more secure than that of banks that have failed to restructure their capital.

Arab International Banking

The recent growth of Arab banking has been dramatic. Up until the mid-1960s, almost all Arab banking was domestically oriented; small-scale commercial banks operated alongside money-changers, with most foreign trade financing being handled by branches of foreign banks. The first sign that Arab banks were emerging in the international market came in the late 1960s with the formation of European-Arab consortia banks in Paris and Brussels. Their establishment coincided with the development of the Eurocurrency markets. Given the instability of currency, Arab nations realized that they needed to protect their growing economic interests by a direct presence in the international financial community. In Paris in 1968 there were only two banks wholly or partially owned by Arabs; now, there are more than thirty-five. In London there are currently more than fifty Arab banks with an operating presence. In the United States the first noticeable Arab entry took place in 1976 through the creation of UBAF Arab American Bank, but in 1980 and 1981 many of the larger Arab banks either opened representative offices in the United States or were granted licenses to open branches. Several Arab banks are in the process of establishing, or have already established, operations in Singapore. Smaller Arab investment banks and companies are well represented in Luxembourg and the Caribbean offshore centers. In Bahrain, a very fast growing banking center, Arab banks have more than a 50 percent share of all offshore assets, which stand at present at over $50 thousand million.

In terms of activities (other than trade and deposit taking), the real emergence of Arab banks has been even more recent. In the first quarter of 1982 more than forty Arab banks led the management of one or more Euroloans. In 1979 there were no Arab banks in the top fifty lead managers. In 1981 Arab banks led or co-led 26 percent of all Euroloans.

In the mid-1970s a new kind of consortium bank with a more compact shareholding structure began to spring up. Many of these banks sought to encourage investment and banking in specific geographical areas. Almost all were formed by Arab countries with surpluses. Examples are the Bank Arab Español, the Arab Latin American Bank, the Arab Turkish Bank, the Arab Hellenic Bank, the Saudi International Bank, and the Gulf International Bank. By 1979, however, although Arab banks and consortia had become well established in international centers like Paris and London, several of the original objectives of Arab shareholders in the early consortia banks remained elusive. In particular, Arab banks were still not managing a significant proportion of their own funds. The capital base of Arab banks operating in the international market in 1979 was estimated at just over $2 thousand million, while assets totaled a mere $30 thousand million of the $300 thousand million of Arab money identified as the accumulated gross foreign assets of OPEC members. Arab banks had yet to convince their own national governments that they offered as secure and well-managed an outlet for OPEC surplus funds as the large U.S. and European banks.

But it was also in 1979 that a new phase in Arab banking began. The renewed availability of substantial surplus oil revenues within the Arab world coincided with a new understanding of the needs of Arab banking to concentrate large-scale resources in order to forge a more permanent and prominent position in the international banking community. A sizable proportion of new Arab long-term investment was directed toward the creation of new banks or toward increase in the capital of existing banks. The formation of the Arab Banking Corporation (ABC) in 1980, with a capital base of $1 thousand million subscribed by the Kuwaiti Ministry of Finance, the Libyan Treasury Secretariat, and the Abu Dhabi Investment Authority, was a clear indication of a new trend in Arab banking. It was also an indication of the seriousness with which this was to be undertaken. Since 1979 a large number of other Arab banks operating in the international market have also increased their capital. During 1981 alone, ten of the top twenty-five Arab banks increased their equity from between 20 and 100 percent. New banks establishing themselves in Bahrain since 1980 have started with an initial capital averaging $150 million. And the banking system in Saudi Arabia has been injected with a large volume of funds as the process of Saudi-ization is completed. As official reserve requirements are relaxed, many of these banks for the first time are building up foreign assets and a place in the international market.

As a result of this new wave of capitalization, by the end of 1981 the position of Arab banks vis-à-vis Arab accumulated assets on the international market was decidedly stronger in nominal terms. It has been estimated that the combined capital of the twenty-five most active Arab banks in the Euromarket probably doubled from an end-1979 total of $2.4 thousand million to nearer $5 thousand million, giving these banks a capacity to support assets in the region of $100 thousand million. To take the case of ABC, within two years the bank has been able to build up $4.7 thousand million worth of deposits because of its healthy capitalization, which is not only subscribed but actually paid in.

The Arab Latin American Bank—ARLABANK

Established as a multinational bank (wholesale dollar base institution), it has its headquarters in Lima, Peru, where it has been operating for four years as an offshore mechanism for cooperation between Arab and Latin American countries. Its capital, which is fully subscribed, has been raised from $100 to $200 million, and as of 1 July 1982 the total paid-in amounts to $150 million. The breakdown by shareholders is 60 percent Arab and Arab-international and 40 percent Latin American, composed of twenty-nine important banks and financing institutions of twenty countries. To carry out its corporate purpose, which is to enlarge the volume of economic cooperation between Arab and Latin American countries, it is authorized to perform all kinds of banking, financial, and promotional activities and to participate in investments and in the development of commercial, industrial, and service businesses.

At present it maintains units in five countries (a branch in Bahrain and representative offices in London, Argentina, Brazil, and Colombia), participates as a member of the Latin American Association of Development Financing Institutions (ALIDE), and maintains close operating links with the development and commercial banks of the region. It has furnished resources for a variety of projects, especially in Latin America, and encourages actions to identify possibilities for investment of Arab capital in the countries of Latin America.

At the close of 1981 ARLABANK's total assets had risen from $1,524 million to $2,088 million; its operating profit had climbed from $11.2 million to $20.1 million. It had attracted $1,838 million (compared with $1,369 million in 1980) in deposits from the Arab and international markets, and its loan portfolio grew from $706 million to $1.2 thousand million. It had also participated as manager/comanager and acted in other leading positions in fifty-five international syndicated loans totaling $5.9 thousand million, most of which were allocated to the financing of projects in Latin America.

Other Aspects of the Internationalization of Banking Activities

While not a new phenomenon, the internationalization of banking activities has accelerated sharply in the past ten years. The major place of establishment for banks engaging in international finance, centers such as London, New York, and Paris, has more recently moved to financial centers located in developing countries such as Singapore, Panama, and Bahrain. The growth of the latter is of particular interest, to the extent that it represents a "delocalization" toward the Third World of institutions that tap and reallocate loanable funds. The inclusion of certain developing countries in this international circulation of capital is favored by the recent introduction of original methods such as offshore banking. As a result of legislation enacted in Peru, Lima too is becoming an important offshore banking and financial center in Latin America.

Parallel with the growing share of private loans in the debt of developing countries, the role of private banks in these countries has increased considerably. In the most dynamic developing countries, such as Brazil, Mexico, and South Korea, the level of loans from these banks is greater than that of loans from multilateral and bilateral sources. Their growing involvement has led the banks to closely scrutinize the development of "risk countries."

Banking activities in foreign countries are carried out by banking units with various forms of links to the head office. These banking units are in direct contact with the local clientele, which may include, in addition to individual depositors and/or borrowers with host country nationality, foreign commercial (import-export) and industrial firms. For this diversified clientele, the foreign banks offer a variety of services, ranging from traditional banking operations (deposits, credits, foreign exchange, transfers) through investment operations (by the purchase of shares in local firms) to the most sophisticated services such as consulting, franchising, leasing, licensing, and engineering.

The activities of foreign banks can compete with those of local banks. The result can be to promote the competitiveness of the latter through a transfer of technology, to reduce the informal monetary sector (usury), and to mobilize local savings more efficiently. But this competition can also restrain the development of the activities of local banks in certain sectors (e.g., wholesaling or operations linked to international trade). The effects of the competition among foreign banks themselves as they penetrate a particular market or increase their share in it must also be considered. Finally, it is important to examine the way in which national banking systems supervise the activities of foreign banks.

The Case of Latin America

To a growing extent over the last decade, Latin American banking has become more internationalized through its presence in other countries, both within and outside the region, and its participation in consortium or multinational banks, established in traditional financial centers or in such new, emerging markets as the offshore banking centers. The following factors have been cited as some of the most significant reasons for the internationalization of Latin American banking:

○ complementing the services supplied to local customers;
○ boosting the growth of banks that might otherwise find themselves held back, either by expanding the domestic financial market or by speeding up a process of financial disintermediation;
○ searching for a variety of financial areas that are restricted locally, such as the market for bonds in different foreign currencies, their buying and selling, and so forth; and
○ financing foreign trade operations. (In this connection, it has been recommended that the banks of Latin America cooperate more closely in the foreign market, both in the traditional foreign trade operations and in regard to international services and financing, with an active participation in the Eurocurrencies exchange market by those banks with offices in the financial centers.[1])

It has also been stated that although the Latin American foreign debt is adequately guaranteed by its economic development (with growth rates above those of the industrialized countries, natural resources, and potential labor), the region, on its own, does not have enough resources to meet its energy needs and produce sufficient food products. For that reason it must continue to turn to foreign financing. The Latin American institutions are qualified not only to enter the world money market but also to guarantee the loans and raise funds that may be allocated, directly or through syndicated loans, to the economic and social development of the Latin American region.

The area as a whole has some 400 financial channels abroad, which include operational, representative, and branch offices, affiliated companies, and consortium banks. Argentina, Brazil, Colombia, Mexico, Panama, and Venezuela occupy the foremost positions in private Latin American banking participation abroad. Brazilian banking, with 130 varying financial concerns, is at the forefront, followed by Argentina, with 58; Venezuela, with 46; Mexico, with 26; and Panama with 22. According to data compiled by ALIDE, Latin American banks make their presence felt in international financial centers of the first order. In London there are twenty-seven financial institutions of the region participating actively, while in New York a significant number (forty-one) of Latin American banks maintain different types of presence.

On another level, the banks and financial agencies of Latin America have also heightened their degree of internationalization through equity participation in consortium banks, of which mention can be made of EULABANK, EURO-BRAZ, INTERMEX, and LIBRA BANK, as well as ARLABANK and the Banco Exterior de España y de los Andes (EXTERBANDES).

The Coordination of Financial Actions for Development

For quite some time there has been cooperation among the development banks, the international financial system—which has been directing a significant amount of funds of the OPEC countries—and the financing institutions that operate with OPEC resources as well as funds from other sources. This cooperation has made an important contribution to development. The logical hope is that this contribution will become more efficient and more extensive, without at the same time causing unfavorable conditions for those supplying the funds.

The growing capacity of the development banks of the Third World is reducing the margin of risk in investment projects, with each success making better the terms of operation with the commercial, national, and international banks. It is the action of the national banks that enlarges national markets to the extent that they become attractive to the international financial system. The provision of resources so that national banking may fulfill its mission is the responsibility equally, or should be, of the national as well as the international financial system. This is not a vicious circle that must be broken in order for progress to be made. Rather, it is a cycle of growth that should steadily be enlarged and strengthened for the primary purpose of arriving at an efficient communication.

Both the international financial system and development banking exert a demand in the capital markets in which loans are offered on soft terms. The future effect of a policy in regard to duration and risk, stability and emergency may hardly be defined by a single kind of banking. The choice must essentially be shared in the light of the financial requirements and in accordance with experience and the outlook for the changes and emergencies, which have become increasingly pronounced in both the developing and the industrialized nations. As a result, there is an ongoing need for the sharing of cooperative activities. Such sharing has been expressed in a variety of arrangements such as the following.

Regional Associations and World Grouping

Because of their objectives and the role they play, the regional associations of development financing institutions thus far constitute positive advantages for their member development banking institutions and in favor of multinational cooperation. Those advantages should be extended to the regions that do not yet have such associations. The exchanges among the associations of Africa, Latin

America, and Asia and the Pacific have demonstrated the need to strengthen regular and continuing contacts in order to coordinate their actions and unify their efforts. This is best accomplished by a body that would take the objectives that inspire the regional associations and establish them at the world level. Because this is the best way to encourage the formation of new regional associations, it is natural that primary emphasis be given to the world organization.

Such an organization (World Federation of Development Financing Institutions, or WFDFI) could have many benefits, of which the following are worth mentioning: (a) equitable and balanced development, contributing to a new international economic order; (b) more intense regional activity at the service of development banking; (c) encouragement of development financing institutions of the developing countries; (d) support for the institutions that supply and channel resources; (e) more thorough studies and better skills in development banking; and (f) support for the enterprises interested in development and its financing.

The new world body should be, both now and in the future, exactly what those who comprise, sustain, and direct it wish it to be. Careful planning would be required to turn it into a motive cell, with a sober structure and broad goals, working with a minimum of highly qualified personnel having previous experience. This would combine institutional and individual capacities in a flexible, effective, and operational system that would result in general advantages for development financing and for the activities of the regional associations, their natural ordinary members, and, through them, the financial institutions of other kinds and their executives and managers. Direct services might also feasibly be furnished to the development financing institutions that, no matter what their category, are members of the regional associations. Furthermore, until specific regional associations have been established, regional committees could be set up to carry on temporary relations with the world grouping and to advance the idea of the regional association and garner support for its creation.

The major objectives of the World Federation include: a more effective buildup of development banking throughout the world; the individual and collective strengthening of its regular members; encouragement of development banking's interrelationships at the international level; the acquisition of in-depth knowledge of the true situation of development banking and its dissemination at the world level; the development and continuous reinforcement of training; and the performance of actions enabling the development financing institutions, grouped according to the conditions in their respective regions, to carry out their tasks with the greatest degree of efficiency, in the largest amount possible, and with the most promising prospects for the progress of the developing countries. By its very nature the federation should be an apolitical, nonprofit body representing development banking at the world level.

The federation should, at the world level, support the development financing institutions by supplementing the work of the regional associations. An organizational plan would enable the federation from its very initiation to perform fruitfully and become stronger without exaggerated bureaucratic requirements.

Both in its responsibilities and structures, the group is conceived to serve as an active focal point for the pragmatic achievements of its membership.

Now that WFDFI is embarking on its operational life, it is possible to implement its agenda for action. But this cannot be achieved without effective coordination of the national institutions, the renewed support of the international organizations—United Nations Industrial Development Organization among them—and of the World Bank, the regional and subregional banks, and the active interest of countries and governments.

Note

1. See Institute for Latin American Integration (INTAL), Inter-American Development Bank (IDB), "Integración Latinoamericana," Mar. 1981, note on the Fourteenth Assembly of Governors of the Latin American Banking Federation, held in Puerto Vallerta, Mexico, 10–14 Nov. 1980.

Funding Economic Development: Tapping New Commercial Sources and the Implications for Development Banking

David Gill

Broadly speaking, it is painfully evident that funding economic development, whether in the developed or in the less developed nations, is going to be more difficult in the next decade than in the last. All are aware of the problem the international development institutions are having in obtaining additional funding on acceptable terms. Likewise, most of these agencies are now asking borrowers to augment loans by arranging for parallel loans or cofinancing with private lending institutions at market rates.

One significant implication for development banks is that, as they become more dependent on commercial sources of funds, especially from foreign markets, the development banks themselves will be expected to meet international private sector credit standards, and as a consequence, their own on-lending policies to their private sector borrowers will also be scrutinized more carefully. To some extent, those banks benefiting from national government guarantees or those that are owned by national governments may fare better than development finance institutions that are controlled from the private sector. However, even this may not be much comfort, as some of the former had grown used to paternalistic government support and thus may be less prepared than the private banks for closer scrutiny.

Among the many issues that development banks will have to consider under these circumstances are: (a) prudent debt equity and interest coverage ratios for their own institutions and for the companies in their investment portfolios; (b) the quality of their independent audit and financial reporting system; (c) the extent to which they are matching maturities, floating and fixed interest rates, as well as currency risks; and (d) the extent to which they are maximizing their access to funds from their domestic financial markets. A review of the important role of the U.S. credit-rating agencies and their policies and standards can be instructional in this regard.

As has been evident recently, lenders are shunning high returns in favor of low risks. Thus, borrowers of marginal quality are now paying a higher "spread" over whatever the international "bench mark" rate is, and borrowers with conspicuously weak credit standings are lucky to obtain funds at any price. In any event, the prudent borrower must assume that from time to time in the coming years we may run into a similar period of financial crisis. This only goes to say that, in easy as well as tight market conditions, commercial lenders look to the quality of credit and charge borrowers with strong credit ratings less for funds than those with weak credit ratings. Consequently, development bankers must accept that the rule of survival of the fittest will apply in obtaining commercial funding.

The Importance of Equity Finance

The importance of equity finance in the light of the foregoing is evident. Everything else being equal, the higher the ratio of equity to debt, the better the quality of the borrower. One can only express grave concern over the steady deterioration over the last decade of debt-equity ratios seen in almost every country in both nonfinancial and financial corporations. For instance, major international bank debt-equity ratios have moved from about 15:1 to about 30:1 in this period. Nonfinancial corporations in most European countries have moved from the 1:1–2:1 debt-equity ratio range in the 1960s to about 3:1 by 1981. In the United States, the trend also has been adverse, albeit debt-equity ratios are still typically less than 1.5:1. With the decline of bond markets in the last decade, even in the United States, and the move toward dependence on commercial bank floating rate loans, interest coverage, even among U.S. nonfinancial corporations with AAA credit ratings, has declined from over five times the average earnings available to meet interest expenses to approximately three times. The situation is generally worse for European countries and much worse for companies in many developing countries, which are used to even higher gearing levels.

Regrettably, governmental policymakers, bankers (be they from international aid agencies, commercial banks, or development banks), and academicians generally tend to think of finance more in terms of borrowing and lending than in terms of equity or risk capital. Consequently, little attention was paid to this problem until recently, when bankers in particular became more conscious that increased loans for expansion were becoming dangerous in the absence of additional equity funding. This phenomenon became especially apparent to them when the ratio of nonperforming loans in their portfolios began increasing during this recent period when recessionary declines have coincided with higher interest rates.

All of this points to the importance of planning ways to obtain additional equity funds to maintain reasonable debt-equity ratios and to reduce interest expense burdens, both for development banks themselves and for their customers.

The Role of Fiscal Policies to Encourage Flows of Domestic Savings into Equities

As mentioned earlier, in many countries governmental policymakers and people in the business community at large tend to attach insufficient importance to the role of equity finance, which has made achieving this target difficult. In many cases this has led to tax policies that have tended to penalize equity investors and, conversely, to encourage the flow of savings into short-term deposit-type instruments.

If the priority of government is to mobilize domestic savings in whatever way is easiest, it is only natural that bank deposits and government debt instruments will be favored by tax exemptions, while earnings from corporate debt and equity remain fully taxed. This is true in the absence of a significant industrial sector, since such tax policies do not make a substantial difference to the economy. Unfortunately, these policies, while quite reasonable when first established, are frequently continued even when the country's level of wealth and financial sophistication is well beyond the point where tax-related advantages for these instruments are needed.

The opposite policy extreme has been seen, curiously enough, in such politically and economically diverse countries as the United States, Sweden, and Egypt. Until recently in the United States, the individual tax rate on "unearned" (investment) income was substantially above that of "earned" (wage and salary) income. Until four years ago, the capital gains tax rate in the United States exceeded that of most other OECD countries. Egypt went even further and until recently had an effective tax rate on all types of savings income (except for certain government debt issues, which were tax free) of 97 percent for individuals in high tax brackets; the tax on savings income was 40 percent, even for individuals whose earned income was deemed so low that they paid no income tax at all.

Conversely, some countries such as Brazil and Korea even in the early 1970s provided strong incentives for individuals and corporations to invest in equities by having a lower rate of tax on income from equities than on ordinary income. In the case of Brazil, an actual tax credit is allowable to be charged against tax liabilities to offset part of the cost of new equity purchases. In recent years, France (which has continued this tax regime under its new government) and Sweden have both emulated the Brazilian practice of allowing credits against tax liabilities for the purchaser of equity; in 1981 the Mexican government did the same. In these cases, government policymakers recognized the need to encourage the flow of savings into equity, not only by eliminating past higher taxes on income from securities compared to income from various deposit and government debt instruments, but also by providing positive incentives for such investment.

In both countries this came about only when it became evident that the efficiency of enterprises, and to some extent their financial health, as well as national economic development policies were being hampered seriously because of punitive tax policies that discouraged entrepreneurial activity. There have certainly been positive benefits from strengthened equity markets in these countries. However, although some observers will say the economies of these countries have not really improved, others will suggest they might have done worse in the absence of these policies.

The Significance of the Institutional Structure

It follows that, besides fiscal policies and, for that matter, monetary policies, the institutional structure of the domestic financial system is also very important when it comes to the direction in which savings flow, as well as the volume of savings. On the latter point, it is now recognized that "marketing" is very important in competing for the disposable income of individuals or institutions. Households are encouraged to buy consumer goods by media advertising. (In addition, in some countries, including the United States and Sweden, tax policies also favor consumption by permitting interest on personal debt, even for the purchase of consumer goods, to be treated as tax-deductible expenses.) Thus, unless there are financial institutions making similar "marketing" efforts to encourage savings, there will likely be a less-than-optimal level of savings regardless of the tax situation. In turn, if banks are marketing only deposit instruments and no institutions are marketing securities (long-term debt and equities), savings will tend to flow more into short-term bank deposits than into securities. Put another way, if one is concerned with encouraging the flow of savings into equity and other long-term instruments such as bonds, it is essential that there be financial institutions and financial experts focusing on marketing these instruments and related services.

It is clear that in both the old world and in the emerging world there are two broad-based patterns of institutional structure. At the one extreme is the so-called universal banking system, where all financial services can be provided by one class of institution. At the other is the specialized system exemplified most specifically by the United States under the Glass-Steagall Act of 1934, which specifically segregated banking from securities market activities and encouraged specialized financial services through a wide spectrum of specialized institutions.

Most countries, especially in the developing world, have financial systems structured somewhere between the two extremes. The smaller and poorer the country and the less financial management skill available, the more likely and rational is a universal banking system. Otherwise, among the semi-industrialized countries, the evidence seems to show that the usual economic benefits of division of labor normally apply. The developed countries with the strongest securities markets are Canada, Japan, the United Kingdom, and the United States, all of which have specialized systems, whereas the wealthiest countries with the weakest securities markets appear to be France, Germany, the Netherlands, and Sweden, all of which have had the classical universal banking system approach.

This is not to say that a specialized financial system, including a legally segregated securities market system, is sufficient in itself to ensure an adequate flow of savings into long-term securities. Clearly, tax policies, political and economic stability, and the perceptions of individual savers as to whether they will be fairly treated as minority shareholders or purchasers of securities all can have a stronger influence individually or cumulatively under different sets of country circumstances. Nevertheless, in many cases there does appear to be a clear connection between specialization and deeper securities markets and financial efficiency.

National Policies and Regulations to Encourage Foreign Portfolio Investment

It is an interesting phenomenon that in many developing countries governmental policies concerning foreign investment are designed, on the one hand, to encourage direct investment, notwithstanding the implications as to foreign economic and political control, and, on the other hand, to discourage portfolio investment in the local securities markets in spite of the fact that portfolio investors have no interest in exercising control or influencing local management. If countries or enterprises wish to optimize both the amount of foreign finance they can obtain and the conditions under which they receive it, it is hard to see why there is so much resistance to opening domestic securities markets to foreign insurance companies, pension funds, investment funds, and other sources of long-term finance outside of the international commercial banks. It should be noted in this connection that the resources of the international banking system, as vast as they are, still represent only a portion of private sector sources of funds potentially available.

For example, in the United States pension funds alone had estimated year-end 1981 assets of over $900 thousand million, of which about $10 thousand million were invested abroad, including over $5 thousand million in equities. Assuming that this was invested on a market capitalization weighted basis, 8 percent of this amount or about $400 million could be invested in LDCs. However, it is generally anticipated that a much larger proportion of pension funds will be invested abroad in the future, with the LDCs again taking a growing share of this amount. European, Japanese, and Canadian pension funds, which are close to the same size in total (including some $300 thousand million in private pension funds), have a history of investing more aggressively in international (and even LDC) stocks than their U.S. counterparts. They could be expected to commit even more, were acceptable securities available. In addition, insurance companies and mutual funds in the United States are becoming more active in investing internationally, again following the example of some of their major European counterparts.

In the course of discussions in the Development Committee of the IMF and World Bank some years ago, it was suggested that the principal problem for developing countries and companies in gaining access to such international capital markets was the restrictions imposed by the capital-exporting countries. In practice it has turned out that restrictions have been more on the side of the recipient countries.

In a recent study the International Finance Corporation conducted on this subject, only Singapore, Malaysia, Spain, the Philippines, Thailand, and Jordan can be considered to have tax, foreign exchange, and capital importing and exporting laws and regulations suitable for foreign portfolio investors, although even in some of these there are complex administrative regulations to cope with. Most other countries that have securities that would be potentially of interest for such investors have various restrictions to make foreign portfolio investment impractical. They include restrictions on repatriation of sales proceeds, an inflexible minimum investment period, restrictions on investment in a broad portfolio of shares, taxes on dividends and capital gains at levels substantially above international averages and, in some cases, even above the levels of tax that nationals would pay from such income in their own country. In addition to these restrictions, a few countries completely prohibit foreign portfolio investment.

Innovative Financing Instruments

The current tight and often chaotic conditions in international financial markets are bringing pressure to bear on investment bankers as well as borrowers (including development banks) to find new methods to obtain funds. As a consequence, a number of innovative instruments have been developed, while a number of old ones have been resurrected.

Old instruments that have been revived are convertible debt instruments, debt instruments with warrants to purchase common stock, "extendable" and "retractable" bonds and loans, "two-pay" debt instruments, and commodity- and currency-linked bonds. Newer instruments include "zero coupon bonds," "pass through" bonds and loans, issues of warrants to purchase common stock as entirely separate offerings for cash, unconnected with issues of bonds or other obligations, and issues of short-term bonds with warrants to purchase long-term bonds.

In more affluent times, when lenders chase borrowers, such innovations have ordinarily been considered as a means of financing appropriate only to rather speculative enterprises and they thus have been somewhat looked down upon by conservative lenders and AAA-rated borrowers. Nowadays, however, even the most prestigious national governments are issuing debt instruments with innovative features, and the most highly regarded international banks are offering instruments such as Convertible Subordinated Capital Notes with complex fringe benefits so as to encourage conversion. Regrettably, many of these instruments are not well known in developing countries and hence not often used. In some cases company laws or banking laws, accidentally or otherwise, actually prohibit their use in domestic financial markets or in international markets.

Conclusions

These concluding comments are addressed principally to policymakers and to development bankers in countries where there is potential for improving access to international financial markets, or for making domestic markets stronger, or both. In the International Finance Corporation we have worked with governments and with development banks to assist them to develop their domestic financial markets, as well as to improve access to international capital markets. Among market practitioners, development bankers are in a particularly good position to help their governments in this. They can do so (a) by providing the benefit of their practical experience, in particular by focusing on the need for improving funding arrangements, and (b) setting a good example through their own actions. The first means is self-explanatory. The second consists of practical steps that development banks can take.

First, development banks can organize their own internal financial affairs, particularly their auditing and financial reporting systems, by emulating the standard approach used in international markets as exemplified by the criteria used by credit-rating agencies. From this base, development banks can establish and execute policies to ensure that they have a broad base of equity shareholders, both domestic and foreign. This could be important not only in order to maintain an adequate capital base, but also to ensure ongoing support from the national and international financial communities, to obtain debt funds on attractive terms, and to develop new business proposals.

Second, banks can also, to the extent laws and regulations permit, experiment with innovative financing instruments and encourage portfolio companies to expand their sources of finance and improve the terms on which they attain finance. Finally, and probably of greater importance, development banks can help establish new specialized financial institutions such as investment banks, leasing companies, and venture capital companies in their domestic markets to increase marketing possibilities for new methods of financing.

As they do all these things, development banks can encourage government planners to establish the most practical and effective infrastructure and environment for the overall savings mobilization and investment process, both domestically and from abroad.

Finally, in some countries political policies and established mores inhibit some of these possibilities. In other cases, wholly government-owned development banks may have other limitations. The arguments presented here have tended to emphasize a private sector approach. Fortunately, the experience of institutions like the International Finance Corporation has shown that this has worked quite well in tapping commercial sources of funds in the past. In the future, particularly with the continued collaboration of governments and development banks, only greater progress should be anticipated.

Note

The views expressed in this paper are those of the author and do not necessarily represent the opinions of the International Finance Corporation.

Background papers

Available on request from the International Finance Corporation's Capital Markets Department: Conference reports—"Development Banks and the Mobilisation of Financial Resources" (1979); "Some Thoughts on the Implications of Different Financial Institutional Structures on Securities Market Development" (1979); "Fiscal Policies for the Development of Equity Markets" (1981); "The Role and Funding Strategies of DFIs in a Changing Economic and Financial Environment" (1982); "Securities Commissions as Developmental Agencies" (1982); and a supporting document—"Country Financial System Profiles for Selected Countries" (1980/1982).

Dialogue: Money Talks: Sustaining the Monetary System

Cesar Virata
William Cline
Mark Leland

Cesar Virata

Let me briefly describe the current situation in the international monetary system and outline some of the issues before us in the international monetary field. I will not go as far back as the establishment of the Bretton Woods system, because the system has evolved along the way. Now we are largely governed by what is known as the Jamaica Agreement of 1976, which made fundamental changes in the articles of agreement of the IMF. These revisions in the articles of agreement were ratified in 1978 and now define the agreement that governs the member countries of the IMF.

International reserves are dominated by the U.S. dollar, with other reserve currencies becoming an important component of reserve holdings—a multiple reserve system, one might say. The share of the SDR, which was rather insignificant to begin with, has dwindled further, amounting now to about 3 percent of international reserves. On the other hand, while gold was formally demonetized, it continued to be widely held as a major part of reserve portfolios of central banks. Exchange rate fluctuation too has become a common phenomenon in financial markets in spite of the undesirable complexities that brings to bear on financial and trade transactions. Interest rates increased to historic levels both in real and nominal terms. The textbooks, one may recall, suggest that real interest rates should be about 2 or 3 percent. Now, however, we witness rates of up to 8 or 10 percent. A further dimension to the situation of high interest rates is the fact that inflation rates are going down while interest rates have remained quite high. Balance-of-payments adjustments continue to weigh heavily and unevenly on different groups of countries. The non-oil-developing countries' current account deficit has changed only in magnitude and in 1982 was expected to be in the neighborhood of 100 thousand million U.S. dollars. The present structure of the financial system seems unable to promote or to adequately assist the adjustment process. The recycling of surplus funds through the banking system is available only to a limited group of countries, and at the same time the official balance-of-payments assistance that the IMF was established to provide is limited by resource constraints and subject to conditions that fail to take into account the exogenous nature of deficits for many developing countries.

On this basis, one can probably define the issues confronting us in the monetary field and suggest ways to promote a sustainable monetary system. One issue is evidently the exchange rate system. The volatility in exchange rates has added an undesirable element of uncertainty and costs to trade and finance. This is not conducive to promoting investment and production, so the question then arises, can the volatility be minimized without hindering the process of exchange adjustment necessitated by underlying economic forces? Should there be more active intervention, which would imply some perception of appropriate rates or a range of rates? Is this feasible? Can international consultation assist in this process? Finally, how effective has the IMF's surveillance been, particularly with respect to reserve currencies?

Another dimension to this issue of money and finance pertains to international liquidity and reserve assets. The adequacy of international reserves and liquidity has been a contentious issue between surplus countries and deficit countries, the latter being predominantly developing countries. Underlying this problem is the distribution of reserves whereby those who most need reserves have the least while those who need it least have accumulated large surpluses. Furthermore, reserve centers have the option of generating unconditional liquidity to meet their own requirements. The elasticity of the system therefore favors primarily the reserve centers. The system in turn is highly sensitive to the domestic policies of the countries of the major reserve center. Clearly, such a system does not operate in the interests of the broader community, for it does not serve the need of a large number of countries, and it makes them vulnerable to policy action in reserve centers. The basic question may then be posed as to whether liquidity increases should continue to be determined primarily by the reserve centers. Does such a situation promote adjustment? If not, should the SDR be pushed or should the basis for distribution be on the present quota system, which is invariably disproportional to needs? With reference to conditional liquidity for the nonreserve centers, this is the only source from which they may finance their balance-of-payments deficits. Unfortunately, the conditions and terms of such financing have become very stringent, which leads one to question whether this is really appropriate. Can the developing countries sustain their economic growth on such terms?

Finally, the issue of recycling: the private institutions definitely have played an important role in the recycling of surpluses. Their capacity to continue to do so is being questioned, and if deficits continue to mount for a group of developing countries, we can then ask the question whether these institutions can be expected to accommodate such increased demand.

William Cline

Nowhere is the concept of economic interdependence more relevant than in the area of external debt; here, too, one perhaps is reminded of the real vulnerability of the financial system. Today, lending to developing countries represents simultaneously a vehicle for further LDC growth, a lubricant to industrial country exports and growth, and a hostage that increasingly will make it impossible for the North to walk away from the South without jeopardizing its own financial stability. The external debt of non-oil-developing countries has grown from $97 thousand million in 1973 to $473 thousand million in 1981 and to about $530 thousand million if short-term debt is included. The public is increasingly aware of the implications of this debt for financial stability in the North. For the nine largest American banks, LDC debt represents over 200 percent of capital. Bank loans to Mexico alone amount to 41 percent of bank capital and Brazil represents another 39 percent. A default by either country would be a devastating blow. A general default by developing countries would cause financial chaos for the North. But large figures for LDC debt do not mean necessarily that there is a pending disaster. Much of the increase in debt has been inflationary, not real. Moreover, the exports of developing countries have grown along with debt, and by and large exports have equaled debt over the past several years. Nevertheless, there are growing signs of a worsening debt burden for the South, primarily in the middle-income countries. First, the ratio of debt service, in other words interest and amortization, to exports has risen from 14 percent to 21 percent between 1973 and 1981. In the late 1970s much of this increase was illusory in the sense that it really represented an increase in interest rates caused by an increase in inflation, and what the developing countries were paying in interest they were receiving the benefits of from inflationary erosion of their debt. But by 1981, high interest rates meant high *real* interest rates —minus inflation—and the real burden of debt servicing is now higher than in the 1970s and will remain so unless real interest rates fall sharply.

Second, if short-term debt is included, the debt service ratio rose from 32 percent in 1977 to 50 percent in 1981, a much more impressive increase showing a more severe deterioration than is indicated by traditional long-term debt figures alone. Moreover, the shift toward a higher emphasis on short-term debt means an erosion in the solidity of the debt and increased vulnerability to short-term reserves in the balance of payments.

Third, the fraction of the current account deficit of non-oil LDCs that is absorbed merely by debt service rose from 46 percent in 1974 to 93 percent in 1981. In other words, new lending today goes almost wholly for the servicing of old debt rather than for the infusion of new resources for growth. The near-term prospects are not favorable for a major turnaround. The decline of the OPEC surplus will provide little relief. Because of slow world growth and ongoing development needs, the non-oil LDC deficit can be expected to continue at approximately $90 thousand million annually even if the OPEC surplus disappears. In short, the aggregate trends do give some cause for concern, although not as much concern as might be caused by a simple glance at the debt figures by themselves. However, individual countries, not aggregates, get into trouble. If one examines the key debtor countries, the picture is once again basically reassuring but with possible storm clouds on the horizon.

The three largest debtors are Brazil, Mexico, and Argentina. Each has its own problems. Argentina may need to reschedule its debts because of the Falklands war. But each has the underlying economic strength to avoid a truly serious debt crisis. Other major borrowers include such reassuring names as Korea, Spain, Venezuela, Israel, India. The list also includes perhaps some riskier clients: Indonesia, Turkey, Chile, Egypt, Pakistan, the Philippines. But no single one of these countries or even two or three together have debts large enough to threaten the system. In short, when examining the major individual debtor countries, one again comes to the conclusion that LDC debt appears sound at the present time but that it needs close watching.

In recent years, however, it has become clear that the most immediate risk is from eastern European debt. At about $80 thousand million, this debt is equivalent to an extra Brazil in the system. But, this debt has unique political features. In Poland, debt rescheduling has been hindered by the understandable but potentially costly desire to use debt as a lever for political liberalization. If Poland formally defaults on its debt of about $25 thousand million, banks in Germany and Austria will be under severe strains. Already, the political climate has caused a red-lining of lending to the socialist countries, and Romania has been forced to request debt rescheduling, mainly because of the cutback in short-term credit from the banks. The umbrella theory of Soviet banking for eastern European debt has been thrown into serious doubt, and the private banks are freezing or reducing exposure. Because of Poland, and conceivably because of the Falklands war and the reduction in OPEC loanable funds, the international credit market has turned from a borrower's market to a lender's market. Eastern Europe is already subject to a lending cutback, and interest rate spreads paid by developing countries may be on the rise. The danger now is that the private banks which play such a crucial role in recycling petrodollars will cut back their lending and precipitate debt crises. One bank may rationally seek to reduce its own exposure, but if all banks do it at the same time, they will precipitate a crisis. A related phenomenon is that banks react to political pressure and political risk by shifting from longer-term lending to short-term lending. Thus, they cause a greater structural vulnerability for the developing countries. At the very least, the net impact of the change in financial markets seems likely to be a downward pressure on LDC growth as they attempt to tighten their belts in response to reduced availability of lending.

How secure is the world financial system in the face of pressures from LDC and eastern European debt? Why cannot central banks simply deal with any crisis as it arises? Perhaps they can, but there are doubts. Central banks cannot in principle, for example, bail out insolvent banks (those with a negative net worth), only illiquid banks (those whose funds are sound but tied up). It is true that even an insolvent bank, if large enough for systemic effects, might have to be bailed out somehow by the government. But at the outset, one should recognize that the financial system is under strain from domestic pressures. Many thrift institutions face possible bankruptcy. The number of corporate bankruptcies such as that of Braniff Airlines is growing and the recent cases of

Dreysdale Securities and Penn Square National Bank showed how large the shockwaves could be from the failure of even small actors. In the case of Penn Square, only 45 percent of deposits were insured, indicating that deposit insurance even in the United States is not a complete solution.

International lending adds an entire layer of additional problems to a multi-financial structure that already is showing some cracks. First of all, in the international area there is what may be called the "gray area" of lender of last resort. In the Eurodollar market and other offshore centers, there is ambiguity over which central bank bears the responsibility for support. In principle, foreign branches and subsidiaries would call on their parent banks in a crisis, and parent banks would call on their central banks. But it is not legally binding for a parent bank to support a foreign subsidiary although there would be strong pressure to do so in order for the bank to preserve its reputation. If the parent bank is from an Arab country or is not from a Group of Ten (industrialized) country, or if the subsidiary is a consortium with unclear parentage, the matter is even less certain. Moreover, even in clear-cut cases, it is not wholly certain that parent central banks would provide support in the foreign exchange that is needed. Second, there is the phenomenon of the interbank market. Much of the vast Eurodollar market represents loans from one bank to another principally for the purpose of parking funds on a short-term basis until the next long-term loan comes up. But the heavy interbank exposure carries a risk of domino effects. Banks not lending directly to a Braniff or a Poland can be affected by crises because they have lent money to other banks that are directly involved.

Third, capital ratios to lending vary by country, and in some countries, including the United States, capital may be overstated by valuation at book rather than market value. Some countries do not impose capital requirements on foreign lending.

Fourth, provisioning practices vary and may be inadequate. In the United States the size of provisions set aside for dubious loans is to a large extent at the discretion of the bank and its auditors. One profitable bank has made large provisions for Polish loans but most of the others, with their profits dismal because of mistaken predictions on interest rates, have not done so. Typically, rescheduled loans are carried at the full book value even though rescheduling in itself is evidence that the loans have not met expectations.

In the light of these circumstances, what kinds of reforms might be possible to shore up the system? A crisis of large proportion with massive external defaults and banking collapses on the scale of the 1930s is highly unlikely. But, as in the case of military strategic planning, it is necessary to consider low-probability but high-cost events and to see whether the system has adequate defenses against them. The following suggestions are very tentative, but might be possible reforms in this area.

The first would be that parent banks would have a mandatory guarantee that they stand behind subsidiaries in the offshore markets. At the present time, the closest thing to this provision is that the Bank of England requires so-called Letters of Comfort from foreign banks for the subsidiaries in the Eurodollar market, but these are not legally binding. They could be made legally binding, and it would be possible to make similar requirements for all the other offshore centers in order to avoid a flight of banks from the Eurodollar market to other centers.

A second reform concerns provisioning and capital ratios. Continued work, which has already begun in the Cook Committee of the Group of Ten central banks plus Switzerland, is necessary on possible changes in loan provisioning and capital ratio requirements. Provisions set aside on rescheduled loans would be one possibility, and national tax treatment could be reformed to remove tax disincentives to realistic provisioning.

Rescheduling is a third area for reform. Private banks could form a group to better ensure their capacity to respond to rescheduling situations. Private bank response has largely been drawn out and very much ad hoc.

A fourth area for reform concerns insured loans. The World Bank could greatly expand the use of its authority to insure private loans. It could adopt a more liberal and realistic gearing ratio for insured loans relative to capital, and it could begin a program in which only countries judged to have appropriate economic policies would be eligible for the insured loans, that is, a concept similar to the conditionality provision in the IMF.

Fifth, the resources of the World Bank and the IMF should be expanded to enable them to make a growing contribution to financing and, ideally, to make it possible for a mid-course correction, reducing the share of private bank lending relative to official lending, in the light of high private bank exposure.

Other proposals for reform have included private bank safety nets and comprehensive depositor insurance in the Eurodollar market, but these schemes have not generally been considered realistic. In any package of financial system reforms, it is necessary to preserve a balance between those reforms that reduce and those that increase financial flows. For example, tighter banking practices on provisioning and capital ratios would tend to reduce lending to developing countries unless accompanied by measures such as loan insurance or expansion of World Bank and IMF lending. Financial system reforms could help ensure against catastrophe, but the broader threat for the medium term remains that growth in the developing countries will be forced by world economic conditions to slow down. In 1981 LDC growth already fell from 5 percent in the 1970s to only 2.5 percent. The outlook could be still worse if industrial country recession and high real interest rates continue and if trade protection increases. The one source of relief currently, moderating oil prices, is always subject to political shock. Because their own financial health is at stake, it behooves the industrial countries to give closer attention to the impact of their policy actions on the economies of the South.

Mark Leland

Let me address myself to the role the United States plays in the world monetary system and in so doing focus on a few specific highlights.

The relative size of the United States in the world economy has declined over the last three decades. U.S. domestic financial markets do not dominate the world financial scene to the degree they once did. Events in other countries now have at least as great an effect on the global economy as events in the United States. Likewise the U.S. economy, in turn, is much more sensitive to foreign economic developments. It is also true, however, that the U.S. economy still remains the world's largest and the U.S. dollar is still by far the central currency of the international monetary system.

The SDR has to an extent become less important, but the hope is that other currencies, the yen primarily, as well as the mark can increase their role as usable currencies. There is perhaps a better chance of that happening than there is to increase the role of a new currency such as the SDR. However, we still recognize the fact that the role of the dollar is crucial, and that is why it has basically been argued that we have to implement policies for sustainable non-inflationary recovery of the United States economy. In shorthand, the most important thing we in the United States can do is to get our own economic house back in order. In talking about the problems of high interest rates, Prime Minister Virata referred to the problem we face with the relationship of inflation and interest rate, that is, in bringing down inflation, because of the role of the dollar. This is not only an international fact, it is equally a fact in the United States—those who had lived on the basis of inflationary expectations are going to suffer. So one is faced with the difficult choice between accepting ever-increasing inflation that was doing enormous damage to the international financial system and to our own domestic economy or trying to do something about it.

The last decade saw a declining confidence in the dollar; we feel that price stability in the United States will go a long way toward permanently restoring confidence in the dollar. As we move into a durable recovery, a stronger and more stable growth will make us a more reliable export market for others, and, likewise, a dynamic U.S. economy will help to ease the pressures for protectionism. It is our view that the assistance and the growth of the developing countries as well as that of the developed countries depend upon trade. The benefits provided through building up the market for that trade can do a lot more than concessional flows, which is not to deny the value of concessional flows but to say that the other really does play a bigger role. The program of the United States is designed, thus, to give us a more stable economy.

Over the last decade there has been a pronounced deterioration in world economic performance, both in terms of growth and in inflation. At the same time, we have indeed seen a great deal of exchange rate turbulence. I do not believe that either of these facts is due to the structure of the monetary system as such. Rather, I believe they were caused more by incorrect economic policies, incorrect domestic economic policies in many countries, and by divergences in economic performance between countries with sound policies and low inflation rates and those with high inflation. The problems are also being caused by the oil shocks. The oil shocks were what may be called an exogenous event and one that had to be dealt with by all countries, the United States included. They were beyond our control at the time. Most oil-importing nations have since taken actions to conserve energy and to diversify energy resources, thereby lessening dependence on imported oil and fostering economic structures less wasteful of scarce energy resources.

But other difficulties, I feel, were caused by wishful thinking in the formulation of domestic economic policies. We have made our policies over the last two decades as if we could have our cake and eat it too. This is a luxury we now realize we cannot afford. We have relied on the existence of a lasting trade-off between inflation and unemployment. Nations, including the United States, have permitted inflation to rage unchecked and have even at times adopted deliberately inflationary policies on the assumption that inflationary policies would lead to faster real growth and higher employment than noninflationary policies. Such policies have done just the opposite. The heritage of our attempts at this kind of short-run growth stimulation has been both higher inflation and higher unemployment.

Similarly, most of our countries have used widespread government intervention in the marketplace to suppress or replace the workings of market forces and to redirect economic activity. We have sheltered domestic industries from competition and from change. This is a fact in both the developed and the undeveloped world. But such intervention has left us with unsustainable economic distortions in our economies. We face a growing burden of adjustment and it is not by recreating or restructuring the system that this will come about. Under these circumstances we can see that the blame for deteriorating growth and the inflation performance lies more with policies than it does with the system. Exchange market turbulence is primarily a problem of national economic policies. We have had great fluctuations since 1980. Indeed, we have had great fluctuations over the past several years. If one looks at the dollar in 1973 and then at where it is now as against many of the major currencies, one finds that the dollar is still—despite the fact that it is considered so high—below where it was then. Most of our trading partners have been expressing recently their concern over these large exchange rates movements and also the short-term volatility, which was to a large extent simply a matter of the market's correcting itself. The economic factors have favored the dollar, particularly when markets have compared U.S. policies and performances with many of those in Europe. High U.S. interest rates have been a factor, but if one looks at the evidence, one finds that this has not been the only factor. In fact, interest rate differentials have frequently moved against the dollar even as it appreciated. Everyone would agree to the desirability of greater stability in exchange markets. But the conclusion that we have drawn from recent experience is that such stability must stem from greater stability and convergence in the underlying economic policies and performances of the major trading nations.

There are differing views about the role which exchange market intervention could play in the stabilization process. U.S. policy has traditionally reluctantly favored any such intervention. Other governments have believed otherwise, and we are at present studying to see what kind of evidence supports their belief, or if there is sufficient empirical evidence to support it. Our belief is, however, that given the size of the market and given the resources available to governments, the most healthy thing one can do is to strengthen the markets and not try again to call on government intervention, which is to some degree tilting against the wind. This is not to say that there are not certain things that can be done as, for example, in the case of the yen. Further internationalization of the yen or greater use of it as a reserve currency—now that there is a greater demand to hold it and not simply to get it and convert it into dollars—can be very beneficial to the system, and it is something that we could work on. But basically the problems will not be solved by intervention. What may help, however, is an attempt at the kind of coordination proposed by the 1982 Versailles Summit of leaders of the major industrialized nations whereby these nations would develop a program of closer cooperation in pursuing medium-term economic and monetary objectives. This would suggest an attempt by governments to follow the same type of responsible fiscal and monetary policies that will give stability to the exchange markets in their currencies because they will all be following the same policies at the same time.

Finally, the worst thing that could be done would be to try to turn the IMF into a development aid institution. That would undermine everything that the IMF was supposed to be and undermine the basic support that it has always managed to get.

The United States is itself undergoing a certain form of contraction. We are cutting back in our own budget, in our own expectations. We are a very big part of the world, and it is true that how well we do very much affects how well everyone else does, though less so than before. How well the European community does is also very important, likewise with many of the more advanced developing countries. They all play a very important role in the adjustment and recovery. The most we can do is to try to get our economy vital again, and obviously when you are having to cut back domestically on the expectations that people have, it is very difficult to increase anything that you are doing externally. So one finds a process of international adjustment, aided very much by the IMF but also by individual countries—an adjustment to the oil shock, an adjustment to inflationary policies. The role we should play in the monetary system is to try to carry out the most sound financial policies we can.

Part 3

In the Year 2000

Introduction: Helping Them Help Us

Emilio Colombo

Today we sense even more strongly interdependence among industrial societies and societies on their way to development, especially because public opinion in all countries is more and more sensitive to the problem. World peace is the ultimate goal of our thoughts and of our actions, and it cannot be based on the balance of terror embodied in reciprocal fears of the catastrophic consequences of a nuclear conflict among the super powers. New horizons are open to us as peoples of the Third World proceed toward emancipation. We have to redefine the North-South relationship on a more just basis. We have to call for cooperation among all peoples in order to reach a better and more equitable distribution of world resources, to contribute to the stability of emerging nations, and to arrive at a better understanding of their problems.

Individual countries and international organizations have in recent times engaged in efforts to tackle development problems more concretely and to reach beyond vague statements of principle. This increased sensitivity to the development problem shown by public opinion in industrialized countries has coincided, not by sheer chance, with a period of deep crisis in the world economy. This has led us to understand that the difficulties of industrial societies can be overcome *only* with the establishment of an international order that is more just and more responsive to the needs of LDCs. In fact, the world crisis *contributes* to the definition of concrete solutions to development problems as governments —notwithstanding the very many economic and social difficulties—appear to be more ready than in the past to direct resources to the solution of the really urgent problems of less advanced countries. Among these problems, the fight against world hunger is certainly in the forefront.

The Italian government has promoted a plan of action in this field at the Ottawa Summit of Heads of State of the seven major industrial countires. Our objectives were concrete. The plan of action entailed specific initiatives for development of given functions in agricultural production, such as the protection of crops, the fight against parasites, the increased availability of seeds and fertilizers, and the increase of local storage facilities. This initiative represents, therefore, a program for integrated intervention, within individual national strategies, aimed at solving problems of underdevelopment in a realistic and efficient way. It is not by chance that one of the central components of this plan is the attempt to develop autonomous production in the food and agriculture sector. Above all, we have, so to say, to fuse the evolving initiatives in the area of food aid and the structural interventions in the agricultural sector. No doubt, we have an urgent and immediate problem—that of saving millions of human lives. But there is another problem no less urgent—that of preparing the necessary tools and structures so that millions of human lives can be saved, not just on a single occasion, but once and forever.

We are also aware of the need to create solid structures in new nations that receive aid. This is a condition for real development which respects sociocultural traditions in each country. Only if we favor this type of development will it be possible to insert emerging nations in the productive circuit. The modernization of their structures is imperative, not only to improve their present receiving capacity and streamline the implementation of integrated aid programs, but also to assist these countries to become, over the medium term, stable partners within a balanced system of international economic relations.

The Italian government intends to be actively present on the international scene. But our intentions would not be realistic nor credible if they were not supported by a pledge of direct action. To this end, the Italian Parliament has allocated for the three-year period 1981–83, 4,700 thousand million lira, equivalent to about $3.5 thousand million, for international cooperation. Additional funds will be allocated for emergency situations. We are deeply committed to this course of action. Beyond ideal and humanitarian considerations we are impelled by the need we see to better integrate Third World countries in the world economic system and to increase their participation in the benefits derived from active trade among nations. Only in this way shall we be able to assure a balanced and harmonious development to the society of peoples. This we must understand not only in social and economic terms but also in a political sense if peace is to be guaranteed and preserved. In the years to come we expect to meet the challenges ahead with the help of nongovernmental organizations in, among other areas, making widely known to the Third World the availability of countries such as Italy to establish cooperative relations.

Development in Context

Francis Mading Deng

Some years ago an African-American Conference took place in Khartoum. During a reception in honor of the participants, one prominent Black American pulled me aside discreetly and expressed concern over what he had just seen during a sightseeing tour of the city. On a farm where prisoners were working, he had noticed that most of them were Blacks. I wondered what he meant by Blacks, thinking that he might have assumed the Arabs of the Sudan were White. But our friend was well informed and knew precisely what he was talking about. Most of the prisoners he had seen were tribesmen from the south. Did this indicate racism in the Sudan? Certainly not! What then could have accounted for the large proportion of southern tribesmen in prison?

I had not thought about the issue in precisely those terms, but some speculations from a different perspective came to mind. Those southern tribesmen were among the people who flooded northern towns, and particularly the capital city, following the postcolonial removal of the restrictions that had kept the south "Closed Districts," left to evolve slowly along indigenous lines with minimum, if any, external inputs or stimulants for development. Isolated and insulated from the mainstream of the cross-cultural currents prevailing on the national level, the traditional members of these communities remained rather self-sufficient in a subsistence economy, proud of their ethnic and cultural identity, ignorant of Arabic, the national medium of communication, and scornful of urban conditions. Yet, those conditions offered modern advantages that were lacking in the tribal context.

Once the barriers were removed with independence, many people from these communities began to flock to northern towns and cities, some to escape the civil war that was raging in the south, but most to labor for cash, largely motivated by the values of their traditional society, such as the need to acquire cattle, their ideal of wealth, or to supplement their agricultural produce, which in the past they had done through various modes of gathering, fishing, and hunting.

Because the objectives of their urban labor remain grounded in their traditional setting, they work hard, spend very little, eat only what they need for mere survival, and stay aloof from the cultural environment of the city, clustering in ghetto-like conditions, segregated more by choice than by discrimination. As a relief from the pressures of work and alienation, these young warriors dance, sing, drink, and fight along the lines of their traditional divisions back home, sometimes extending the divisions into feuding or warring units. But to be arrested and thrown into jail does not require such obvious offenses. Loitering at night, getting involved in a drunken brawl, or simply being unable to communicate, combined with the quick temper of a sensitive outsider, could trigger a confrontation with the police, and into jail the tribesman would go. Once in prison, there would be little if any supporting system for help. The observation of our American friend was supported by various reports I received from informed individuals about the number of southerners in prisons around the three towns that constitute our capital.

It is not necessarily the utterly poor or the very needy person who leaves his tribal setting to seek opportunities in town. A young man of known social background, reasonable family wealth, and a respectable status may leave for town labor to seek personal sources to augment the family fortune or to establish an independent base that should enhance his autonomy in deciding his future over such matters as when and whom to marry. Once a young man goes into the city, he is among the lowest of the urban low, and his tribal emphases on respect and dignity are sharply confronted with the realities of indignity. The saying goes among the Dinka of the Sudan, "Dignity remain; indignity, let us go," for they realize that the conditions of labor in town plunge one into a status of servility that is tolerable only because it is experienced far away from normal society and in surroundings where it does not really matter, because one is unknown.

Rural-urban migration is a universal phenomenon, with consequences that may well be similar throughout the world. What I am stressing, however, is that there has been a tendency to view development in terms that dislocate individuals and even communities from their natural social and cultural setting, to be utilized as mechanical devices or physical inputs for the development process, viewed in terms of growth and growth statistics. There is a conspicuous failure to build on the existing values and institutions, not so much as constraints to be overcome, but as dynamic potentials that could facilitate and aid a development process that is sensitive to the human worth.

The Abyei Project

Many years ago, propelled by my concern over the dehumanizing trends of change in the Third World, I embarked on a study aimed at exploring ways and means of guiding development to be more harmonious and less disruptive to traditional societies. I pursued the subject in my doctoral dissertation for Yale Law School, using a "law, science and policy" approach. The outcome was *Tradition and Modernization, A Challenge For Law Among the Dinka of the Sudan*, published by Yale University Press in 1971.

The study presents the organization of the human resources of Dinka society along territorial, kinship, generational, and sexual lines and the extent to which it determines the political, economic, social, and cultural roles of the various participants. The study also demonstrates the extent to which a new educated class has emerged that constitutes not only a potential force but also a pressure group for modernization of development. The study highlights, besides these group dynamics, the striking emphasis on the individual within the collective identity, a point about traditional society that is often overlooked.

This participational map of Dinka society is then seen in the context of the fundamental values that constitute the overriding bases for distributing resources, the extent to which these values permeate the social fabric to determine who gets what through the normal channels, and the implications of the stratification in terms of conformity to, or violation of, the social norms.

The recommended strategy for orienting social and cultural development is essentially a method of mobilizing the various participants of Dinka society in a positive and constructive way, building on their distinctive characteristics, whether traditional or, as in the case of the educated, modern. The idea is to enhance their cooperation and mutual accommodation to ensure a functional balance and harmony in the process of development. Along with this participational synthesis is the conceptual integration of the value systems, represented by the traditionals and the moderns, with a manipulation of the integrated model to be forward-looking and favorable to development.

Even in material terms, this orientation could tap more resources than are usually expected from the tribal context. These words from a Dinka chief are quite revealing, if only because of the self-confidence they convey.

> Let me tell you what we have to do to improve ourselves. This wound you see on my hands is a wound from making roads. Ever since the government came my people have been building their own roads. I have always built the roads. Money has never come into my tribe to be paid for working on the roads. And if you need money for development, the cattle at home are all in your hands. Many of the things in the tribe are in your hands. Just show us what we can do with them. I collected money before I left and put it into a box. I came and asked, hoping that the government would secure for me a truck which I would buy and take to build my own area by myself. That is all I want. I just want a truck and I have the money for it. I don't want any financial help. I want a truck and I want tools and I want axes. I want to build schools and I want to build hospitals. And we need the thing that cultivates the ground for crops. When we cultivate the crops, part of the produce will be sold for cash and part will be eaten. Those are all the things I am asking for. And I have the money for them.

After having satisfied myself with a theory of bridging tradition and modernization, I began to look for avenues of implementation. It was then that the Harvard Institute for International Development (HIID) was brought to my attention as suited for such an academic-action combination.

Political developments in the Sudan brought about a favorable climate for initiating the project. The civil war was ended. The area on which my studies had focused, Abyei, was disputed between the south and Kordofan in the north and had a prime value for both. Although ethnically and culturally the Ngok Dinka form part of the southern complex, for historical reasons they had administratively been linked to Kordofan, one of the then provinces, now regions, of the north. The area itself remained a crossroad for the herding nomadic and seminomadic Arab and Nilotic tribes in the north and the south, meeting there or alternating seasonally in search of water or to escape floods, as the case might be. The peace and harmony that had prevailed between the Ngok Dinka and the Missiriya Arabs were being eroded by the civil war, until in 1965 the area erupted with hostilities that sharply divided the people along south-north ethnic and cultural lines, forcing the people of Abyei even more into the war. The Addis Ababa Accord, which brought peace to the south, left the issue unresolved, supposedly to be decided by plebiscite. But it soon became obvious that the problem was far more complex than that, for the stakes of the various interest groups in the area were, and remain, high.

That was when I came to the conclusion that instead of suffering the strains of a disputed territory, the area could more advantageously build on its positive history of linking the north and the south and on the prevailing postwar climate of peace, unity, and reconciliation. I felt sure that if the grievances of the people of Abyei were addressed by granting them control over their local affairs within Kordofan, and if, in addition, they were provided with basic services and a development program that would recognize and build on their distinctive features, their aspirations would be satisfied and they might become reconciled to the positive aspects of their new situation. Their area could again become a peaceful border in which the neighboring tribes could meet and interact in a harmonious atmosphere, reinforcing national unity and integration.

The idea was well received in the relevant decision-making circles on the national level, including the president himself. The momentum reached its peak on both the national and international levels when President Mohammed Gaafa Nimeiri reiterated in Kadugli, the provincial capital, in his Independence Day speech on 1 January 1977, the government policy over the area, solemnly pledging his personal responsibility for the development of the Abyei area. Placing it in the context of the overall development of the province, President Nimeiri stated,

> I would like development in this rich province to be an overall and integrated development. I direct the Ministry of Finance, Planning and National Economy and the People's Executive Council of the Province to co-operate in the setting up of a comprehensive plan for the development of the province by promoting the traditional sector, indicating the contributions of the four economic sectors, and the share of the local development and self-help in this effort which we want to be an example to be emulated by all provinces. If this is what we want for your province, I want the area of Abyei—where the great Dinka and Missiriya tribes meet and co-exist—to be an example of the interaction of cultures. Abyei is to the Sudan exactly what the Sudan is to Africa. This project will be

implemented under my personal supervision in cooperation with all the institutions of the state, universities and international organisations.

Armed with that high-level interest, I approached HIID to undertake the implementation of the project, giving the political rationale as justification for the national support the project would receive and offering *Tradition and Modernization* as a theoretical model for experimentation.

HIID's approach to the development of Abyei turned out to be different from what I had envisioned. Using the argument that the financial and human resources available for the development of the Third World, especially such rural areas as Abyei, were scarce, their main objective was to experiment in search of the least expensive techniques that worked, especially in agriculture, health, water supply, transport, construction, and animal husbandry. It was also important that the results be capable of replication elsewhere in the Sudan and the Third World. Because of the political rationale of the project and the need for positive action that promised quick returns, Harvard was urged to combine experimentation with action. That was what they undertook.

But so modest and research-oriented was their view of the project that from the time of their initial field visit in 1976 to the termination date in 1981, the funding for the various aspects of research and action, both foreign and local, never exceeded $3 million. In a project which, according to Harvard, received "the highest ratio of faculty participation relative to the size of project of any HIID undertaking," with Cambridge retaining the main coordination and direction and a considerable traffic of research experts between Harvard and Abyei, no wonder the local people hardly benefited from this financial input, except for some modest results accruing from research.

Evaluating the Project

My main objection to the project was its lack of social and cultural orientation. Initially, the people of Abyei were asked to identify their needs, in many respects quite obvious; and that was the extent of their involvement. A locally based organization was to have been established but was never realized for a variety of reasons. With considerable effort, we succeeded in seconding to the project a group of fairly senior government officials from Abyei. But although they became a useful link with the people, they were soon to express considerable frustration over not only the burden of their operational responsibilities but also their lack of participation in decision making, especially on matters of policy. Sharp differences began to develop between them and their American counterparts on a variety of issues.

One issue of disagreement on which the American field manager carried cultural insensitivity to an extreme was the use of cattle for animal traction. Anyone with the least idea of Dinka society would realize that cattle are central to their social, moral, and spiritual values, in many respects far above their utilitarian value. They have seen their Arab neighbors use cattle as animals of burden for centuries but have never entertained the idea of subjecting their cattle to what they consider an indignity. The Dinka, including the educated, made it emphatically clear to HIID that such use of cattle was totally unacceptable on cultural grounds. The American field manager, dedicated to the idea, threatened that he had the key to the money and that if the Dinka did not accept the use of cattle, the project would be terminated. This of course touched on Dinka pride and the calls for the termination of the project began to pour in. The American field manager was eventually replaced by another American, who succeeded in winning the confidence of the local people. But much damage had already been done.

Even the argument that the Dinka are too poor to sustain more than the most modest concept of development totally missed their proud self-image as wealthy cattle owners who, far from being pitied, are envied. Consider for instance the following words of a Dinka chief:

> It is for cattle that we are admired, we the Dinka. The government likes us because of our cattle wealth. All over the world, people look to us because of cattle. And when they say "Sudan," it is not just because of our colour, it is also because of our great wealth, and our wealth is cattle. . . . It is because of cattle that people of all the tribes look to us with envy.

As we saw in an earlier quotation from another chief, the Dinka believe that with their cattle and their labor, they could indeed afford development, with appropriate guidance and channels for procuring their needs. After enumerating the many institutions that should be established, including schools and hospitals, yet another chief posed and answered the question of financing.

> And with what money will they be built? They will be built with the money of our people. The Chief must collect the money. The Chief must establish cooperatives. The Chief must hold meetings and ask his people to collect money and build houses and then say to the Government, "We want a doctor to be brought."

I am not suggesting for a moment that the Dinka are wealthy enough to afford their own development. I am merely stressing the issue of perceptions and their relevance to the orientation of development. It is, however, interesting that according to the findings of HIID, "Analysis of transactions in the livestock market in Abyei indicate that roughly one million Sudanese pounds of cattle sales occurred in that market in 1980." I should add that these transactions take place mostly during the dry season of six months only.

Even the political rationale for the project was viewed as a complication and a constraint that it would have been better to avoid. Nevertheless, it continued to spotlight the project, giving it a high visibility that contrasted sharply with the results and encouraging local rivalry, ultimately rendering the project vulnerable and precarious. In retrospect, it would now seem that had the project worked to convince all those concerned about the common interest behind the political rationale, it might have at least fostered some appreciation among the authorities of Kordofan and the Missiriya Arabs. But, as it was, the outcome of the project turned out to be the exact opposite of the intended results. Political problems over Abyei and the project itself soon mounted, erupting into a series of violent conflicts between the Arabs and the Dinka and among the Dinka themselves.

Indeed, apart from myself and the central government authorities, who shared my vision, most of the significant political elements in the area seemed unhappy with the project, largely because of its political connotations. Vocal elements of the educated youth of Abyei, who were politically militant, saw the project as a way of neutralizing pro-south nationalist movement in Abyei. Some of these differences reflected long-standing rivalries between factions of the tribe. Beyond the Dinka, the Arab tribes and Kordofan authorities saw it as a favoritism to the people of Abyei, a circumvention of provincial authority through individual connections with the center, and perhaps a step aimed at ultimately severing Abyei from Kordofan and annexing it to the south. Strong presidential statements in favor of the project went virtually unheeded by the provincial authorities, who probably saw them as merely a manifestation of connections with the central government. So entangled in the political conflicts did the project and the institute become that absurd allegations were being made to the effect that the Dinka were receiving arms through the project.

It was with the compounding of all these problems that USAID eventually decided to terminate its funding and withdrew from the project. Harvard, too, left. The project was declared a failure.

The experience of the Abyei project of course raises a whole range of questions, some of which may be unique to Abyei, others of which may be common to rural development in remote areas. But over and above these questions is the most important issue: unwillingness to orientate rural development to the social and cultural context of the recipient people. I had hoped for a creative use of the traditional human resources within the context of existing social and cultural conditions to promote a self-sustaining process of development from within.

The problem I am addressing is real. Those of us who come from rural areas feel the agony of the indignities our people suffer to earn insignificant material gains outside their contexts. And we are not talking about a group of disaffiliated and detribalized individuals or rebels against traditional society. We are talking about massive numbers of people who belong to communities that are identifiable ethnically, socially, culturally, and territorially, but who are being forced to go adrift because of the lack of alternatives within their natural environment. In the years ahead, this must surely pose a challenge for a human, people-oriented approach to research and development.

The Marine Revolution

Elisabeth Mann Borgese

If the world is one global village, then the main road of that village, the artery of global communication, is, and has been throughout history, the ocean. The ocean always has been of very great economic and strategic importance, but during the last quarter of a century the uses of the ocean have undergone a transformation, which can be rightly termed a "Marine Revolution." In the future the economic and strategic importance of the ocean to the members of the world community will be far greater than it ever was before.

First, our generation is witnessing a development that is not only of economic or historical but of evolutionary importance to humankind: that is, the transition from an economy based on gathering and hunting in the oceans to an economy based on cultivating aquatic plants and husbanding aquatic animals—the large-scale introduction of *aquaculture*. Aquaculture is growing by leaps and bounds, while fisheries are stagnating or decreasing. Today about 15 percent of aquatic food production is cultured, and it is an easy prediction that within about two generations world fishery will be transformed into a culture in the sense that there will be human intervention in the life cycle of any commercially fished species. The oceans, which in the past have made a minor contribution to world food stocks, may make a major input in the future.

Second, over the next fifty years we may witness a shift from land-based mining to ocean mining, with significant consequences for the structure of economic international relations and the relations between industrialized countries and developing countries. At present three sectors of ocean mining are scientifically and technologically almost ready for commercial production. These include the manganese nodules of the deep seabed, the metalliferous muds in the middle of the Red Sea, and the polymetallic sulphides along the rifts near the Galapagos Islands and along the west coast of the United States. The future may bring many other possibilities. The shift may be explained by the desire to avoid conflicts with competing land use and for lower labor costs, cheaper transportation, and less environmental impact—although this latter needs a lot more study. Humankind will have to learn to handle this new sector of the international economic order with far greater care than it has handled the land-based sector; otherwise, the results may be even more catastrophic than they have been on land.

Third, the oceans are capable of making a significant contribution to the world energy supply. Here again, science has already prepared for an industrial take-off. Energy from tides, waves, currents, thermogradients, salinity gradients, and marine biomass may provide alternatives to today's options, which are either near exhaustion or not viable.

Legislating the Marine Revolution

The Third United Nations Conference on the Law of the Sea adopted in April 1981 a Convention on the Law of the Sea. While it has undoubtedly many defects, it is a unique document—a "constitution" for the oceans that is path-breaking in many respects.

To summarize very briefly, the Convention on the Law of the Sea—consisting of 320 articles in seventeen parts plus nine technical annexes—defines delimitations and jurisdictions, rights and responsibilities of states in various traditional and innovative ocean zones: (a) a Territorial Sea of 12 miles, a contiguous zone of 12 miles, an economic zone of 200 miles, a continental shelf of up to 350 miles; (b) the high seas beyond the limits of national jurisdiction; and (c) the seabed beyond the limits of national jurisdiction—perhaps the greatest innovation, since the seabed, together with its mineral resources, has been declared the common heritage of mankind.

The convention deals with all major uses of the ocean but provides an institutional framework for only one of them—the International Seabed Authority. The authority will manage the exploration and exploitation of the mineral resources of the international area. The convention does not create an institutional framework for other oceanic uses but is satisfied with references to "The Competent International Institutions." The sixty-two references necessitate many changes in these institutions to enable them to cope with their own responsibilities.

Incomplete though it is, the convention is an extremely important document and signifies the transition from an obsolete and untenable system of laissez-faire in the oceans to a system of management. It also creates international environmental law and a dispute settlement system that is the most comprehensive and the most binding in existence, thus contributing to the maintenance of peace.

An Irreversible Process

The ratification and application of the convention cannot be stopped—not by any nation or group of nations, no matter how powerful. Long before its adoption, the convention triggered a series of developments so broad as to be irreversible. One example of this is the concept of the economic zone. So many countries have declared, unilaterally, economic zones of their own that this is already being recognized as customary international law.

A further example is national legislation and the building of national infrastructure: Coastal states are increasingly occupied with the drafting of national legislation to regulate and manage the utilization of their economic zones and to implement the new Law of the Sea even before it is ratified. Thus the international law made by the convention is being internalized much faster than is usually the case with conventions.

Yet another example of the irreversibility of the convention lies in the field of regional cooperation and organization. The provisions on the management of living resources, the protection of the environment, marine scientific research, and technology transfer have triggered a global movement toward regional cooperation and organization, articulated in the Regional Seas Programme of the United Nations Environment Programme (UNEP). There are now ten such programs with their conventions, protocols, plans of action, and financial arrangements covering one ocean region after another. All this is a consequence of the convention, although it anticipates and explains the convention even before it is signed.[1]

Two final examples of the entrenchment of the process are evidenced in the restructuring and strengthening of the United Nations' specialized agencies and institutions dealing with the oceans—the "competent international organizations"—and in the management of seabed mining. Within the United Nations one can envision three new directions in restructuring the organization. They will become more operational, less merely coordinating. Second, for this they will require higher levels of funding, which may conceivably be achieved through systems of international taxation as provided for in the case of the seabed authority: this, obviously, is going to exercise some influence on the rest of the U.N. system. Third, there would be better coordination or integration of policies among these organizations, considering that the problems of the oceans are closely interrelated and need to be considered as a whole. Here too, responding to historical necessity, this evolution is already in course, anticipating and further developing the Convention on the Law of the Sea.

Here something very surprising and very paradoxical has happened. It was feared that while all other matters would take their due course, nothing could be done about seabed mining until the convention would come into force. Requiring sixty ratifications, this might have taken quite some time.

However, resolutions adopted as integral parts of the convention package radically change this situation. Resolution I established a Preparatory Commission; Resolution II established an Interim Regime for Seabed Exploration, Research and Development, including protection of preparatory investments, on the one hand, and development cooperation including transfer of technology, on the other. Resolution II also bestows considerable functions and powers on the Preparatory Commission, enabling it for all practical purposes to function as an interim regime.

It is interesting that for the establishment of this regime only fifty signatures are necessary rather than sixty ratifications. The fifty signatures will undoubtedly be obtained immediately and without any difficulty.

It will be the task of the commission to adjust from the legal concepts of the 1970s on which the structure and functions of the Seabed Authority in the convention are based to the economic and technological realities of the 1980s and 1990s. This I am sure can be done.

Note

1. On 6 Dec. 1982, 119 nations signed the convention at a meeting in Montego Bay, Jamaica. The final act of the conference on the Law of the Sea was signed by 143 nations. Being signatory to the final act but not the convention entitles a nation to attend future meetings of the Preparatory Commission as a nonvoting observer. Some industrial nations, including the United States and the United Kingdom, did *not* sign the convention but did sign the final act.

Monetronics and Informatics

Frank Feather

I propose that we look at the world money game with a slightly different perspective and seek the possible connections between a new international economic order and the new world information and communications order.

In the microelectronic computer revolution, which is as significant as the agricultural and industrial revolutions, the impact on international banking is phenomenal. We have created an international banking or gambling casino where billions change hands daily around the clock. This electronic money chases its own tail around the globe with changes in time zones, searching out the highest interest rates on a minute-by-minute basis and increasing the velocity of money exponentially. Most international bankers do not understand this phenomenon, but they are caught up and cannot get out of playing the game. The system is in motion and cannot be stopped.

Every banker knows that when you accept a deposit and on-lend it, that money soon comes back in the form of another deposit. In domestic banking there is a restraint on this in that reserves have to be kept against deposits, so eventually the money dwindles and cannot be recycled in that fashion. In international banking there are no such reserves. The money is lent out at electronic speed and is ballooning on the Eurodollar market, the Asiadollar market, and so on. How high it will go nobody really knows. The microelectronic revolution has precipitated the rapid growth in the so-called information-based society. Information or knowledge workers now make up about 70 percent of the work force in North America. Information or knowledge, I would venture, is the new stock in trade of the majority of postindustrial enterprises in North America. It is the new economic good. Yet, the value of all this information does not appear in any company balance sheet, unless it is in the form of a patent or a copyright. Only the cost of producing the information exists, and yet we know that that information is actually worth much more than that cost. Consequently, neither does it appear in any government's national account figures, and this anomaly comes on top of the discussions about human resource and inflation accounting, topics with which the international accounting profession have been unable to come to grips during the past decade. It seems to me that a company's two most valuable assets—its human resources, which are written off at cost, and its information knowledge, which is also written off at cost—do not appear on its balance sheets. Yet these balance sheets record assets acquired at historical costs: costs since discounted through depreciation at a time when the world is being ravaged by price inflation. Such company balance sheets and profit-and-loss statements are simply not worth the paper that they are printed on, and yet they are the basis of our international economic system. As a former banker, I myself have lent millions of dollars day after day based on balance sheets that are not structured according to the real world situation.

Let us also not forget that money is only a score-keeping system. It was created when people felt the need for a medium of exchange, a medium that has changed with human evolution. When we learned to write, we moved to paper money, to writing checks, bills of exchange, promissory notes, and so on. We are now in the world of electronic money, which is blip money. It no longer actually exists on a piece of paper. That "money" is still founded on trust that there is value behind it and that it exists; if you see a balance sheet or a bank statement of your account, you believe that there is money behind it sitting in a bank. More and more transactions are done electronically, and unless you actually have money in your pocket to spend, you never see the money that you are actually using. It would perhaps be healthy to pause for a moment to reflect on the real meaning of money. It is nothing more than a psychological score-keeping system that we have invented and which is now in danger of collapsing as an international system.

In the new electronic world, big corporations are driven to invest and borrow in any currency on an overnight or even minute-to-minute basis. Some firms now make more paper profits or horrendous losses from currency and investment speculation than they do from producing actual material goods. Many even find that the best available investment is to invest in themselves, not through capital investment, but by buying up their own shares. Money has clearly diverged from being the same as real world production. We are now dealing with a system of information about money. This new money is speeded up at electronic velocity and is now so difficult to track that national agencies are revising their methods of counting it. Thus, the U.S. Federal Reserve board and others seem to repeatedly revamp their money supply indicators. Against this somewhat chaotic background, the various players of the world money game try to change the rules of that game in their own favor. The countries of the North raise protective trade barriers to protect themselves from imports from Third World debtor countries. This action, on the other hand, forces the industrialized countries to keep extending loans to the LDCs in a fool's game in which it is easier for an industrialized country to meet an unrepayable loan with printed money than to shut down one of its own uncompetitive industrial plants. OPEC redirects its petrodollars at will, much to the consternation of banks in the developed world that either chase the petrodollar through the ballooning Eurodollar and Asiadollar markets or are forced to roll over LDC loans. Many LDCs can never repay their loans under existing circumstances. The industrialized countries will either have to write these loans off, collect on the debt by "repossessing the country," or seriously try to create a new global monetary framework.

In a world where money and information flow around at an electronic speed, it is necessary to create new or substantially changed institutions that will recognize this fact. A new global management system to control both money and information—which are equally intangible—in the interest of all the players of the world monetary game, the information game, and the information about money game, is vital. We need a new international economic order. We need a new world information order. But they are so intertwined that they are one and the same. This is the direction that we must pursue in the years to come.

"I Think I Can . . . I Think I Can . . . ": New Engines for Development: Assisting Small and Medium-sized Economic Units

Luigi Coccioli

In the last few years the importance of the role played by small and medium-sized firms in countries with a longer industrial history has been rediscovered because of the special features that characterize them. Mainly, these are their essential role in increasing the flexibility of the structure of industry; their good industrial relations; the wide range of opportunities this situation offers entrepreneurs to acquire the skills and competence that will enable them to take the initiative and accept responsibility. In more recently industrialized countries—to use the definition given by Fua in his report to the OECD on the problems of late development in Europe[1]—there is yet another still more important reason for the interest shown in small industries: the vital role they play in creating employment.

According to Fua, the proportion of jobs presently provided by small businesses compared with the total number of employed in the countries we are referring to is so great that the highest feasible growth rate of large industry would not compensate for even a modest decline in the number of jobs provided by small-scale businesses. It must also be remembered that the amount of capital required for each person employed is significantly lower in small and medium-sized firms. A few facts will suffice to demonstrate the enormous importance of small business in every industrial system.

Small Business in the Larger Industrial System

A survey carried out by the EEC as far back as 1966 has already shown that small and medium-sized businesses produce a very high percentage of the total product in all of the most industrialized countries and employ a high percentage of the labor force, a percentage that is not undergoing any decrease.[2] By 1971 this was confirmed by an OECD report that estimated that in EEC countries more than 75 percent of industrial firms employed fewer than fifty people. Furthermore, the report underlined the fact that the importance of small and medium-sized firms in a country's economy cannot simply be measured in statistical terms: they produce a range of specialized articles in relatively small quantities and satisfy many of the needs and services of their local communities rapidly and cheaply; they can take decisions more quickly than large business and their overheads are not so high. In this period of increasing concentration of economic power, they offer great opportunities for individual initiative.

A closer examination of Italy's experience in this field reveals three fundamental elements: (a) the high incidence both in terms of employees and in terms of gross product that small firms have in the industrial structure of the country; (b) the determining role played by small industry in the development that occurred in the 1960s; (c) the fact that many vital sectors of Italian industry owe their strength to the role played by small industries. A historical analysis of the role of small-scale business in the development of the Italian economy in the twentieth century reveals that the growth and spread of small firms constitute one of the main factors in the first phase of the country's industrialization.

Small and medium-sized firms penetrate backward areas, introducing the methods of industrial production that act as the stimulus that sparks the evolution of local craft industries. This process of industrialization consists in setting up a vast number of new businesses and the conversion of small craft industries into modern capitalistic industries.

Another aspect of this type of growth is that areas in which industrialization occurred at an earlier date develop more advanced forms of production and productive sectors with a higher technological content, while economic activities that are less innovative are transferred to peripheral areas. In so doing, first, the traditional centers of industrial development reach a higher level of maturity. Second, industrial activity in the peripheral areas expands to cover even greater parts of these areas. Moreover, the increasing industrialization of these same areas increases the rate of expulsion from the more advanced centers of activity, thus intensifying the development of the aforesaid peripheral areas. When the capacity for expansion reaches its apex, rationalization takes over to consolidate the progress that has been made.

Small Firms in the Modernization Process

A great deal of the literature on the economics of underdevelopment has examined the problem of small firms, and the numerous writers have come to very different conclusions. One current of thought, which draws on the models of unbalanced growth (Hirschman, Streeten, Dobb) and polarized development (Perroux), sees the small production units as the typical expression of the "traditional," "backward," or "subsistence" sectors.[3] This school of thought maintains that small firms have a very low level of productivity and that their sole contribution to potential development is as reservoirs of low-cost labor to satisfy the growth needs of the modern capitalistic sector, which consists of large and medium-sized firms.

A second school of thought, which draws on the models of balanced and gradual growth (Nurske, Rosenstein-Rodan), takes the opposite viewpoint, seeing small and medium-sized firms as the principal source of entrepreneurship and as the ideal base for the process of modernization and the gradual spread of industrialization over the entire territory, exploiting principally local natural and human resources.[4]

Although the first interpretation—which emphasizes the view that big industry has the greatest "pushing effects" on the rest of the economy—could explain the dynamics in some Third World countries, especially those that are least industrialized, it is totally inadequate for describing the transformation in and the role of small firms. This is especially true for countries such as Brazil, Mexico, Argentina, Nigeria, and South Korea, in which the process of industrialization—though not yet very advanced—has gone beyond the phase of exclusive concentration on the exportation of raw materials to a situation whereby these countries now produce goods they previously imported. Here, the foundations have been laid for the use of and the conversion of the preexisting traditional small firms into small "modern," competitive units that can introduce technological innovation in the economic structure.

Two further models can be useful for the interpretation of the rise and growth of small-scale production units: "satellite firms"[5] and "international subcontracting."[6] The presence of small satellite firms in an area in which peripheral traditional firms operate in light industry is of greater importance in those areas (especially in South America) where the process of industrialization by import-substitution has reached a higher stage of development. This has resulted in the creation of small, highly specialized, and innovative firms that are especially active in industrial subcontracting: for example, parts in the automobile sector in Brazil and Mexico.

International subcontracting, however, seems to be concentrated in specific geographic areas and economic sectors: in the former, certain Southeast Asian states (Hong Kong, Singapore, Taiwan, South Korea, the Philippines, and Malaysia), some Mediterranean countries (Portugal, Turkey, Greece, Morocco, and Tunisia) and parts of Latin America (Jamaica, Mexico); in the latter, certain "traditional" economic sectors (textiles-clothing, toys), "mature" sectors (electrical household appliances, industrial vehicles, cars), or "new" sectors (electronic). These three sectors have a common feature—they require a large labor force, at least during certain stages of the manufacturing process.

In recent years several governments of less developed countries have attempted to stimulate international subcontracting and export-oriented investments with the aim both of improving their trade balances and of accelerating the rate at which jobs are created in industry to meet the sharp rise in their populations. It must, however, be pointed out that such strategies have very precise limitations, especially because a situation arises in which the national economy is difficult to control because it is dependent on external decision centers. It is not by chance that such models are to be found in small or extremely small states (Hong Kong is the classic case) whose only resource is labor and whose economic and political autonomy is virtually nil. This has created the basis for a possible conflict between the attempts that many LDCs are making to improve and specialize their functions in international subcontracting by converting to more skill-intensive manufacturing processes, and the tendency of the multinational to decentralize manufacturing processes that offer less added value and require lower levels of technology.

In addition to the small-scale firms involved in international subcontracting, we must also consider those small firms with an entirely different role, namely, introducing in the agricultural sector the use of appropriate technologies that both gradually modernize the old crafts industries and lay the foundations for creating the first forms of new industrial organizations. This model draws on Gadgil's proposal on "intermediate technologies" for small firms in LDCs, which he put forward in a seminar on the problems of small-scale rural industries held in India in 1964.[7] The proposal was later developed by Schumacher, the founder of the Intermediate Technology Development Group in London, who ascertained the negative effects involved in transferring technology to the Third World: sectorial and territorial imbalance; imbalances in the incomes and consumption structure; unemployment caused by the destruction of many crafts industries; the difficulty in operating sophisticated technologies in industrial environments with inadequate experience; the increase in the import of raw materials and semimanufactured products while products and raw materials available locally were not exploited to the full.[8]

Consequently, it was suggested that technologies be developed that would require low capital investment per product and labor unit, would use local human resources, whose use could be easily introduced all over the country, especially in rural areas, and which would guarantee higher productivity compared with the traditional processes of production. With the assistance of international organizations such as IDA and OECD, whose interest in these problems was increasing rapidly, these principles were applied to concrete industrial initiatives in sectors such as foodstuffs, agricultural machinery, traditional semicraft activities, energy production, and public works.

It would be fair to say that the existence of a tight network of small-scale firms in LDCs is a *conditio sine qua non* in revitalizing the more traditional sector of the economy and reducing the gap that divides it from the modern sector.

Policies in Support of Small Business

Once one recognizes the essential nature of the role of small businesses, the key problem undoubtedly is to identify the best policies to stimulate the vitality of small firms that already exist and to promote the creation of new ones. There are two sides to this issue. What part should national government play? What role should the international development cooperation agencies, international financial institutions, and the major banks that operate at international level be called upon to play?

National governments, wishing to achieve a rapid take-off, often favor large firms and capital-intensive technologies, thus creating new distortions as well as aggravating old ones. The realization of the importance of the development of small firms must stimulate new directions, i.e., induce governments to adopt policies that will help by acting as incentives to small-scale businesses. Possible solutions could include granting aid, tax reliefs, low-interest loans, and cut-price energy. But apart from financial help (which is often necessary, given the difficulties small firms encounter in gaining access to monetary and financial markets), if a policy to help small-scale production units is to be far-seeing, it must provide for a whole series of services that are essential to the needs of small business.

On the basis of the experience of certain industrialized countries, we must underline the importance of the existence of appropriate bodies, be they public or private, that carry out given functions at an optimum scale, which it is impossible for small-scale businesses to do because of their size. Such services can include bookkeeping, financial advice, legal advice, the buying of raw materials and other goods as well as marketing, including international marketing. The weakness of small and medium-sized firms in creating their own sales network might be countered by creating cooperative organizations or trading companies that carry out such functions on their behalf. Two further factors of great importance are professional training and the spread of technological innovation. But a discussion of these two aspects also involves a discussion of the role of international organizations within the framework of North-South relations.

Small Business and North-South Relations

Balanced development and adequate growth in the South depend to a very large extent on the cooperation that will be provided by the North. Quite obviously, interdependence and international cooperation are absolute necessities. All the organizations involved in this field (international financial institutions as well as commercial banks operating at an international level) must make an ever-increasing effort to ensure the flow to LDCs and, above all, to the smaller business in those countries, of the resources that are necessary for their economic take-off and development. Various bodies have already made proposals to help developing countries obtain larger amounts of long-term capital: the Brandt Report, in particular, has been one of the most recent attempts to formulate hypotheses on a new approach to financing development and transferring capital to LDCs.

Among these proposals is a request that the World Bank, the regional development banks (Inter-American Development Bank, African and Asian Development banks, and the Arab Fund for Economic and Social Development) play a more decisive role; it also suggests the setting up of a World Development Fund in which all countries will participate and in which the decision-making process will be more equally divided among lenders and borrowers. With particular reference to small and medium-sized firms, the following proposals are advanced.

A first observation concerns the International Finance Corporation (IFC), an affiliate of the World Bank that was established in 1956 to promote the growth of private investment in the LDCs. IFC's principal tasks are to provide and bring together financing, technical assistance, and management needed to develop productive investment opportunities in LDCs, especially in the least developed of these. IFC is therefore one of the very few international organizations that can make both equity investments and loans without government guarantees.

Among the many types of operations IFC can carry out, one that is of particular interest to small businesses is the setting up and financing of joint ventures between small and medium-sized firms of industrialized countries and LDCs. Such initiatives have played an important role in the spread of technological innovation in the Third World.

IFC's activity has developed enormously in the last few years. Suffice it to say that the value of investments approved during the fiscal year 1981 exceeded the total approved in the first fifteen years of its history. In spite of this, the financial contribution of IFC to the development of LDCs is still modest: it is estimated that in 1980, IFC and its associated investors and lenders accounted for about 6 percent of the flow of direct investment, net of reinvested earnings, from OECD countries to developing countries.

This body's potential to finance the private sector must be increased, with an emphasis on small and medium-scale industries. To satisfy the requirements of mobilizing the flow of external capital, a system of cofinancing among international financial institutions has been developed in recent years, involving especially the World Bank, IFC, and the Inter-American Development Bank, and their financial partners. These include official sources (governments, their agencies, multilateral financial institutions), export credit institutions, and private financial institutions. A greater contribution on the part of commercial banks in particular could effectively provide more financial and technical assistance for the development of firms in LDCs.

On this subject I would like to underline the importance of the operations carried out by EEC bodies, including those of the European Development Fund in the African, Caribbean, and Pacific (ACP) countries and by the European Investment Bank (EIB). In the last few years the latter has paid particular and ever-increasing attention to financing the projects of small and medium-sized firms within EEC member countries. The same attention should be paid to small and medium-scale businesses in the Mediterranean Basin, ACP, and overseas countries, where the EIB is constantly increasing its commitments. Even in this case, the recourse to cofinancing could lead to the mobilization of greater flows of resources.

Finally, a proposal concerning Third World banks and the financing of small businesses: just as precise sociocultural conditions are necessary for the rise of entrepreneurship in small businesses, a high degree of sensitivity is required of financial bodies if they are to help small-scale business. Another quality they must possess is the imagination necessary to work out specific technical forms of financing that will satisfy the special requirements of agriculture, industry, and construction.

The experience of commercial banks in industrialized countries can and must be made available to banks in LDCs, in order to improve the quality of the help given to a sector that can play a vital part in the development of the Third World.

Notes

1. G. Fua, *Problems of Late Development in Europe* (Paris: OECD, 1980).

2. EEC Commission, *Survey on the State of Small- and Medium-sized Industry in EEC Countries* (Brussels, 1966).

3. O. Hirschman, *The Strategy of Economic Development* (New Haven: Yale University Press, 1958); P. Streeten, *Unbalanced Growth* (Oxford Economic Papers, 1959) and *The Frontiers of Development Studies* (New York, 1972); M. Dobb, *An Essay on Economic Growth and Planning* (London, 1960); F. Perroux, "Economic Space: Theory and Applications," in *Regional Development Planning* (Cambridge, Mass.: MIT Press, 1964).

4. R. Nurske, *Problems of Capital Formation in Underdeveloped Countries* (Blackwell, 1953); P. N. Rosenstein-Rodan, "Note on the Theory of the Big Push," in *Economic Development for Latin America* (London, 1961).

5. Perroux defines "satellite firms" as those small firms that operate in the area polarized around a large-scale leader firm.

6. According to M. Sharpston, this term denotes all commissioned export marketed by the purchaser.

7. D. R. Gadgil, "Technologies Appropriate for the Total Development Plan," in *Appropriate Technology for Indian Industry* (Hyderabad, 1964).

8. F. Schumacher, *Social and Economic Problems Calling for the Development of Intermediate Technology* (Cambridge, 1965).

Food Security for Nations and People: Rapporteur's Report

Martin McLaughlin

Presentations by the Panelists: A Summary

Although Chairman Maurice Williams, executive director of the World Food Council, was glad to see food issues raised to the top of the global agenda, both at the Cancun Summit of world leaders and elsewhere, he was distressed by a trend toward pseudo-pragmatism with respect to social problems that he found among some government officials. Poverty, hunger, and injustice, their argument goes, have been with us always and will continue to be with us, no matter what we do. We should therefore stay on the present course, apply the orthodoxies of the past, and preserve the status quo. Williams said this makes complacency a virtue and institutionalizes protectionism of the status quo. It is a philosophy to feed bureaucrats, not hungry people. It is idle to speculate whether this kind of system can be maintained; it cannot.

Sartaj Aziz, assistant president of the International Fund for Agricultural Development (IFAD), discussed food security at three levels:

(a) Global: The international food system is characterized by jagged fluctuations in the production and prices of grain, the basic staple food; this means a reserve system must be created, food aid must be made available for those who cannot buy commercially, and some kind of arrangement for emergencies must be devised.

(b) National: Sixty countries did not increase their food production as fast as their population grew, but the potential of forty or fifty of these countries is much larger than has been mobilized so far. Aziz pointed out that developing country food inputs increased from 40 million tons in 1972 to 103 million tons in 1981, compared with a 1974 prediction of 80 million tons in 1985. Since nearly half of this importing is done by low-income countries, ways need to be found to help every nation to increase its potential.

(c) The people level: National food security does not guarantee food security for people. They have to have income. The most important premise of the food debate is the clear recognition that the food crisis of 1973–74 was not caused by food shortages as such, but by poverty. In that year 400 million tons of grain were fed to livestock; 2 million of those would have been enough to feed malnourished people. The link between poverty and the food problem came through very clearly and underpins any food security program.

But while the link between poverty and hunger is simple to present, tackling that issue is much more difficult than was thought at first, because it involves the whole complex of the political, social, and economic aspects of the development problem. The first major principle of remedial action to emerge from IFAD's analysis was that in any situation where 40 percent of the land is owned by the top 1 or 5 percent of the population and 40 percent of the population may own only 5 percent of the land, it is not possible for the agricultural system to continue to feed the people. Outside support will almost inevitably worsen their problem because benefits will accrue according to the land-ownership pattern and will therefore increase the gap. Second, no trickle-down approach or program based purely on technology will work; projects have to start with people, not with technologies and analysis. Third, projects cannot reach the target poor unless those people are organized in some way; there has to be a minimum organizing unit such as a marketing association or a water management group. Fourth, once these people are organized, they have to receive a technological package that they can understand because it is related to their experience. The project has to fit their own perceptions. The experts can often come up with a solution that meets the problem but that is not necessarily related to the people. In that case, knowledge is not passed on—the government cannot sustain the project—and dies, leaving a bad odor in its wake. What is required is that the initiative of people be used in a situation that is technologically and socially harmonious.

The most difficult problem in this respect is land ownership. Land cannot be moved around, but one can create assets and stimulate economic activity on the land. But the assets created by the system must be made available to the landless; for this, software, not just money, is needed. Local leaders are important, since they appreciate the problems and can work with the people who most need to be helped. Outside aid must help to create new units that are creditworthy. Poor people are not likely to be thought creditworthy, but they are more likely to be good risks because they know they will suffer more if they do not pay.

It is ironic that just as the link between poverty and hunger is clearly established, the resource base for, e.g., IDA and IFAD is shrinking. The acceleration of these programs, which offered such hope, has now been drastically slowed. The resource base is threatened by further reductions in upcoming years. We can only hope that it is a temporary lull and that the food problem will come to the fore rather soon. But governments do not give the poor very much priority, and their participation is essential.

Lester Brown, president of the Washington-based Worldwatch Institute, emphasized that the basic problem is how to devise development strategies to get at the lowest-income poor. That is where the game will be won or lost, and we are far behind where we should be. The 1974 projections have been borne out; in fact, the food deficit is running ahead of schedule. The loss of momentum has continued and for the same reasons as prevailed then. Food production has fallen below population growth, especially in Africa; per capita income growth there is down 14 percent. It is in Africa that the lack of skills and institutions is most obvious. Citing the World Bank's prediction of a sustained decline in per capita income for 186 million people in Africa during the current decade, Brown noted that this is the first time that a major region has gone into such a decline and that it will be very difficult to turn this around. Three things are undermining Africa, he said: rapid population growth, the world's fastest rate of physical deterioration in the countryside, and the lack of priority for agriculture among the governments of the region. Other regions may follow Africa, because their problems are serious and similar.

Although in the development field we tend to focus on social and economic factors, ecological factors like the loss of soil are also very important. This is not just a Third World problem; we have it in the United States, too—it is less visible today than it was in the 1930s, and there is no leadership today, as there was then, to handle it. Civilization as we know it cannot survive the loss of topsoil at the current rate.

Another very serious problem is the growing competition of the industrialized countries, especially the Soviet Union, for available supplies of grain. The Soviets are thinking of importing 44 million tons of grain in 1982–83, financed largely by their oil and gold exports. This presents a very serious concern for the food-deficit developing countries. There seems to be no prospect of the reduction of the Soviet food deficit in the foreseeable future. Two ships leave the United States every day loaded with grain for the Soviet Union, and Soviet crop forecasts have just been reduced again.

But the single force that will shape agriculture in the next two decades more than any other will be the energy transition from nonrenewable to renewable sources of energy. Since 1950 agriculture has become much more energy intensive; 113 million tons of chemical fertilizer were used in the United States last year. The demand for renewable energy, however, will shape agriculture, the economy, and society generally over the next decade. In the early industrial period, the location of industry was tied to the availability of energy sources, mainly coal and iron; but as oil gradually replaced coal, that link broke because the oil was, in the main, located far from where industry was being developed. With the move to renewable energy, however, this relation will shift back because renewable sources are generally not transportable (or did not need to be transported). Industries like the very energy-intensive aluminum industry are already moving toward sources of cheaper energy.

We have to think about how all this will affect land-use patterns and land values in the future. We will be using this energy either physically, as in the case of solar collectors, or biologically, as in the case of agriculture. Rural projects will acquire an energy collection value as well, and we will become much more aware of population-land-food ratios. We will begin to look to agricultural wastes as a source of energy (e.g., the stalks left over after sugar cane is refined), and food processing will become a source of energy as well. Fuel will be added to food and feed as a product of agriculture. We may see new varieties of plants domesticated when we move away from the food concentration. There may be some very efficient sources of energy among plants because they are high in starch, sugar, or oil; Brazil, for example, is already meeting about a fifth of its motor-fuel requirements from agricultural sources. There is an African palm tree that produces an oil that may be able to replace a good part of the diesel fuel required: Brazil hopes to get 60 percent of its fuel requirements from this source. Moreover, the marketing of firewood is becoming a second source of income for farmers, including some in the United States; some farmers say they get as much income from their winter harvesting of wood as they do from their summer harvesting of food and feed crops. The United States gets about twice as much of its total energy from firewood as from nuclear power.

There is also competition between the food and energy sectors for water, especially in the case of synthetic fuels. The Soviets, too, are concerned about the food and energy problem and have therefore moved the management of dams into the ministry of agriculture. The United States has not used water efficiently and will have to think much more seriously about that in the future. In some poor countries the water systems are mostly unlined and are losing a great deal of water through seepage and in other ways. Populations have to be more scattered as we move toward improved water use; as concentration in urban centers declines, we may achieve a reduction in the population growth rate. Another interesting matter is the shift in terms of trade between the countryside and the cities as the former begins to supply energy as well as food. This, too, has implications for land-use patterns.

Moving toward renewable energy will result in more jobs in the energy field in the countryside. There is a whole set of new research issues coming out of this: multiple cropping of food and energy crops in an annual cycle, nutrient recycling (which cannot be handled with urbanized populations), multiple cropping of food crops, minimum tillage (32 percent of U.S. crops are now grown this way), and the growing of more perennial crops and fewer annuals. Perennials increase the crop and reduce soil erosion because cultivation does not have to take place so often. An emphasis on perennials would reverse the trend of the recent past; annuals have been favored becaused they can be produced through intensive agriculture and because each year they produce a great number of seeds for the next year's crop.

Rick Gilmore, of Washington-based Gilmore International Consultants, pointed out that developing-country purchasing power has suffered from the general economic situation and that this is a major problem unlikely to be solved by elaborate multilateral schemes. He was not enthusiastic about the World Food Council's scheme, felt that the IMF facility would not be adequate to solve the problems of the poor countries, and said that the farmer-held reserve in the United States is not really available for purchasing and is in any case not a mechanism for price stabilization.

Global food indicators this year, Gilmore said, are extraordinarily positive: world stock positions are up for wheat, coarse grains, oilseeds, and rice; wheat stocks were almost 10 percent higher than in the preceding year and are more than 7 percent greater for coarse grains; carryover stocks for the current marketing year, notwithstanding new estimates of a greater shortfall in Soviet production, are more than adequate for security. All categories increased at about the same rate last year, thereby widening the margins of supply over demand two years in succession.

Reflecting these stock accumulations, export prices went down even faster. U.S. wheat export prices are off 13 percent, and corn is down roughly 20 percent from the 1981–82 marketing year. These differences are repeated for every grain-exporting country but are particularly dramatic for U.S. varieties. Other important indicators are in the same slump. For instance, ocean freight rates on the U.S. Gulf–to–Rotterdam route reached $6.75 per long ton, the lowest figure recorded since September 1978 for vessels in the 50,000-ton and over class. Declines were also registered on the lower volume routes to developing countries, and the lower demand of the recessionary economy, together with plentiful supplies, also reduced the cost of most agricultural inputs—especially phosphate and potash fertilizers.

For those who are skeptical about the reality of the world food problem, these indicators point not just to conditions of global food security but to world food glut, and they eliminate the need for price stabilization measures to enhance international food security. Developing countries, along with competing high-income importers, can cover their food deficits in the short and medium term from existing food supplies. There are, moreover, untapped lines of credit that surplus-producing countries are offering in their efforts to promote additional foreign sales, and the IMF's new compensatory food financing window is still another means of ensuring that needy people have access to food.

There are, of course, variations on this theme that allow for disparities in the allocation of these global food resources to individual countries. Accordingly, the argument runs that multilaterally secured trade liberalization can do more for global food security than international reserve initiatives, particularly when handled in conjunction with national policies affecting domestic production and consumption. The United States under President Reagan has espoused a policy that emphasizes "self-reliance" (in lieu of self-sufficiency) through production and consumption efficiencies assisted in large part by the American private sector, and the United States has disavowed past efforts to establish a multilateral reserve system on the grounds that the market can achieve the same objectives more effectively.

Although it would be convenient to dismiss this argument by citing evidence to the contrary, Gilmore felt it would be a mistake to revive old solutions without considering current conditions from a different perspective. For the developing countries the top problems are exchange rates and national balance of payments. Although the nominal price of grains is at its lowest point in three years, the dollar is at an all-time high. With a high debt burden worsened by low, if not negative, returns on their raw materials and manufactured products, developing countries have seen their potential gain from low world grain prices evaporate. Their currencies have fallen relative to a U.S. dollar that is sustained by high interest rates rather than real increments in productivity, which could use their materials. In 1981 African currencies depreciated an average of 29 percent against the dollar, Latin American currencies 18 percent (except the

Mexican peso, which dropped 73 percent), and Asian currencies 14 percent. As a result, the purchasing power of developing countries has suffered, impeding their access to food resources from abroad.

Paradoxically, this trough in international agricultural prices, stemming from competition by exporters trying to reduce expensive surpluses, hurts those developing countries attempting to accelerate domestic production through an array of often protectionist incentives. Both food aid and commercial sales can undermine the agricultural economies of aid-recipient countries at the same time that the prices of inputs have increased worldwide. Under these circumstances, total food production in developing countries is not expected to increase more than 2 percent, whereas consumption requirements will continue to grow along with population and income.

Finally, available supplies of free stocks must be distinguished from end stocks in any realistic calculus of food resources that can be obtained on the open market. Here, the big unknown is U.S. domestic programs designed to curb production and bolster prices. In 1981–82 and again in this marketing year, only those farmers participating in acreage-reduction programs designated for each crop can be eligible for deficiency payments. Because of low prices, farmer enrollment for the first year reached a national average of 81 percent, but certified compliance is likely to be closer to the 35–50 percent range, given the income constraints that American producers now face. Even at these levels, government-held and farmer-owned reserves are at record highs. Crops under reserve in the United States are held for three years and generally can be released only when they reach levels between 20 and 35 percent above the current market price, depending on the individual crop. In other words, these reserves are not working stocks in the sense of their being readily accessible for domestic or foreign purchases. The purpose of the program, indeed, is to raise and sustain domestic and, hence, international prices by removing a significant portion of supply from the market. It is not to serve as a price-stabilization scheme or a backstop to international food security.

Under the Reagan administration the incentives offered may not induce enough farmer participation to attain the price objectives. On the other hand, there may be a surge in compliance the closer the farmer comes to the official enrollment deadline without any increase in demand. In the first scenario there may be unmanageable levels of free stocks, which could force Washington to resort to export subsidies; in the second, more supplies could be locked up than anticipated, creating temporary shortages for spot buyers such as developing countries. Certainly another contributing factor to any short-term shortages would be massive Soviet buying in response to forecasts of probably ever-dwindling harvests for the current crop year. Thus, government policies in the United States and elsewhere may work against food security in developing countries.

The private grain trade can also detract from food security. There are a host of efficiencies accompanying economies of scale and commercial technologies that the six major grain companies emphasize, but there are some less obvious inefficiencies rooted in their oligopolistic structure. In theory, developing countries, just like other importers, can select out the inefficiencies, but their market power is weak and they cannot provide high-volume sales, rapid handling, multilateral sourcing, or large-lot transactions delivered in large vessels, and they do not engage in active hedging operations.

In these circumstances, Gilmore urged political and economic readjustment in an effort to help developing countries achieve an acceptable level of food security at minimum cost. He rested his case on the following propositions:

○ Present international agricultural conditions, marketing systems, and institutions offer new means of achieving international food security for developing countries in the next decade.

○ Concessional food resource transfers can be less beneficial to aid-recipient countries than to surplus exporters.

○ The political climate and current economic conditions do not augur well for new initiatives requiring substantial additional expenditures by principal food exporters.

○ Increased political and economic sophistication among leaders of developing countries enhances the prospect for maximizing the benefits from current market conditions and introducing measures appropriate to longer-term national food security and self-reliance.

○ Exporting countries have a tangible self-interest in promoting more equitable allocation of existing food resources and in improving market stability.

Discussion ranged widely: the problem of eroding forest land and the alleged suppression of reports on renewable energy sources by energy companies; the urgency of reducing the population growth rate; the question of poverty and misallocation of resources and benefits (food does not get to hungry people); the mixed-blessing character of food aid—as a disincentive to agricultural production but a spur to other sectors; the possibility of a U.S. national food bank and a world food bank (Gilmore's proposal made elsewhere, cited by one of the participants); the sad termination of successful programs by irrelevant politics (an Israeli complaint); the problem of dietary changes induced from outside the developing countries (e.g., wheat for rice, Coca-Cola—criticized as unnutritious); the skewing of internal prices against the rural sector; and the U.S. grain embargo against the Soviet Union.

Gilmore noted that questions had linked the positions of the panelists more than their own presentations had, meshing macro and micro issues and getting right down to basic political and investment decisions. The embargo has an impact on trade. In the United States there has been a flirtation with the "food weapon," and it will happen again; there will be price gyrations, structural distortions, windfall profits, etc. But the long-term trend does not suggest long-term shortages; we have not begun to reach the maximum yield even in the United States, for even with surpluses we do not have decreases in production. He thinks that the soil erosion and other problems mentioned by Lester Brown will play a big part eventually. With respect to Coca-Cola in Kenya, Gilmore saw this, too, as a political problem, but of a different kind: tastes are subject to very strong influence from powerful market forces like Coca-Cola, but the multinational company is interested in profits and should be judged on that basis; it is not in business to achieve social justice. It is the Kenyan government that welcomes Coke to the country and gives it tax breaks, favorable exchange rates, special labor exemptions, and the like.

Brown agreed that food habits are being shaped by various forces. He noted that after the sugar export to Japan (which had been criticized as unhealthy and antinutritional by a Japanese participant) there was a very large push to get the Japanese to eat wheat and then raisins. Now Japan imports both wheat and raisins for raisin bread, and it exports rice. He thought there would be more conformity internationally in diets as energy uses shift; he finds that there is already some shifting in diet patterns in the United States—e.g., less consumption of beef and more consumption of poultry, which is a more efficient converter of grain into animal protein.

Aziz said that small farmers make up two-thirds of the population but have only one-third of the cultivatable land. In some cases the average farm size is one hectare or even half a hectare—in China and Bangladesh there are ten people per hectare. In countries where the population growth preceded the change in economy, the increase in urban areas that followed will be very difficult to reverse; the investment requirements are too high, and it is not feasible for other reasons. We have to start from where we are, and it is hard to move forward from a small base; but the productivity potential in some poor countries is very high. The small farm in the United States is 500 acres, in England perhaps 80, compared with numbers listed above. There are other difficulties: even when the pressure on land is not so severe, traditionalism is often a brake on modernization because no investment is going into the traditional sectors. There is also a problem of migration as a result of ecological deterioration and slash-and-burn agriculture; seasonal problems are obstacles in many countries. Both man-made policies and geography can become the problem. We have to attack all the constraints: poor farmers do not get subsidies; services do not reach them; research is not about their crops; processing facilities are in the cities. As land-tenure patterns are modified, however, these things, too, can be changed; then the rural economy can be diversified into new crops and new jobs can be created. This is the real measure and meaning of integrated rural development.

The world food problem—the problem of hunger—is how to ensure that people are enabled to obtain their food on a continuing, dignified, self-reliant basis through a sustainable food system in which they participate equitably.

Success *is* possible. Nearly everyone agrees that hunger *should* be eliminated from human experience. Many argue that it *can* be done—that it is a feasible objective for the end of this century, provided the necessary political support is rallied to the task. The question is whether we will meet that responsibility.

Part 4

We've Got the Power

Harnessing Political Will

Joan Lestor

I doubt if in Britain in January and February of 1982 more than a handful of people had ever heard of the Falkland Islands, let alone the Malvinas. But a few months later, we had a war; a task force sailed out to save a territory that most people had never heard of and did not know where to find. We had a prince, the son of a ruling monarch, going with them, and we had all the ingredients for crisis atmosphere in which the campaign to defend the Falkland Islands was conducted in the United Kingdom. I am not commenting on the rights or wrongs of the situation. But it is remarkable that when a government wants to create an atmosphere of popularity, of urgency, and of sacrifice—because there *was* human sacrifice involved—it has the means to do it and can do it to perfection. Those who raised their voices to question the Falklands action, who looked at the problems and all that was involved and sought other solutions, were of course dismissed and decried as antipatriotic, as traitors, and as wanting victory for the Argentinians. I give this example because it points to something that as a politician, who believes in rational men and women, I found extremely disturbing. That experience pushed me to think a great deal about how we mobilize public opinion and whether things are not indeed often stacked against us. It goes without saying that the campaign that was mounted in Britain did assist the government greatly—at a time of enormous economic difficulties and rising unemployment—to mobilize support in other areas.

Let me relate another, perhaps contradictory, experience with this business of political will and atmosphere. I came into Parliament in 1966. I fought five campaigns and retained my seat each time. In Britain in the late 1950s and throughout the 1960s there was an enormous racist lobby. My own party, the Labour Party, was profoundly affected by that, and those of us who were, to use a loose phrase, "good on race"—that is, those who were defending the rights of Blacks not only to remain members of our community but to bring in their children and their families, to stand equal in relation to the law—were in the minority. We were told we would lose votes if we advocated those rights, and my own party was saying that we must curb immigration, we must do this, and we must do that because "people won't like it."

Britain is racist. Britain is xenophobic. Most countries are, I find, but Britain may be particularly so. Many battles over such issues were fought in the late 1950s and 1960s. While not for a moment suggesting that everybody is now emancipated from those 1950s' views, I would hold that today you could not become a candidate for Parliament in my party if you held those views on immigration and race. The atmosphere, as a result of all sorts of events, but particularly because of the involvement of large numbers of Blacks in the movement, both in trade unions and in politics, is that you have got to be "good" on the issue of race if you wish to be a public representative.

I relate these two contradictory stories because those of us who despaired in the late 1950s and 1960s that the labor movement would ever face up to its responsibilities on the question of race relations are beginning to see a slow yet quite dramatic change in the whole atmosphere and presentation of the situation. There are many deep-rooted problems on the question of race, but what I see here as being significant is the fact of being able to at least change an atmosphere in a political party so that it becomes *acceptable* now to say the things that were *unacceptable* to some fifteen years ago on the complex issue of race relations. There are many other such instances. So when we talk about political will, we have to look at some of the means of propaganda, the means whereby people's opinions are changed, and perhaps the courage of individuals to stand up against the tide of attitude that is temporarily flowing against them. That is the first important element.

International Development and the Politician

The Labour Party in the United Kingdom is trying to make its members responsive to and to stand up on matters of principle that we believe are imperative for the survival of the world. We therefore have a responsibility, as politicians, to get into party programs the policies that are related to aid and development and that encourage a positive and progressive global atmosphere, all of which are vital to the future. There are people in Britain who would say, "Look, you're right, you're absolutely right, but don't say anything about it because, you see, people don't understand. Just wait until you get there and do it." That is absolute rubbish, because if you have not carried at least some people with you in the electoral process, then you are going to have quite a job of implementation when you are elected and in decision-making positions. It will be said that those policies were not part of your campaign platform, that they are not in the manifesto. We must get both the politician and the party that (s)he represents committed to the aims and aspirations embodied in the aid and development policies. We must not introduce them by the back door and do it very quietly; we must be very unambiguous.

Politicians are sometimes two-faced about this sort of thing. A politician might say to you, "Well look, it's very unpopular in my constituency because trade will be affected or it may affect the industry locally; I'm going to be very careful on this. I agree with you, but I won't say too much." That same individual will be saying to his constituents, "I'm having nothing to do with that at all because I don't believe in it, and if you don't like it, you must lump it, don't vote for me." So everybody, unless he or she is a complete cabbage, will eventually stand up on an issue and will, in fact, resist the pressures that are pressing him or her to do what may be considered the wrong thing. It is important to recognize that the behavior of a politician is to a large extent determined by the pressure that he or she is under to behave in a certain way; that is very important.

Changing the Politics of Development

The lobby for a change in atmosphere and a change of approach in aid for development and disarmament is only beginning. The disarmament lobby seems to be winning much more than the aid for development lobby. In Britain today, because of the upsurge of the campaign for nuclear disarmament and the whole upsurge of the peace movement, the government is now embarking upon a propaganda campaign to convince the people that they do need the bomb, that they do need nuclear weapons for survival and safety. This clearly demonstrates that the lobby for peace and against nuclear weapons is beginning to have some effect, that it is beginning to take off in Britain. A measure of its success is the government's response to try in some way to stem the tide.

We have got to develop a new approach, a whole change of attitude in the atmosphere for aid and development whereby, first of all, it is considered antisocial not to recognize the connection between the survival of the North and the survival of the South. We shall need to use key people, wherever they may be, in a propaganda venture in order to put pressure on members of Parliament and indeed on political parties. All sorts of people must be engaged, not necessarily those connected with politics, but people who are prepared to stand up and identify themselves with these issues. The numbers of these people are not so important. It is the most articulate people, the people that can be very visibly identified with a proposition, who attract the attention of the member of Parliament and in turn will force pressure on the political party. We must therefore engage people and move into areas that perhaps we have not yet explored in creating a strong lobby for aid and development.

There are many different sorts of people in a country and in politics, each taking a different viewpoint as to the best way of dealing with a government or policies with which one may disagree. Much of it is very negative: "Let's go out and bash the other person"; "let's go out and hold up the person to ridicule"; "let's just go out and show how abortive their policies are." That's fine, but in the pessimistic atmosphere of today's world, one also has to offer people alternative possibilities. People in my own country and in many other parts of the world have lost hope. People do not believe that there are any alternatives. People do believe that the rising unemployment and the despair in the Third World are here forever and that there is nothing they can do about it. The more we simply point to the errors and the misbehavior of those in power, whatever color they may be, the more we reinforce that feeling of pessimism and that feeling of hopelessness that people have. But if we were to put forward attractive alternatives such as a global approach on aid and development, the more we link up issues like the survival of your child and getting a job with what takes place in the Third World, the more hope for the future we may stimulate.

It is imperative now that we, members of the development lobby, reach out to the people who do not believe in what we believe in, to the people in positions of influence and power, that we convince and convert them, and if they do agree with us, that we use them in the areas where they operate to try and spread the word, to create a positive, hopeful atmosphere for change. People will often say, "I'm not political." In other words, they do not want to be regarded as left wing, right wing, or whatever. "I'm not political but I agree with you on A, B, and C," they say. That's fine. We must recognize and build into our strategies the fact that political prejudices can be broken down to create a lobby of people from different areas and of different constituencies, working together toward a common goal. We must make the connection between *our* survival and the survival of the South, or the other way around, if viewed from the South. We must emphasize that it is possible to mobilize public thought, public attention, and to change people's attitudes, almost overnight, about all sorts of subjects, if the media, the politicians, governments, and others choose that it should be so. The job of the development lobby is in part to ensure and create a wider awareness and make a case for the urgency of development problems so that politicians, political parties, and others can no longer afford to neglect the lobby because it is in their interest, above everything else, to participate in it.

People Meeting Other People: A Challenge and a Chance for a New Interdependence and International Cooperation

Ronald Leger

It was in large part the oil crisis that triggered the beginning of a necessary awakening in the international community; this in turn has forced a deepened awareness of the need for enlightened and inspiring leadership, partnership, and cooperation among all. In essence, the two previous international development decades—established by the United Nations to set goals and formulate strategies for international growth and development—have been characterized by a "we-they" philosophy. The associations and institutions created or recognized during these years have largely reflected this "apartheid style" of development. The future should witness the development of new associations based on equality, mutual respect, interdependence, and a better knowledge of each other's problems or, at least, their respective viewpoints.

A mutually beneficial interdependence can best be achieved through mutual consent among strong autonomous institutions and associations. In large part, the industrialized countries have their own autonomous associations and institutions in all fields of social and economic activities. The flourishing NGO development community is a testimony to the willingness of large segments of citizens of industrialized countries to have meaningful human relationships with others. However, to develop these relationships into truly meaningful forces will necessitate the development of a more active dialogue among the developing nations themselves. In other words, the so-called North-South dialogue will not develop so long as those living the same problems do not talk better among themselves. This means, therefore, that the North-South dialogue is dependent on a more intense South-South dialogue, which the North should not fear but rather welcome and encourage.

The nongovernmental associations have a unique role to play in fostering the South-South dialogue. Some developing countries are perhaps in unique positions to play a pioneering leadership role. Some have long-standing traditions in citizens action groups for development. What we call the NGOs (which are, in reality, citizens associations) are both very numerous and diversified. Other developing countries need to learn more how to count on their citizens groups and not solely on government initiatives. They will better do this by learning from others living in similar situations.

Intellectual and technical talent and technologies are relatively abundant in some developing countries, and these are often more appropriate than their counterparts in more developed countries. Their industrialized and technological bases are often more easily adapted to other developing countries. In fact, some nations, while remaining developing nations, are capable of equal partnership and dialogue both with the industrialized as well as with the least developed countries. In certain sectors of their economy and research they are at par with the most advanced. However, in other sectors they live the same problems and dilemmas as the least developed.

In some developing countries the problems of development are experienced especially intensely—unmet basic human needs, population growth, water, desertification, energy, urban slums, deep-rooted effects of colonialism, etc. Yet they have the knowledge base and infrastructure—often greatly lacking in other developing countries—to tackle them from within. Most developing countries' populations have a traditional and active religious respect for life and afterlife and a profound respect for cultural diversity—the foundations of dialogue among nations and a precious antidote to materialism.

There is a great need for strong, dynamic, permanent, and well-organized dialogue associations created by and for the developing countries at the nongovernmental level. The kind of interdependence based on mutual respect and cooperation that is now emerging and needed is far too important and too complex to be left to governments or official international bureaucracies alone. Governments are not usually capable of being agents of change. They are of course necessary, for they can question, analyze, discuss, coordinate, study, and process. However, they can seldom create and innovate. Only people with vision and imagination can do so.

Change requires the active participation of all citizens motivated by leaders. Great and complex change will require vision and cooperation but above all outstanding and courageous leadership. In the past, many Third World leaders have mobilized their own citizens and world opinion to bring about major changes in the world through nongovernmental associations. Some of these changes include decolonization and political independence of hundreds of nations, the abolition of slavery, and the fight against apartheid—all major problems challenged by courageous individuals who mobilized citizen groups. More recently we have witnessed the efforts of the peace movements.

In all cases, the first real thrust came from courageous leaders with the backing of committed and organized citizens. To mention but one, Gandhi remains one of history's most outstanding visionaries in this field, even though his work is not yet completed precisely where it all started: against apartheid in South Africa. One should also remember that the Bandung conference was primarily a nongovernmental movement for the political independence of the colonies in the 1960s.

A Renewed Commitment

Once again the time has come for courageous, concerted action and cooperation among developing countries. The so-called New International Economic Order and the North-South dialogue are in an impasse because both North and South are divided among themselves, but more importantly because the citizens of the world are somehow expecting their respective governments and the U.N. system to create the necessary institutions for dialogue. So long as these initiatives are left to governments and intergovernmental institutions, the North-South dialogue will be dominated by the East-West political considerations and power games. Instead, South-South, North-South, East-West fruitful dialogue and cooperation are both necessary and productive among those nations that feel the same problems, live the same hardships and frustrations, and dream the same dreams for their present and future citizens.

In many developing countries there exists a reservoir of young men and women, both urban and rural, who are filled with a fascinating mixture of self-confidence, dedication, realism, professionalism, and spirit of teamwork. These are the essential ingredients for the formation of strong dialogue associations. These young men and women will provide the leadership for an active and courageous dialogue movement among the developing countries. The Canadian International Development Agency is prepared to assist in this process, but we cannot nor should we initiate or organize it.

The challenge to the developing countries lies in the development of strong, dynamic, and inspiring dialogue associations, first among themselves, which they will have created in accordance with their own needs, values, and ingenuity. The challenge to the industrialized NGOs is to better understand and to inspire the important social changes evolving in our own countries. One of the important tasks ahead will be to enable Third World citizens to speak directly to the citizens of the industrialized nations and to financially encourage the emergence of Third World NGO associations that would not simply be copies or affiliates of those in the industrialized countries. A tremendous power of the citizenry lies yet to be exploited in the years ahead.

Book II

Across the Borders

Introduction: The Crisis of Multilateralism

Mahbub ul Haq

We have used the term "crisis" with such reckless abandon that there is a real danger that we may not recognize a real crisis when one comes along. But it is far from crying wolf to acknowledge that we are now facing a real crisis of multilateralism, a deep crisis of the international spirit. Precisely at a time when the emerging global village demands global cooperation for its very survival and development, we are going back to bilateralism, to unilateral actions, to the selfish go-it-alone policies of nations. The tide in human affairs for global cooperation and for more cooperative decision making—once so strong and powerful, once taken so much for granted—is running against the forces of internationalism.

It is useless to bemoan each individual event. It is irrelevant to lament every temporary setback. We must understand the overall pattern. We must fight the underlying trend.

We may yet avert the dangers. One clutches these days at every hopeful sign. First, we must consider the recent experience of nations. Despite their desperate unilateral actions they are not emerging from their economic recession. They may yet recognize—one hopes in time—that a successful world economic recovery is simply impossible without world economic cooperation. There is a whole literature on this subject—from Brandt to many learned treatises. But where words have failed, experience may teach.

Second, all other nations may begin to defy the political and economic arrogance of power by the two superpowers and come to their own workable accommodations. But though the prevailing wind is all against us, can we really afford the luxury of pessimism? Lord Keynes, we will remember, stood alone in the 1930s, preaching a new economic philosophy when the economic realities were all against him. Jean Monet stood on the rubble of a shattered Europe and declared that there would be a united Europe one day. George Marshall did not even wait for the bitterness of the war to die down to announce his plan for the reconstruction of Europe.

And our own Barbara Ward, fighting failing health and growing international cynicism, declared just before her death an abiding commitment to headstrong optimism. This is not easy. It takes rare moral courage. Such persons are not mad idealists. They are the only real hope. Indeed, rather than dwell upon the past, we should roll up our collective sleeves and try to shape the future. It is in that spirit that the following articles are presented.

The Future of International Cooperation

Simon May

Let me begin by making three points about the kind of case we in the development community have been putting forward. The first is that it will be essential to define far more carefully the mutual economic interests that so patently exist between North and South, if these interests are really to galvanize initiative and action in the North. For example, almost never have I seen any protagonist of aid argue *why* public money can benefit industrialized countries more if it is given to the South than if it is spent in their own underprivileged regions. We must not pretend that aid spent by the South on imports from the North will always benefit the Northern economy more than tax cuts or increased public spending in the North itself would.

When the North, together with no more than a handful of developing countries, is the major determinant of food prices, and when nearly every Northern country possesses intervention mechanisms designed to protect those prices from either rising or falling, we must not pretend that a major problem for the North is that food shortages in the South can push up food prices and therefore inflation in the North. In Britain and other European countries even nonspecialists are beginning to question some of the arguments for mutual interests that have been put forward.

Second, in putting across its message to the public, the development fraternity too often assumes that once the case for mutual interests between North and South is accepted, the kinds of policies that are needed to uphold these interests follow with such inexorable logic that they need hardly be justified or defended against their critics. The Brandt Report, in retrospect, was guilty of this omission. For example, the political feasibility and economic costs of the proposed deal with OPEC on oil prices were never discussed in the report, let alone defended against criticism. Nor did it seriously take on the powerful brigade of free marketeers whose ideological tenets or plain unfamiliarity with conditions in developing countries have caused them to dismiss as ineluctably socialist any intervention in the economy by governments, whether in the promotion of investment, in the provision of finance, or in stabilizing commodity prices. These are defects that will need to be remedied in the new Brandt Commission document.

Third, I wonder whether we have not given undue primacy in our arguments to the *economic* interests shared by North and South. In particular, it would seem to me that we have excessively downgraded the political and moral arguments for supporting development in the Third World.

Politically, it is hardly controversial to propose that serious economic decline in a society, at almost any level of income, is likely to feed popular resentment and unrest. In almost all societies, except those whose people are so unorganized or weak with poverty that they cannot protest, these resentments are likely to foment violence and endanger peace. Events in Jamaica, Costa Rica, and the Sudan all support this thesis. In all three countries recent violence is clearly correlated primarily with economic decline, and not with repression or growing gaps between rich and poor. This is an argument to which I believe people in the North will listen.

Important though these economic and political interests are in mobilizing support for good development, it would be wrong to underrate the power of the moral argument for development on the Western mind. Yet, too many have prematurely assumed that moral objectives can no longer seize Western society with the will to act. Too many believe that materialism and ideological confusion are making the West increasingly indifferent to the search for moral fulfillment.

Moral Rearmament

I do not believe that the West as a whole is becoming morally more indifferent. Those who make such judgments are failing to notice a profoundly significant and deeply rooted trend, although still a minority trend, that is creeping in on most Western societies. It is the growing rejection of the search for personal expression without limitation and of the notion that all absolute standards and judgments are evil—so characteristic of the 1960s. Instead, the search is growing among this minority for a more ascetic and socially responsible way of life in which personal expression, while still great, is more limited, and absolute standards in social behavior as well as in the arts, science, and the economy are rediscovered. We are seeing this not only in the ecologist, conservationist, and alternative parties that are springing up throughout the West, but also in the more orthodox mainstream of Western politics and society.

To the extent that this new trend is far less self-indulgent than what came before it, it provides a more hopeful basis for kindling a renewed sense of moral responsibility toward the Third World. It is true that in its search for moral revitalization, the West is looking far less to Third World societies for inspiration and far more to its own heritage of moral values. However, I would maintain that at least as far as continental Europe is concerned, this is less a sign of greater inward direction than it is of disillusionment with the ability of most Third World societies to generate superior ideologies and ways of life. This is why we perhaps need not fear that the trend will cause the moral energies of Western society to be focused entirely inward, away from poverty and underdevelopment in the Third World.

Despite all the West's materialism, principles of justice usually motivate its great social movements, not the impulse to accumulate surplus income. None of the great movements of modern days—disarmament, ecology, the peace movement of the Vietnam era, civil rights, women's liberation—were economically inspired. Even Marshall aid, the precedent we often urge Western governments to follow, was not primarily a response to demands by Americans for higher living standards. It was motivated above all by the threat to Europe's freedom posed by Soviet communism in the immediate aftermath of 1945. If the U.S. Congress had been asked to adopt the Marshall Plan as a countercyclical measure, it would almost certainly have been defeated. Today, in relation to the Third World, it is far easier for a Westerner to understand the plight of individuals than to be motivated by the economic benefits of increasing their purchasing power. For all these reasons, let us have renewed faith in the moral arguments for development and in the moral energies of Western societies that remain to be tapped.

Improving the Negotiation Process

There are two new areas that those in a position to influence governments urgently need to address. First, how can we help devise a more effective process of negotiation between North and South? Second, what sort of leverage can the South possibly mobilize to bring about the changes it needs and wants? It is a fact (which historians will surely one day ponder with amazement) that the overwhelming majority of leaders have failed seriously to consider either of these issues, even though the outcome of North-South negotiations is vital to their survival and to that of their people.

In the negotiating process we are faced with a very real dilemma. On the one hand, we cannot continue indefinitely to rely on a process of negotiation that literally has failure built in. This results from three serious shortcomings: first, the organization of participants into blocs of countries means that they either move together or they do not move at all; second, those who do most of the negotiating tend to have little say in the decision making of their governments, except perhaps when they represent weak and poorly organized states; and third, the sheer visibility of the process makes concessions unnecessarily conspicuous and therefore problematical for governments.

Of course, there are ways in which this method of negotiation could be improved. It is absurd, for example, for delegates to make speeches at the outset of their negotiation which stake out demands in so public and so unyielding a fashion that any compromise is then seen as capitulation. However, the drawbacks of this process are so fundamental that it is doubtful whether any procedural reforms that can be made will greatly improve its lamentable inefficiency.

On the other hand, we must also recognize that the forces for Third World unity and therefore for bloc bargaining are neither transient nor fickle. We cannot ignore the pervasive feeling among developing countries of being unjustifiably weak in international decision making, notably in the world's financial institutions. Nor can we neglect the desire common to the overwhelming majority of Third World countries to distance themselves from the superpowers and to assert their individuality. For these largely psychological reasons, it is essential to preserve universal forums such as the Group of 77 in which every Third World country feels that it can have a modicum of international status. Nor is it only the weaker countries such as Tanzania that find this important. It is desired even by a country the size of China—a fact about which top Chinese leaders are becoming increasingly candid. It would therefore be both foolish and futile for the West to try to bring to an end the Group of 77 and other forums that embrace the Third World as a whole.

The only way of escaping this dilemma is to create alongside the traditional forums a process of negotiation that is really capable of delivering results, and of delivering them rapidly. If such a process of negotiation is to tackle the three fatal flaws of existing forums, it must be selective in its membership. It must leave out those who are unprepared for progress where possible; it must ruthlessly limit the number of subjects with which it deals; and it must be able to count on the regular participation of heads of government, senior ministers, and top officials. The Cancun Summit is not a model of what is needed because it lacked two vital ingredients: careful preparation beforehand, and sustained follow-up by both heads of government and ministers.

We now need to think in terms of erecting a structure of decision making for North-South negotiations on the lines of that in the EEC, where specialized and general councils of senior ministers convene on a regular basis, punctuated by meetings of heads of government, whose job it is to give an impulse to the whole process of decision making. If this is necessary for a community of ten countries of roughly equivalent stages of economic development and closely related traditions of culture and politics, how much greater is the need for such a process of decision making among the infinitely more diverse participants in the North-South dialogue.

The same kind of process is needed for negotiations between Third World countries. At present, the "South-South" process is a shambles. With a handful of notable exceptions, meetings are attended by officials of insufficient status working on ludicrously broad agendas. It was shameful that even at the New Delhi meeting in February 1981 called to discuss South-South cooperation, no more than two heads of government and a handful of foreign ministers felt able to come, although forty-four developing countries were represented. It is simply not good enough merely to talk in terms of creating a Third World secretariat, timely though that is. The whole structure of South-South negotiation needs to be radically overhauled, much on the lines argued above in the sphere of North-South negotiations.

These are points that we need to put squarely to governments. For too long we have shied away from instituting a more streamlined process of negotiation because many mistakenly believed that this would endanger, or even necessitate the abandonment of, global methods of negotiation—something most leaders from the Third World are understandably reluctant to countenance. In fact, fruitful linkages can be forged between forums of universal membership and negotiation conducted by a more limited number of countries, to the benefit of both.

This then raises the question of the influence that the South is able to exercise in relation to the North. It is almost incomprehensible that this issue has been so superficially addressed by most Southern leaders, including many of those who have the greatest stake in the outcome of North-South negotiations. It is also incomprehensible that so many of them persist in believing that the surplus countries of OPEC are really in a position to use oil on their behalf as an instrument of power vis-à-vis the West. Every indication suggests that OPEC countries will not use their oil as a stick with which to beat the West—by embargo or by drastically cutting back on production—unless circumstances force them to do so. And as we have seen over two decades, such circumstances are likely to be created only by the Palestinian question and not by the economic fate of the South.

But if they cannot use oil as a stick, can they use it as an incentive to the West to be more cooperative in the North-South dialogue? Could they agree to restrain their pricing policies when the market for oil is tight again, as it may well be, in return for concessions by the West? I firmly believe not. No OPEC leader could possibly justify such restraint on oil prices on the grounds that he has bound his country to an agreement made previously with the West, or on the grounds that he is responding to some economic incentive provided by the West. To do so would be seen as mortgaging to the industrialized countries the very source of his nation's real sovereignty in international affairs—the ability to influence the price of oil. Such restraint on oil prices can be pursued only if it is undertaken unilaterally and if it is ultimately justified on its own merits. This is why Saudi Arabia, for one, has repeatedly refused to negotiate with the West on the price of oil. That is why Saudi Arabia has pressed OPEC to adopt a unilateral formula on oil prices even though the producers would get nothing in return from the consuming nations for such a formula.

We should disabuse Third World leaders of the illusion that they can safely harness the many and varied interests of their countries in the North-South dialogue to the negotiating power of OPEC's oil. Rather than looking to OPEC's oil as their trump card over the West, these leaders should be encouraged to examine alternative sources of power.

Sources of Power Yet Unexploited

One such source of power would be what might be called "geostrategic power"—that is, influence over other Third World countries that are of key importance to the West. To give just one example, Mexico has considerable geostrategic power through its ability to influence those countries in Central America and the Caribbean whose policies are perceived by Washington to be vital to North American security. In fact, this geostrategic power looks as if it will be a still more important source of influence over the United States than Mexico's rapidly growing reserve of oil. The second and what may ultimately be the most important source of power in the South is its ability to create alternative institutions and centers of international organization. These might provide effective alternatives to those institutions now dominated by the North.

In no sphere of affairs would the evolution of such institutions more power-fully sting the pride and impinge on the consciousness of the North than in international finance, for its dominance in the system of international finance is one of the great symbols of the West's perception of its own primacy. This does not mean, however, that the South would be wise to create such institutions to the exclusion of all Northern countries, even those sympathetic to its aims. To do so would be as shortsighted and small-minded as those Northern countries that want to keep the South subservient and isolated. Southern-led institutions would be far more effective if they were fortified by the great expertise and the added creditworthiness that can be gained from the support of one or two major Western governments. France, Holland, Canada, and Japan—all of these have governments and people who perceive their interests in the Third World with increasing clarity and who can make a vital contribution to developing the financial and political influence of the South.

Moreover, the psychological impact on those Northern countries that still want to exclude the South from the governance of international affairs will be far more painful and worrisome if they see other Northern countries, which are allies and friends, participating in these institutions. They will then see countries that have so far helped them to maintain their dominance over the international system branch out to create additional alliances and build the foundations of new systems of international order; in due time, they may well see these same Northern countries begin to discuss with their Southern partners vital issues of policy such as oil or access to minerals—issues that may be quite separate from those with which these new institutions were originally designed to deal. All this would have a profound impact on the minds of those in the North who are dedicated to preserving the present structure of international economic affairs—an impact perhaps as powerful as any material leverage the Third World is capable of exercising.

It would therefore be a great pity if the so-called ECDC (Economic Cooperation among Developing Countries) discussions that are now gathering momentum were to become an occasion for closing ranks against the North as a whole. This would only feed that perfidious belief that has damned practically every negotiation in the United Nations to date—the belief in the unbridgeable divide between North and South.

Areas of Influence, Avenues of Power

A Third World International Finance Corporation that co-opted a few Northern members, such as the countries previously mentioned, would be a good start to institution-building by the South. If a small minority of Southern countries are opposed to such an institution for ideological reasons, they must not be allowed to veto it. It is perhaps possible to minimize the chance that this will happen by making any such initiative as technical as possible in purpose and appearance. The more technical or utilitarian an initiative appears to be, and the less it looks like a radically new departure in the organization of Third World economic cooperation and diplomacy, the more likely it is that its supporters in the Third World will have the political confidence to go ahead without the Group of 77 as a whole.

Merely to map the objectives of the North-South dialogue or to discuss them purely in economic terms is not enough. Perhaps because economists have had the monopoly on North-South debate, we sometimes forget the crucial importance of understanding the political factors that determine the success or failure of our aims.

Finally to the question of how to influence. If we are going to exert long-term influence over governments and other major decision makers in society, bodies like the North-South Round Table of SID and the Brandt Commission are simply not going to be adequate. There are two major shortcomings in these high-level groups. First, they lack a secretariat led by a major figure of world standing who is not subservient to the members of the group but who has the personal authority to constantly cajole them into discussion, initiative, and action. A technical or administrative staff, however competent, does not have the status and authority to perform this task.

The second shortcoming of the kind of groups we have had until now is that almost none of their members actually sat as representatives or delegates of the major, organized forces in society, such as trade unions, employers' federations, the banking community, or political parties. Since they sat in a private capacity, most of them could say anything they liked without first obtaining the agreement of others in their countries. This reduced the incentive to fight and fight hard in their own organizations and countries for the action they came to realize was necessary. In addition, the expression of a personal view by a set of individuals, however eminent, inevitably reduces its weight. Authority is almost always precarious in the extreme if it is wielded by an individual only in his own name. As it happens, Barbara Ward was the exception that proved this rule.

It has become urgent to create a commission for international development that rectifies both these shortcomings. We need a top-level committee whose members are delegated by the most powerful organs of society, and we need an equally top-level secretariat, led by a major figure, to guide its deliberations and actions. If its members represent their organizations rather than themselves, their views may differ greatly, at least initally. However, continous exposure to the real facts of poverty, to the real *problematique* of development, to the real interests at stake for both North and South will promote a gradual convergence of views to an extent that no amount of lobbying or edicts from eminent bodies could ever achieve. The only caveat is that members of the commission must be committed in principle to North-South cooperation.

There is a powerful precedent for this kind of commission that we should remember if we are tempted to believe that it will not work. It is the Action Committee for the United States of Europe, conceived and founded by Jean Monet in 1955 to pursue the task of uniting western Europe. Monet's Action Committee was built on exactly the two principles just outlined. And it paid off. Within two years of its founding, it played the major role in creating both the EEC and the European Atomic Energy Commission and therefore in laying the basis for the economic and political regeneration of Europe.

The Long March Ahead

The task before the development fraternity is now to broaden its reach beyond the converted and the committed. It must seek to implant in a far wider constituency the unyielding desire to achieve the economic emancipation of the billions who still linger in poverty and intellectual starvation. As we embark on this monumental task, our conviction and our energies must be restrained only by the knowledge that self-righteousness can so easily destroy the power of our sincerity. With that constantly in mind, let us remain, in Barbara Ward's memorable words, "headstrong" and "profoundly convinced that we shall overcome."

The Imperative of International Economic Cooperation

Javier Perez de Cuellar

At the United Nations, "interdependence" and the consequent imperative of "international economic cooperation" have inspired debate and discussion for a number of years. When the General Assembly adopted the Declaration on the Establishment of a New International Economic Order in 1974, it stated unequivocally that the momentous events of that time had thrust into prominence the "reality of the interdependence of all members of the international community." It also recognized the asymmetric nature of this interdependence between developed and developing countries and called for measures to redress structural imbalances in the world economy. The General Assembly had stated further that the interests of the developed countries and those of developing countries could no longer be isolated from each other. It is fully recognized that international economic cooperation is essential to ensure the removal of the inequalities among nations and promote the political, economic, and social well-being of all peoples.

The growing integration of the world economy in the years that have followed has served only to further confirm that assessment. If the solemn commitments to the goals embodied in the United Nations International Development Strategy for the 1980s are to be made meaningful in this interdependent world, then the way forward must lie in greater national efforts as well as strengthened international economic cooperation.

There is a pervasive sense of gloom with respect to the prospects for growth during the rest of this decade. There is disagreement and uncertainty about the value and effectiveness of past policies, as well as strategies for the future. A certain intellectual disarray with regard to the interpretation of the functioning of the economy and society played a part in weakening international economic cooperation, and in eroding support for multilateral development institutions.

The current downward spiral comes at the end of two or three decades of exceptional growth and development in both the industrialized countries and developing countries. In the 1950s and 1960s the developing countries recorded growth rates that surpassed those of the more dynamic among the industrialized countries during the formative stages of their economies. The economies of industrialized countries also grew at unprecedented rates and entered the era of mass consumption and full employment. The last two decades saw world trade growing at rates that exceeded past records. Today, the developing countries together are the largest trading partners of the developed countries. The economic and social chaos of the 1930s and the horrors of World War II provided the impulse for the idealism and wisdom that led to the adoption of domestic and international policies conducive to growth and employment everywhere. It was the determined search for innovative ideas and pragmatic policies that also led to the institutionalization of international economic cooperation. The birth of the U.N. system, with its development and financial institutions, was the high point of this postwar period.

It is clear that international economic cooperation has a significant share in the responsibility for the remarkable postwar reconstruction in the industrialized countries. This successful performance in the recovery of the industrialized countries provided the experience upon which international institutions for the development of the newly emerging countries were founded. The relatively high rates of growth recorded by the developing countries were, first and foremost, the results of their own efforts. They have always financed some 90 percent of their own investments from their own savings. However, the developing countries, even if not satisfied with the structure and functioning of some of the institutions, would be among the first to testify to the significance of international economic cooperation and the multilateral institutions in assisting them in dealing with the development process.

However, although the concept of international economic cooperation and the nature and role of international institutions are well understood by those who deal with these subjects directly, it is clear that they are not understood and appreciated by the vast majority of ordinary people. One of our important tasks should be to consider how best we can promote such understanding among a wider audience.

The current world economic crisis makes it more imperative and urgent that we intensify efforts to promote international economic cooperation. The resumption of growth in the developing countries is one of our first tasks. Development, however, should not be treated simply as being synonymous with high rates of economic growth. The fruits of growth cannot be relied upon to percolate down to the poorest strata in society. The development process must also promote human dignity and well-being. As Emerson observed very wisely, "Man does not live by bread alone, but by faith, by admiration, by sympathy." I would also add that humanity needs to be considered as such, not as a collection of numbers in a list of statistical tables, nor undefined data of economic analysis. The victims of the economic crisis we are talking about, the recipients of the coordination and development we are aiming at, are men, women, and children who cannot wait forever. The plans and proposals for improving the present situation cannot disregard the fact that the vast majority of suffering humanity will not be standing placidly aside while a decent life is denied them.

In considering the various aspects of international economic cooperation for development, we should not limit its scope to the North-South axis. Admittedly, the existing international development institutions grew up on the basis of North-South cooperation. But today, the scope for cooperation along the South-

South axis is also increasing, given the vast and hitherto largely untapped potential for cooperation among developing countries. Collective self-reliance of developing countries is recognized as an essential step in the expansion and maturity of their economies. The various initiatives undertaken within the U.N. system for the promotion of economic and technical cooperation among developing countries are slowly but steadily improving their ability to become effective and self-reliant partners in the world economy.

The resumption of relatively high rates of growth in the developing countries should be seen as part of a broad-based and balanced world economic recovery in which the industrialized countries would play a leading part. The effectiveness of the postwar initiatives has once more demonstrated that crisis frequently offers great opportunities. Adversity also generates idealism. The present is therefore the time for imaginative initiatives.

Elements of a Recovery Program

There is now some recognition, at least within the U.N. system, of the need to deal with the problems not only from a cyclical point of view but also from a structural one. This provides us some grounds for cautious optimism about the launching of a global round of negotiations once an agreement on a framework for these negotiations has been reached. Of course, one has to bear in mind that worldwide economic recovery should begin as soon as possible; it should not have to wait for the completion of international agreements on all the long-range problems with which global negotiations will be concerned. There is an urgent need for concerted international action for economic recovery to extricate the world economy from the present stagflation. It is important to recognize the vital role that accelerated economic growth of developing countries can play. Indeed, such a recovery will make the longer term structural changes in the world economy that much easier to achieve.

In a statement to the Economic and Social Council of the United Nations, I outlined some elements of a recovery program. Five of these are basic. First, national and international policies must be changed decisively, to sustain economic expansion. Second, the international trading system should be maintained as openly as possible and recent moves toward protectionism must be turned back. Third, a stabilization and revival of the commodity markets is essential. Fourth, the flow of capital, especially concessional capital, and technology to the developing countries should be stepped up. Finally, international monetary cooperation should create conditions in which the forces for economic development can realize their full potential.

It has been noted that there is a state of anarchy in present international economic and financial policies. Further, one might add that the present state of the world's economy serves to exacerbate economic and social tensions and to accentuate political conflicts. I consider it imperative at the present juncture for all parts of the international community, North and South, East and West, to take concerted action to effectively coordinate international economic and financial policies so that the process of economic recovery can begin. Along with the recovery must come action to correct imbalances through continuing efforts in the major areas of trade, raw materials, energy, money, and finance. The United Nations provides a truly universal institution for this purpose. However, its efforts and those of its member states require the full and sustained support of enlightened public opinion and the stimulus of bold and innovative concepts and plans.

Winning by Bargaining

Michael Allen

Frequently in international forums, people who think they are bargaining are really only talking. Bargaining may be defined as the coherent attempt to resolve conflicting positions on a consciously shared problem. Given that definition, we recognize that all too often real bargaining is not taking place at the "bargaining table." Many times the problems are not consciously shared. Many times the actors are not aware of the specific positions that all the parties have, let alone what the perceptions of others are. Bargaining is an encounter triggered by very specific things: by changes in expectations or benefits, or changes in the capacities for self-determined or autonomous action by the parties who are to be joined in a bargaining situation. "Joined" in this context describes a situation wherein both parties agree on a piece of litigation about the same thing even though their interests conflict. Of course, there are other kinds of qualitatively different encounters besides bargaining. Often, for example, incoherence is the dominant form of encounter in international forums.

People bargain over specific issues. The issues might be prices, quantities, times of delivery of goods, or the rules and principles governing these. That is, the issue need not be economic. The subject or the problem of negotiation can be mechanical or procedural or can have to do with the principle governing or underlying the relationship. It can also have to do with the context or the structure within which the relationship is taking place. In other words, bargaining can be intraparadigmatic or paradigmatic: it can relate to modification within a context of relationships or to the context itself.

Further, parties who need to negotiate usually spring from the network of relationships created by that problem. For example, if the problem concerns making shirts, then all those making shirts come together in factories and need to negotiate from time to time around the specific problems generated by that activity. Bargaining therefore has specific social and structural contexts, and if we are aware of those contexts, it helps to clarify what we are talking about, when, and for what ends.

One of the factors I find neglected frequently in the discussions of North-South negotiations is the absence of clarity as to what particular network of relationships is being referred to. There are so many things happening in the world and so many negotiations about so many different things that we need to be clear exactly what groups are relevant and have competence over any particular problem. A lot of messy thinking has occurred and consequently a lot of messy action because of the conglomeration of persons and concepts. The pressures acting upon people in particular networks conflict with pressures acting on the same persons in other networks. As an example: The pressure on the U.S. government to respond to negotiating demands from underdeveloped countries conflicts with negotiations which the U.S. government is engaged in with local interests within the U.S. over prices of steel or prices of money, etc. This experience demonstrates a common feature in the bargaining process, that is, that parties in particular negotiations within particular contexts are thinking not only in terms of the politics of that network but equally of the politics of other networks in which they participate. We cannot, therefore, make sense of any particular network unless we place it in a wider context and see the overlapping vulnerabilities that are acting upon people's decisions.

Many times we feel that North-South negotiations take place only in global forums. This is not the case. They can take place in government offices between transnational subsidiary managers and a government minister. In other words, the physical location of North-South negotiations is literally all over the world. Negotiations sometimes take the form of litigation within national courts. They sometimes occur directly between foreign managers and local workers. In addition to multilateral contexts, there are also bilateral forums of negotiations, usually within the context of patterns of dominance and dependence.

Negotiations in formal international legal forums such as the United Nations and its various agencies are based on a voting system; that is, they are quasi-legislative. This usually contrasts with the real world situation because the forums are usually based on the one-country, one-vote concept, whereas in the real world negotiations are based on other realities such as the distribution of wealth, power, and armaments. There is a difference between what can be achieved in negotiation conducted within a context of assumed equality and negotiation conducted in the real world of courts and concessions, agreements, and corporate negotiations. If the Northern and the Southern countries are to bargain productively in serious discussions, their reasons for coming to the bargaining table must result from pressures in the real world and not solely the pressures from within multilateral institutions. It cannot be forgotten that the North, because of its position in the real world outside of these negotiating forums, has the power base to fend off calls for negotiation in those forums.

Further, in many instances the diplomats in international forums and the development professionals are way ahead of others in their own governments. International forums thus become a world in themselves, separate realities with their own perceptions, which are often not coherent with perceptions in the respective countries. The problem is compounded by the segmentation within countries of the bureaucratic structure of lines of communication. What often happens is that a representative of a government will vote one way within, for example, the United Nations Development Program and vote completely differently in another forum on the same question—quite apart from what happens when ministries act in a conflicting manner in the country itself. So this process of disarticulation further exacerbates the problem of who negotiates with whom, when, and on what subjects.

Changing personnel also does little to improve the atmosphere for successful negotiations. One of the difficulties, particularly within the Northern countries as they attempt to negotiate with other countries, is that each administration has to go through a new learning process and reinvent the wheel every few years, only to discover that the positions proffered do not necessarily hold in the real world.

The source of power is revealed as another important element in the negotiations. Many times we forget that there is a difference between latent power and available power; many times the difference between the latent and the available is awareness that the power is there to be taken, grasped, or mobilized. The capacity to harness or to exercise power will be a function of elements such as information, location, or role in the network, wealth, technology, creativity, and personnel. In addition, the solidarity found in formal forums, particularly as manifested in South-South contacts, is often at variance with fragmentation in the real world, so that the prophesies of penetration and marginalization that obtain in the North-South patterns of dominance and dependence are at variance with the more advanced vision of the general fraternity of diplomats. These problems have to be taken explicitly into account and worked into the negotiating equation.

Bringing Class to Negotiations

Perceived interests vary; parties perceive their interests in various ways and obviously make conflicting demands on the same set of practices. Benefits can take the form of wealth through trade, power, or the capacity to transform. The struggle for change has been centered largely on the attempt to redefine the interests of various groups within the world as it undergoes transformation. A factor that many analysts and activists seem to shy away from in the North-South discussion is the historical context or the class context of negotiation. The whole idea of class and the dialectic between conflicting groups is avoided, as analysis is attempted purely in terms of structural context, that is, nice, neat, sanitized categories. We must recognize that there are people—not just in the Northern countries—who have a stake in the preservation of the status quo or modification of the status quo who, for all intents and purposes, are members of the same class. Equally, there are those who have interests in moving toward transformation, in the direction of justice.

Discussions in international forums often point to the lack of political will. This idea seems to be somewhat mystical and is perhaps a chimera. Political will is irrelevant unless we identify the class interests of the persons acting. People will not usually act against their perceived interests.

We do not need to engage in an elaborate discussion of the dynamics of the proposals to consider some brief suggestions on ways to strengthen current North-South negotiating processes.

One problem in the North-South negotiations, who will represent whom, suggests an area for fresh analysis and new approaches. The Northern countries argue that "we can't negotiate with all one hundred-odd Southern countries simultaneously; therefore, pick from among you those who will come up to see us and we will talk with them." In reply to this, we need only to reconsider the issues surrounding the point about whether problems center on the structure or on change within the structure. Some problems simply do not allow for a pattern of representative negotiation. Others do. Problems of principle such as indexation in trade or the codes of conduct for transnational corporations can be negotiated by representatives of typical groups. But typical groups break down when we apply the concept of networks. Representatives can negotiate on behalf of categories of groups; for instance, mineral-exporting countries constitute a group that might negotiate over the principles of mineral exportation and transformation for such metals as copper, bauxite, and tungsten; they can send representatives to argue over the generic principles affecting all. When the problems get down to the specifics, however, all parties affected by a particular network of relationships have to be involved, and not only governments. In the case of a particular mineral, not only do the governments have to negotiate, but so do the unions, the industrialists in the North who are consuming the metal, indeed, all parties across the globe affected by the concrete problem are part of such North-South negotiation. Ways must be found to facilitate this kind of contact, discussion, and coherent negotiation.

Finally, as part of a new negotiating strategy, the issues of global negotiation need to be linked with the issues of peace and environment. In this connection also, Third World negotiators need to have a secretariat to organize their thinking and strategies. Further, governments of the respective countries need to facilitate negotiations not only among themselves but among the respective subnational groups that are affected by the various concrete problems.

Canadian Perspectives on the North-South Dialogue

Mark MacGuigan

As the foreign minister of my country, I have no hesitation in saying that Canada's national self-interest is the major determinant of our foreign policy. We are involved in the North-South dialogue—and will continue to be so—precisely because we believe it is important for our self-interest. National self-interest, however, cannot be defined narrowly and parochially: it must be viewed both broadly and over the long term.

For Canada is faced with some inescapable realities. Geography has given us, as our immediate neighbor, the most powerful nation in the world. It has been said that when the United States catches a cold, Canada contracts pneumonia. Having only one-tenth the population of the United States, Canada has therefore tended to look to universally agreed "rules of the game" to help put us on a more equal footing when conflicts of interest occur. Our geography has additional consequences. Without any other close geographical neighbors, we do not fall naturally into any regional grouping. Regional associations that discriminate against nonregional partners can thus have a greater negative impact on Canada than on other nations. So while supportive of efforts for regional cooperation, we have continued to emphasize global solutions to the problems of international economic relations.

Our relatively small population means a small domestic market, and consequently we are heavily dependent on trade for our economic growth. In fact, about 30 percent of our GNP is dependent on exports, compared with 12 percent for the United States. Of the major industrialized countries represented at the annual economic summits, none is more dependent than Canada on its trade dimension for economic growth. Just to illustrate, it is estimated that more than two million Canadians are directly involved in the production of goods for export—that is about 20 percent of our total work force. Our major export industries are also our most efficient producers. They command the best prospects for future growth and, most significantly, for the generation of profitable jobs for Canadians.

Such basic interests have led over the years to consistent Canadian attempts to "multilateralize" our economic relationships. Leaders such as Louis St. Laurent and Lester Pearson were keenly aware that our long-term interests were best served through the development of international institutions that would balance the influence of the great powers and contribute to a broader stability in the world. Canada, like our partners, clearly benefits from an economic system that promotes global and nondiscriminatory approaches and commands the support of all major players.

It is precisely our stake in an open and stable international economic system that has driven home to us the importance of encouraging fuller participation of developing countries in that system. We welcome their input in creating a system more responsive to their needs. Surely it cannot be in anyone's self-interest to deny fundamental economic justice to vast numbers of peoples when we know that the perception of justice denied has so often led to international conflict and violence. Like justice, the system must not only be fair; it must also be seen to be fair if it is to function effectively.

In the light of these national interests, the Canadian government has elaborated two underlying principles to govern our approach to North-South issues. The first is the Canadian commitment to social justice. In a shrinking world, we have had to broaden the definition of who are our "neighbors." With 800 million people living in absolute poverty, we cannot turn a blind eye to the plight of others, regardless of national boundaries or the ideologies that may divide us. Canadians have come to expect that a moral dimension be reflected in their country's foreign policy. Thus, one of the wellsprings of Canada's development assistance program is a straightforwardly humanitarian concern for the welfare of the poorest and the dispossessed on "spaceship earth." But it is not simply a question of social justice. We have come to realize that, in an increasingly interdependent world, it is in the mutual self-interest of all nations to ensure that the problems of developing countries are effectively addressed. This is the second of our two guiding principles.

The extent of global economic interdependence need not be elaborated. All of us are only too conscious of the importance of developing countries to Western economies as well as the inverse. Even for the United States, whose economy has essentially been driven by domestic rather than international markets, the acceleration of interdependence among nations for goods and services has had the effect of eroding the relative isolation of the U.S. economy. By 1979, in fact, one American worker in twenty was employed in production of exports destined specifically for the Third World.

Interdependence is thus no longer an option. Interdependence is in fact a condition of international life today. The challenge for all governments, now more than ever, is therefore to summon the courage and wisdom to avoid shortsighted assertions of national interest which have a "beggar thy neighbor" effect.

As a member of Parliament for a riding that depends upon automotive production, I can well appreciate the real dilemmas involved. The mutual gains that trade can have for developed and developing countries are not always evident to the unemployed automotive or textile worker, although they can be very obvious for a higher paid worker producing aircraft or high-technology products for export. But in these days of severe global economic difficulties, a return to the attitudes and policies of half a century ago would serve none of us well.

It is for these fundamental reasons that Canada has been concerned not only to enhance the development prospects of developing countries and strengthen the functioning of international institutions, but also to play an active and unique role in the negotiation of the whole range of issues that constitute the North-South dialogue.

Canada's Role

Our economy is at once industrialized and resource-based; sophisticated, yet in some ways underdeveloped. Thus, we share many of the perspectives of our industrialized partners. At the same time, our position as a major exporter of raw materials and net importer of capital and technology is similar to the situation of many developing countries. Canada has been characterized both as the world's smallest industrialized country and as its largest developing country. Appreciating the real concerns and interests of both groups, Canada has often found itself playing an "honest broker" role in multilateral negotiations. We have consistently sought to stimulate movement and to conciliate the conflicting views of industrialized and developing countries.

Our capacity to play this bridge-building role between countries of the North and South has also been enhanced by our political ties. We are a member of the industrialized West with strong ties to the United States, Europe, and Japan. We participate in the annual economic summits of the major industrialized countries. Yet we are a middle power with membership in the OECD and the "like-minded" group of Western nations that share common concerns about developments in the Third World.

We also have ties to developing countries in all parts of the world. Given our lack of a colonialist past and of geopolitical ambitions, developing countries are sometimes less suspicious of Canadian motives than they may be of those of some other industrialized countries. Moreover, a number of associations, particularly the Commonwealth and La Francophonie, have provided us with unique windows on the concerns of developing countries.

Finally, there is the impact that a distinctive international role has had on Canada's sense of itself. I firmly believe that because Canada is a widely diverse country with strong regional identifications, and with a bilingual and multicultural society, a strong international presence has in fact helped solidify a national Canadian identity and self-perception in a global context.

The International Scene

There has been no turn-around in the deep economic recession we are all facing. Inflation, unemployment, budgetary deficits, and interest rates all remain high—with pernicious economic and social effects. In response to anxious and often angry publics, many governments are increasingly focusing attention on putting their own houses in order. As a consequence, funds available for concessional assistance are in fact—and regrettably—declining. Total Official Development Assistance (ODA) from the OECD countries actually fell by 4 percent in real terms in 1981, and the average ODA as a percentage of GNP fell from .38 to .35. Amounts available from capital surplus OPEC countries have similarly dropped in the past two years. This means problems in funding current international programs and real difficulty in finding money for new initiatives.

Canada remains committed to reaching a target of .5 percent of GNP by 1985, and to make our best efforts to reach .7 percent by 1990. But we, too, will have difficulty finding substantial new sums of money to support international initiatives that we may regard as important and desirable.

The difficulties in generating substantial additional aid flows, notwithstanding, international economic cooperation will continue to be critical. If prospects for the industrialized world are poor, for the populations of the developing world it is a matter of survival. The economic difficulties of the time argue not for less action but for more.

Basic to our efforts must be the elimination of hunger and malnutrition. But what is the key to these efforts? Projections suggest that the physical and technological constraints to feeding an expanding world population are not insurmountable. It is rather a question of political direction. Developing countries themselves must make special efforts to increase domestic food production and to ensure adequate storage and distribution. I am heartened in this regard by the progress being made on food sector strategies, including the support that is being given to them by the international community. For Canada's part, we are allocating over 40 percent of our official development assistance—more than $5 thousand million over five years—to the food and agricultural sector.

Energy exploration and development in oil-importing developing countries also continue to be of key importance. Canada has made this a priority sector in its bilateral development assistance. Similarly, Petro-Canada International, with initial funding of $250 million to provide assistance for oil and gas exploration in developing countries, is now operational. Exploration projects are planned in Tanzania, Jamaica, and Senegal and are under consideration for a number of other countries. On the multilateral level, while the idea of a World Bank energy affiliate now appears unlikely to go ahead, we will continue to seek other methods to advance increased energy lending.

A healthy international trading system is also vital to prospects for economic growth and development in industrialized and Third World countries alike. The GATT, and policies established by its ministerial meetings, provides a major opportunity to address current problems in trade and to set a trade agenda for the 1980s. We hope that issues of concern to developing countries can be addressed in ways that strengthen and make more relevant the international trading system as a whole. In this regard, it is time for the newly industrializing countries to accept more obligations under the GATT and to make a contribution to the international trading framework commensurate with their stake in the system.

Closely related, of course, is the effective functioning of the international monetary and financial system.

The North-South dialogue will be with us in one form or another for many years to come. The need to encourage the growth of the developing countries, both for humanitarian and economic reasons, will not disappear. Although the world is going through a difficult period, the acceptance of global interdependence by world leaders has been a major accomplishment. The challenge before us is to translate this acceptance into concrete action. Canada certainly intends to continue playing its full part. But in the coming years sustained efforts will be needed from all of us concerned with North-South relations. I would therefore urge that we not allow ourselves to become discouraged. Governments, if we are to move ahead, need the support of and the ideas from nongovernmental forums such as SID. And if we do not hang together, then most assuredly we will hang separately. There is simply no other choice.

The United States and the Less Developed Countries

Peter McPherson

The United States is intensely aware of the problems in the Third World, and we want to continue to contribute to their solutions. But the situation is not all dismal. Take a long view, and progress can clearly be seen. For example, in the mid-1950s only 1 percent of the Nepalese children of school age ever entered school at all. Today about 70 percent at least enter school at some time. The USAID is proud of the assistance that we gave to the government of Nepal to help build that educational system. Another example: in the mid-1950s, India's grain production was about 50 million tons a year. The effects of that could be seen in the pictures of starving people we saw in the past. Last year, grain production in India was in excess of 130 million tons. This established, more or less, self-sufficiency in grain, though distribution problems remained. What an achievement for the people of India and of course for the U.S. and other donors who contributed to that effort over the years. Yes, we have made progress, but enormous problems remain.

Where do we go from here?

The United States believes that we must increase productivity in the Third World, but in doing so we cannot lose sight of our mission of raising the standard of living of the poor people in those countries. The means for helping the poor may be in dispute, but there is no question about the goal. We believe that the means for helping the poor people is to increase productivity in all sectors of LDCs. The United States believes that additional help needs to be given to the LDCs from outside but that the LDCs can do enormous amounts for themselves by, for example, changing various policies within their own countries. For example, food subsidies for urbanites brought about by holding down prices paid to farmers often discourage productivity and in fact may discriminate against the poorest group of people in a country. Foreign aid used for fertilizer and cheap credit to these farmers often does no more than keep down the prices paid to the farmers and accordingly is merely a thinly disguised subsidy for urban food. On the other hand, the world has many examples of what happens when the discrimination against the poor farmer has been stopped or reduced: the farmer has responded with enormous increases in productivity. Such productivity has been to the benefit of everyone, including the urban consumers. Wheat production in Pakistan in recent years is one such case: in just a few years Pakistan doubled its production, in part because of higher prices paid to farmers. In short, we believe that farmers and other people can produce more if they are given a reason to do so and have the tools to undertake the job.

Let me put this interest in production in a broader policy framework. At least six factors are important to growth in LDCs. They are (*a*) trade, (*b*) reasonably strong economies in the developed and newly industrialized countries, (*c*) continued and substantial foreign aid from developed countries, (*d*) foreign investment in the LDCs, (*e*) the right policy environment in the LDCs themselves, and (*f*) continued technology creation, adaptation, and transfer to the LDCs.

First, as to trade. The United States has long been a leader for freer trade. The Caribbean Basin Initiative is an example of our efforts. By this, we are proposing a one-way free trade for the Caribbean countries and Central America to the United States, assuming these countries individually make policy changes needed to contribute to their own growth—a very important assumption, we believe. In addition, the U.S. government has proposed that GATT be opened up to discussions with the LDCs. This can be of enormous importance and in time we believe can far overshadow the struggles over resource transfers.

Second, I mentioned the need for strong economies in the developed countries and the newly industrialized economies. These economies obviously are the key to strong markets for LDC exports. Also, the United States is, of course, intensely conscious of the negative impact high interest rates have on our own economy and on the interest costs of LDCs in other countries. We certainly hope these interest rates will go down in the future.

Third, the industrialized countries need to continue their economic assistance to LDCs. Such assistance will be needed for training and institutional building, for example. We must never forget that trained people and good institutions are usually the most critical link to economic development. Resources rarely substitute for such people and institutions. The U.S. foreign aid program is increasing its efforts in these areas. Among all the needs that the LDCs face, I should mention the important role of outside assistance in building infrastructure in such places as Africa. The United States is continuing its commitment to a strong foreign aid program. Contrary in fact to some of the public perception and despite cuts in most of the U.S. government programs, our bilateral foreign aid program under the Reagan administration has been increased.

Fourth, foreign investments in the LDCs must be encouraged. The United States needed substantial foreign investment during its early stages of economic take-off, and few other countries have achieved such take-off without large foreign investment. An LDC should total up its potential investments—investment revenue from taxes, savings by its citizens, reinvestment of earnings by its businesses, and from foreign aid. Simplistically, that total should then be compared with the capital needs of the hoped-for economic growth in that country. Almost always the LDC is going to find that there will be a major shortfall that can be made up only from outside. We in the United States are not only or even primarily suggesting U.S. investment. The world has a very active investment community that will go where there are opportunities. Of course, an LDC can expect that investors be responsible and take a long-term view. But LDCs cannot persuade investors to come in if their policies effectively exclude or preclude investors from making money. We think there may be things that can be done to encourage foreign investment. The most important, of course, is the environment in the host country. In addition, we support the idea recently advanced by World Bank President Clausen that a World Bank–related entity be set up to insure against certain noncommercial risks incurred by investors in LDCs. The U.S. government has such an entity for its citizens, as do many other developed countries. But investors from some other countries tell us that they could use such an insuring entity.

Fifth, the policies of LDCs are frequently, in our judgment, more important to LDCs than the assistance and the resource transfers that they get from donors. For example, a country cannot expect to diversify and increase its exports if exchange rates and controls are, in effect, a substantial tax on exports. We look at Korea, Singapore, and so forth, and we know that growth can be obtained. Health care is another area where LDC policies are important. In the next few years we believe that many LDCs probably will need to deal with the dogma that health care must be free to its people. We believe that some charge for health care results in better use of health care and also means that resources are available to reach more people. In short, free health care almost always discriminates against poor people, because many poor people end up not being served at all for lack of resources. The United States is proud of its continuing leadership in primary health care. We are in some forty countries with primary health care projects. But there are, we believe, fundamental policy issues that many LDCs must yet face.

As another example of the importance of policy, I mentioned earlier the policy of discrimination against the poor farmer. I doubt that India would have achieved its full grain production of recent times without increasing the prices it paid its farmers. I firmly believe that many subsidies in the LDCs end up discriminating against the poorest people because they are the least politically powerful and because poor people are often most inconvenient and/or impossible for government programs to serve. More and more of the donor community thinks of itself as development bankers who invest their resources in programs where there is a real chance for growth and change as opposed to a continuation of subsidies and of dependency. This consciousness regarding policy, on the part of donors, is now substantially established. It clearly is a wave of the future, especially given the scarcity of foreign assistance resources.

Sixth, technological creation, adaptation, and transfer is critical. We believe that there must be more "green revolutions"—green revolutions in health, in agriculture, in family planning, and so on. The United States has made and wishes to make contributions in various technological areas. We are planning to substantially increase our biomedical research efforts, perhaps as much as double them. We are proud of our contribution to oral rehydration technology, a technology that apparently will have an important impact upon child mortality.

We continue to provide substantial support to the efforts to find a vaccination for malaria, as an example. We continue to be the largest donor to international agriculture research centers and have recently mobilized the U.S. university communities to do additional agricultural research work, such as to increase the productivity of sorghum and millet. These crops are really poor people's crops on which very little work has been done in the past. Such agricultural research is very important because donors have far too often encouraged LDCs to set up extension programs when there really was nothing to extend. The United States expects to make a major commitment to augmenting irrigation technology. Eighty percent of the irrigation of the world is in Asia, and we think additional technology can be created to sufficiently aid the people on that continent in other areas. We are doubling our research on contraceptive technology. We need more breakthroughs to deal with the population explosion of so many poor countries. The United States is proud of the contribution it has made to family planning in countries like Indonesia, Thailand, Colombia, but the need is still so very great. Kenya, for example, witnesses a 4 percent population increase each year. The United States will continue to keep up a current family planning program, but new and safe contraceptive methods are needed to do a better job.

To summarize, LDCs will find strength in aggressively following policies that will produce growth, not dependence. The developed countries need to do their part by giving economic assistance, by promoting freer trade, by keeping their economies as strong as possible, by investing in LDCs, and by helping to create and transfer technology. The mutual advantage of working together in all these areas is so very clear. The harm in not building together is so very great. We simply must meet the challenge.

Privately Aiding Development

Olof Murelius

Development and the Private Sector

Aid policy differs from one country to another. We need not pretend that aid is given for entirely unselfish motives. The opinion one wishes to convey often depends on the audience. In the representative assemblies of some donor countries it has been openly stated that every unit of aid produces more than the equivalent in orders for the home country. Aid agencies may maintain that they are working for the welfare of the developing countries alone. But aid is an integral part of foreign policy, and trade policy is an aspect of foreign policy. In the United States, representatives of the business community have said that without government support the private sector would be at a competitive disadvantage compared with companies in other industrialized countries. In the present international economic climate donors are increasingly using aid for selfish economic motives. One sign of this is that multilateral aid is decreasing and bilateral aid increasing. It may not make much difference if one donor increases bilateral aid and ties it to the national economic interest and another reduces aid but compensates by subsidizing the private sector in its activities in the Third World.

During the last several years leaders in banking, industry, and business have suggested a new and expanded role for the private sector. They have said that the private sector must begin to think in terms of development, not only as a matter of social responsibility, but in their own long-term interest. As one U.S. executive has observed, "If we shut our eyes to the increased interdependence of the world, we do a disservice to ourselves and the rest of the world."

Others have expressed the opposite point of view: it would be best if foreign private investment in developing countries were discouraged. Those who adopt this attitude may be proponents of "delinking" by developing countries from the international system, or members of trade unions in industrialized countries who fear that jobs will be exported to low-wage countries. There are also those who insist that the private sector should respond only to market forces and that any intervention by public authorities is detrimental.

It is important to realize that the private sector, domestic and foreign, is already profiting from development assistance in the sense that all efforts to improve health, education and training, social and physical infrastructure, and development policy and planning indirectly benefits those who lend, invest, and conduct business in the host country. The question at issue is whether business and development assistance should keep strictly separate or collaborate—and how. It is a complicated question that needs to be addressed.

Problems connected with private foreign investment in developing countries have been studied in great detail. The rhetoric at some international meetings attended by official representatives of countries from the North and the South is often inflamed and tends to be misleading. At the practical level the conflict of interest is less serious, even though substantial differences of perception persist. The foreign private sector has accepted the Calvo Doctrine, which affirms the legitimacy of the host-country insistence on the supremacy of the local law and judicial system, and with the exception of the extractive industry this has not been a significant deterrent to foreign investment. Transnational corporations have tended to become scapegoats in the development debate, and there has been much talk of "taming the multinationals." But transnational firms differ significantly among themselves and tend to reflect the views and practices of the industrial sector in which their affiliates operate rather than their status as transnationals or their nationality. Even the conflict between corporate goals and the development objectives of the host country government has less to do with the nationality of the parent company than with the difference between public and private aims.

There is good reason to believe that domestic and external views on the whole range of issues connected with foreign private investment can be reconciled once the essential preconditions and the facts are conveyed and mutually understood. To mention a few examples:

○ Separating the foreign investment package ("unbundling") into its major components (capital, technology, management, and marketing) may give the host country greater control and may in some cases increase the net return. And countries or firms are of course free to negotiate any type of package they desire. According to an international survey by the Committee for Economic Development (CED), most of the firms questioned believed, however, that the cost to the developing country of unbundling would be substantially greater than the cost of the standard package.

○ Most manufacturing firms would be prepared to export from local subsidiaries in order to improve the balance-of-payments of the host country as long as this is economically justified.

○ Renegotiation of contracts is recognized as potentially advantageous to both parties and no longer offers any great difficulty.

○ Most U.S. firms agreed that manipulative transfer pricing was contrary to company policy and that the use of it was explained by legitimate economic considerations dictated by prevailing circumstances in the home and/ or host country.

○ Most firms want the development objectives of the host country to be clearly articulated, since they wish to comply with them as long as this is also in their own economic interest. A stable framework of law and regulation is an important factor in that context. Some foreign firms suggested that methods be devised to measure their social contributions to host-country objectives.

○ Abuse of dominant market power was recognized to be an appropriate subject for public policy, regardless of whether the practice is engaged in by a domestic company or a foreign firm with a local affiliate.

○ Ways should be found to strengthen the negotiating capacity of developing countries. An important task in that connection is to improve and expand existing systems of information.

A great number of questions pertaining to aid, trade, and investment must be considered before an expanded program of collaboration between aid agencies and the private sector can be designed. How can the private sector be made more development minded? The private sector is often more efficient (cost-effective) in manufacturing and distributing goods and services than the public sector. Many international marketing organizations work effectively in widely differing and difficult environments. This is illustrated by the story of how Stanley found Livingstone in the jungles of Africa. When he sees him he utters the classic words "Dr. Livingstone, I presume?" and Livingstone replies "Have a Coke, Mr. Stanley." If Coca Cola can do it. . . . But what exactly *do* they do? Do they transfer any knowledge? Do they increase self-reliance? Do they satisfy other host-country objectives?

How is a greater sense of social responsibility encouraged? Often social responsibility comes as a result of social or political pressure. After the experience in Chile, ITT for example has left South Africa and declined an order from the military and the police to build up a data system. The development effect of transnational corporations varies from country to country depending on the nature of their products and services, on their interest in the economic and social development of the host country, and on the regulations and attitude of the local authorities. While the aim of aid is to make itself superfluous, this cannot be an objective of business.

What incentives are needed and provided for affiliates of foreign firms to identify with local development efforts by expanding their activities through reinvestment of profits? The eight largest accounting firms are established in nearly all developing countries. What have they done to assist? Have they cornered the market? Some officials in developing countries say that these firms "steal" the few accountants whom the government has educated and so badly needs itself.

How can the private sector assist development without special subsidies? It is generally recognized that subsidies should be avoided since they tend to distort commercial activities and reduce the competitiveness of subsidized firms. How does a government select industries and enterprises for joint development efforts in developing countries without being accused of favoritism? And how does it avoid discriminating between developing countries? The United States has agreed to buy and stockpile bauxite from Jamaica; it has allowed tax write-offs for conventions held on the island; it has given unprecedented tariff breaks—27 products were approved for duty-free status, including items that incur tariffs when imported from other developing countries, for example, Mexico.

How can the wrong kind of industrialization be prevented? Even before the fall of the Shah, Iran was referred to by some consultants as an "industrial graveyard." What is the private sector doing now in other rich but vulnerable developing countries? Will these countries be able to sustain the rapid rate of modernization? Who can and will offer objective advice?

Competition among foreign firms helps to secure education and training of the kind of staff they themselves need, but beyond a certain point support must come from the host government and/or aid agencies. Where the interest of foreign private investors is threatened, they tend to withdraw. There is an increasing interest in management contracts to replace risk investment. It has been proposed—and may be worth serious consideration—that aid agencies should provide the funds and let the private sector do the job wherever suitable.

Issues in Programing Assistance for Development

Aid tends to be conceived by bureaucrats and also to a considerable extent to be designed and implemented by them—needless to say, in cooperation with the host government. It is as a rule negotiated from the apex of one bureaucracy to another. This has probably promoted the development of an oversized public sector. Has it stifled the spirit of enterprise? Do the indicative planning figures (financial frames) provided by bilateral and multilateral aid agencies lead to a type of programming that reduces flexibility and creativity? It has been noticed, for example, that during the period of what we refer to as the energy crisis, aid funds were already committed for a period of years and it was hard to stimulate requests for energy projects. Tying aid reduces the value of that aid by prescribing imports from the donor country, and consultants often function as trade promoters. On the other hand, there is also a complaint about the "tyranny of international specifications" when international competitive bidding is the standard procedure. Aid does not easily make itself superfluous, and the dependence of developing countries remains.

Transnational corporations do not seem to find it difficult to establish subsidiaries in developing countries and to make their activities meaningful from the point of view of profits and overall corporate strategy. It is a different matter to stimulate the development of local industries.

In the case of small-scale industry, significant benefits come only after long and patient efforts, which do not easily invite foreign private investment. There are a few interesting examples within the program of development cooperation between Tanzania and Sweden. A number of so-called sister industries have been established as joint ventures between small-scale Swedish industries that help duplicate their activities in Tanzania through contracts negotiated with Swedish legal assistance and including specified supplies, production targets, and training. The scheme has been supported by the establishment and promotion of a

Small Industries Development Organization (SIDO), which provides credit and services to Tanzanian firms. Another related activity is that of the Tanzania Industrial Studies and Consultancy Organization (TISCO), which promotes industrial investment and development of local consultants.

Projects are the cutting edge of development, but domestic capacity to handle the project cycle is still inadequate in most developing countries, and projects tend therefore to be in the hands of foreign consultants and experts. The project cycle consists of a series of activities all the way from preliminary surveys and studies through project identification and feasibility studies to design, implementation, supervision, and evaluation of effects for policy formulation and the generation of new projects. In Latin America these activities have been promoted through the establishment of preinvestment funds that lend money for project studies and monitor the loans. This has in a comparatively short time led to the growth of an important corps of domestic consultants, some of whom have obtained international contracts through competitive bids. This has increased self-sufficiency and the capacity to manage external inputs.

The aid effort should be decentralized and based as far as possible on the concept of mutual interest. This would involve not only the private sector but also public enterprises, agencies, and institutions in direct contact with their counterparts in the developing countries. Such direct contacts among professionals could facilitate the development effort, increase mutual commitment, and make it more cost-effective. But it presumes that the aid agency would retain the power of the purse and the functions of executive policy formulation, information, monitoring, and evaluation.

The question that remains is how to bridge the gap between development assistance and commercial activity, for it is no use denying that there are conflicting interests. It is one thing to make the local environment conducive to private foreign investment; it is another matter to induce foreign industrial and commercial resources and competence to identify with the government and people of developing countries.

The private sector is waiting for signals from governments as to what they expect from business in the development field; this was clearly spelled out in a recent press release from the ICC (No. 664/481). The question should perhaps be turned around and business invited to present its ideas. Any member of the private sector—bank, industry, trading company, consultant, trade association —who could make a significant contribution to development should know that a proposal for assistance to a well-prepared project would be seriously considered and evaluated. Perhaps what we need is a Third World Corporation ("3W Company"), established by persons with experience and competence in business and industry and a firm commitment to assist developing countries in their difficult struggle to cope both with their own problems and with those posed by the external interests on which they are dependent. It is hard to see how a Marshall Plan equivalent for the Third World could be conceived and successfully implemented without the effective involvement of the private sector.

Sources

For the preparation of this material the following sources of information deserve special mention:

Frank, Isaiah. *Foreign Enterprise in Developing Countries*. Baltimore and London: Committee for Economic Development and the Johns Hopkins University Press, 1980.

Hansen, Roger. "North-South Policy—What is the Problem?" *Foreign Affairs* 58, no. 5 (1980).

Jolly, Richard. "Mutual Interests and the Implications for Reform of the International Economic Order." Paper presented to the symposium "The Past and Prospects of the Economic World Order" (Institute for International Economic Studies), Saltsjobaden, Sweden, 25–28 Aug. 1978.

Lindbeck, Assar. "Den basta u-landshjalpen (The Best Type of Development Assistance)," *Ekonomisk Debatt* (Stockholm) 1979:1.

Book III

Insiders' Experiences

Development and Society: An Overview of the Indian Experience

Pran Chopra

India some twenty-five years ago began a very special period in her history. The beginning of that period marked the end of history's largest program of antigrowth, antidevelopment, and state-guided impoverishment, and the first steps toward self-conscious state-guided growth and development. It also marked perhaps the first experiments of this kind anywhere in the developing world outside the centrally planned economies.

Virtually up to the time India became independent in 1947, for a century and three-quarters, British power, which then constituted state power in India, drained away India's economic resources at a rate for which there is no parallel in the history of colonial exploitation. Estimates vary, but one notable one suggests that what was drained away annually from India was equal to about 40 percent of Britain's own domestic product. That is well above the proportion that a country normally needs to invest in its future to reach the take-off stage. If this had not happened the state of India's economy might have been rather different when India became independent, and so too might have been the state of the British economy and ultimately its impact upon world history throughout the nineteenth century. This is not nationalistic lamentation. As the major landmark of the economic history of modern India, it has to be kept in view or else we lose our way as we track what has been happening in the past quarter-century.

There were five main mechanisms for siphoning off Indian resources to Britain. First, Indian exports to Britain, not to be mistaken for a trade balance in India's favor. What Britain required was taken out in large quantities—gold, agricultural products, and minerals needed by British industry—regardless of the effect upon India's own growth. Little of much value to India was imported from Britain, and the balance largely remained unpaid for. Second, large-scale import of British manufactures, unnecessary for India's own industrialization, had the effect of snuffing out many small-scale industries in India. Third, tariffs: Indian manufactures that could have competed in Britain—given a fair chance —such as textiles, had to face prohibitive tariffs and sometimes punishments under the law. Fourth, direct British charges on Indian revenues, known as Home Charges. Fifth, large-scale remittances of the salaries, pensions, and other funds of British personnel serving in India and the profits of British merchants engaged in India's domestic trade. The last two factors drained away almost as much as the first three.

In addition to this drain, India's economy suffered two severe distortions. Food availability per person declined, and thus the effects of poverty were aggravated because production of foodgrains, which were not needed for export to Britain, grew not only slower than the population but three times slower than the cash crops needed by British industry. Further, for the sake of more convenient administration by an alien power, a type of revenue control through rentiers, known as the permanent settlement, was imposed upon large parts of northern India that are still in the throttling grip of its after-effects, unable to obtain the benefits reaped elsewhere in India through peasant proprietorships.

When we assess the state of the present economy, problems of measurement arise when we examine the indicators. The first problem is that it is very difficult to know the true size of the Indian economy, and especially that part of it which is euphemistically described as the parallel economy and more frankly as the illegal economy or the black market. Everyone knows that there is an enormous black market, but some guesses put it as large as half the official economy. Everyone knows it is growing, but some calculate that it is growing faster than the official economy and so is catching up with the latter in size. The importance of this fact here is that it adds a wide margin of error to official estimates of the size of the Indian economy, and therefore to the rate of its growth at any given time—especially to the size and growth rate of some sectors of industry and trade.

Official statisticians claim that whatever is produced in the black-market economy is detected and counted at one or another of their many checkpoints, but there is no convincing evidence to support the claim. The black market pays no excise duty on its product, pays no income tax on its profits, and buys, manufactures, warehouses, and retails in a closed and opaque cycle. It draws working funds from and deposits incomes into accounts that do not exist in visible books. Official eyes would not be able to read them if they tried, but one of the achievements of the black marketeer is that he is always able to persuade the official eye not to try very hard.

Another unmeasured sector of the economy lies at the opposite end, in very small-scale industry, trade, and especially agriculture. It does not hide itself and cannot collude very much with detectors. It is simply that its waters are too shallow for our statistical ships, and even guesses about its depth are impossible. Until a decade or so ago this did not matter very much. The size of this unknown sector was too small to make much difference in national accounts. The situation has changed, however. The recent thrust in agriculture has multiplied many times those minute transactions in the village economy, generally of a barter type, which always were and still are too small to be measured but now add up to a fair slice of the GNP.

These two unmeasurable sectors have produced, between them, the second problem of measurement: It is hard to measure the true incidence of poverty. All calculations of poverty are based, in one way or another, upon calculations of the per capita income. This in turn is calculated by dividing GNP by the population. Only in some respects and on a very random basis is the result cross-checked with physical verifications made in national sample surveys. The per capita income is thus underestimated, and the incidence of poverty overestimated, as the organized black market at the top end of the income scale and at the bottom end the unorganized barter economy of the village get excluded from the national account. The error could be as large as 30 percent. The problem of discovering how poor India is or is not is further compounded by the conventional economists themselves. Their estimates differ widely. So does their reading of the trend, even of its direction.

One of the best-known economists, B. S. Minhas, says 46 percent of the rural population lived below the poverty line in 1960–61 but the proportion came *down* to 37 percent in 1968–69. Others, equally well known, put the proportion between 33.1 percent and 38 percent in 1960–61, with increases between 40 percent and 54 percent by 1968–69. A study by the Planning Commission finds no trend at all. Changes taking place below the poverty line, for better or worse, remain unread, though these might affect the incomes of up to a third or half of the rural population. Also largely left out of account are changes in nonincome factors, such as health and education standards, resulting from good public policies in such states as Kerala or poor policies in the case of many other states.

The Failures

But these are only theological disputations. What is incontrovertible is that India's poverty is massive, ugly, and getting worse—even if the proportion of the population below the poverty line is falling. Many who live above the poverty line are also among the world's poorest. Their proportion is not falling. In fact, it may be increasing. Only a part of the blame for that goes to the legacy of the colonial past. Part also falls upon contemporary society and its politics, including things done and left undone by public authority and things done in the name of social and economic justice. Full note must be taken of them before the more positive part of the picture can emerge, or before some hopeful possibilities about the future can be expected to make a convincing appearance.

The most significant fact about India's economy is that it continues to be what it always was: mainly agricultural and therefore condemned to low rates of growth. Throughout the quarter-century of "development," the public sector, which by definition aims at restructuring the economy, has had a higher than 40 percent share of capital formation. More than 55 percent of public expenditure has gone to large industry, mining, power, and transport, and only half as much, sometimes only a third as much, has gone to items related to agriculture. Yet the share of these agricultural items in the GNP has declined from only about 50 percent to about 45 percent in years of normal production, and of industry and related items has remained at around 23 percent, or half the share of agriculture. Even higher is the share of agricultural labor in the total work force: over 70 percent, against industry's 10 percent. This is one of the main reasons for the low rate of growth of the national product as well as of the per capita product, because India is no exception to the nearly universal phenomenon that the higher the share of agriculture in the national income and of agricultural labor in the labor force, the lower the per capita income and product. Only countries like Malaysia are an exception to this near-rule; their agriculture is largely of the commercial plantation variety, which can be organized very much like industry and commands a very good export market.

The agricultural population is poor not only as a whole; within that group also, the majority is much poorer than a small minority. Those who are in this relatively privileged minority have a very disproportionate share of rural assets and of the means of production, and their share of the gains of the agricultural development that has taken place in India is still more disproportionately higher. Almost one-quarter of the cultivated land is controlled by the top 2.25 percent of the landowning households. One-third is controlled by the top 4 percent, and 60 percent by the top 15 percent. Concentration of the total rural assets is even higher than of land, and it is growing. The top 1 percent have almost 23 percent. The top 5 percent have 47 percent, and the top 10 percent have almost 59 percent. The bottom 10 percent controlled a quarter of 1 percent in 1961 and one-fifth of 1 percent in 1971. The total assets of the top brackets are even higher than their rural assets because they have diversified their rural earnings into nonrural assets. On the other hand, at the lower end of the ladder owners are losing land and becoming farm laborers, whose proportion in the total rural households rose from 25 to 35 percent in the ten years 1965–75; the proportion of landless labor in the total rural work force also rose from 18 percent to 22 percent over the same decade.

In this constantly deteriorating situation the consequence is that small farmers are becoming marginal and the latter are becoming landless, while more and more land passes into the hands of farmers who on the Indian scale have to be classified as medium and big. That they are also good producers is some saving grace in economic terms but not in sociopolitical terms.

The Achievements

However, whether one looks at growth or development, the picture is not uniformly dark. Far from it. Mention India and most people imagine something only unrelievedly poor, stagnant, and backward. Mention ASEAN and the image is of progress and prosperity. Yet areas and populations in India that are as large as the ASEAN countries put together have maintained growth rates as impressive as ASEAN's over long periods of time: that it does not easily show is another matter.

The combined population of ASEAN is about 40 percent of that of India. This 40 percent of the Indian population has, by all accounts, harvested all the benefits of growth attained by the Indian economy as a whole. The average annual growth rate of the Indian economy for the past thirty years or so has been 3.5 percent. Therefore, the 40 percent of the population that has monopolized the benefits of this growth has experienced a growth rate of about 8 percent, which is the same as, or marginally higher than, the growth rate experienced by the combined ASEAN population during the 1970s, and probably higher by a much wider margin than the ASEAN area's rate of growth during the past quarter-century.

Of course, these are only comparisons between rates of growth, not levels reached. The level reached is much lower even in this better-off group because it started lower, thanks to the legacy of looting referred to earlier. Even the level reached is not very visible, and for that there are several further reasons. One, growth is diffused through an agricultural spread and is not concentrated in strong urban centers of trade and commerce. No Indian city is even to this group what Bangkok and Manila are to their respective economic hinterlands. Two, the influx of population into these growth centers has been more significant than into, say, Singapore or Kuala Lumpur. The third reason is prodigious inefficiency.

Less visible, though, than would be the case of an ASEAN counterpart, the prosperity of the better-off Indian is drawn from sources that are more varied, better balanced, and would be more self-sustaining were they better managed. They are less dependent upon external markets; to the extent that they do need external buyers and suppliers, they have more strings to their bows than a few commodities. By the same means that the Indian economy has reached the size of some of the lower-level industrially advanced countries (though it is much less sophisticated and has to be shared by a much larger number of people), it has also acquired greater diversity, stronger internal complementarities, and greater capacity for self-sustaining growth than most other developing countries' economies.

There are anywhere between 50 million and 75 million Indians, perhaps 100 million in years of particularly good harvests, who, if they could contiguously hold their existing farms, industries, commercial enterprises, other productive assets, and the infrastructure that supports them, would form a nation that would qualify for joining the club of the developed countries. About two-thirds of them would be, or would belong to the households of, peasant proprietors of holdings varying in size between 2 and 12 hectares. On the Indian scale these are middle-sized landholdings. In Indian man-land ratios they have proved to be the most productive, and in Indian climatic conditions they have acquired a productivity that is among the best in the world.

These peasant proprietors are the main carriers of India's so-called green revolution, are largely responsible for keeping India's food production growing faster than the population, having freed India from the scandalous dependence during the 1950s and 1960s upon concessional food imports, and have become the foundation of a reasonably successful administration. In spite of them, India still imports food sometimes—no longer as food aid, but mainly to top off the buffer stock that is a key element in the food administration. Because of them, and because of this administration, even though the statistical per capita food availability is lower than during the days of large-scale food aid, steady availability at nearly steady prices is being maintained throughout India; recurring famines, once a familiar specter, have become a thing of the past.

The remaining one-third of these 75 million or so Indians belong to the white collar services and professions (most of them requiring college education and many requiring modern skills well above the average) and to industrial and commercial enterprises. They have built up an industrial structure, which ranges all the way from the traditional consumer industries like textiles through modern heavy engineering industries and the frontiers of elite industries and technologies like electronics, space, and genetics. They and the commercial entrepreneurs of this class are recognized as among the best anywhere.

This extrapolated "nation" of 75 million has average standards of income and performance, education, and modernization that are comparable to those of the less affluent among the developed countries. But probably it also has less poverty than the latter because it has a similar disparity between the income levels at the top and bottom ends of the scale. Its agricultural economy in particular, and to some extent the nonagricultural too, largely consists of the small- and medium-sized entrepreneur. But the most interesting thing about it is that if it were a nation it would be the youngest member of this size in the club of the developed countries. Some enterprises in it are much older, but most came into being in the past quarter-century.

The Context

The people of this nation constitute only about 12 to 15 percent of the people of India. But the Indian sociopolitical and economic system really rests upon them. They have created it just as much as it has created them. Their universe came into being through the democratization, as far as it went, of the Indian society and economy through the processes of political democracy. But this universe, especially its new agricultural society, has now become the main reason why economic, social, and political power is taking so much time to filter down further into the true base of the Indian population pyramid, where more than half of the Indian people live. But it is as likely as not that, just as they could not be stopped by those who would have liked to stop them, they will not be able to stop the power base from shifting further down, and this is as likely to happen if India remains a democracy as it is if India ceases to be one. The process has gone too far to be held up permanently.

India's national movement for independence was engineered and led by the urban middle classes, though the weight of the rural masses was also put behind it by the civil disobedience movement that Mahatma Gandhi created virtually singlehandedly. Therefore, such goals as it had beyond winning political independence did not aim at agrarian revolution or social and economic justice for the rural poor for the sake of such revolution or justice. Its aim for rural India, in any case of a lower priority than its aim for the urban-industrial India of the middle classes, was efficient and productive agriculture as a stable and efficient source of agricultural raw materials for industry and of food for the urban population. Beyond that, its concern for the rural economy was mainly that the village should also become a good market for the products of the town and growers should have enough incentives to produce more. In fact, there is a close parallel between what the town wants of the village in independent India and what the industrial North wants of the agricultural South on the international plane.

That is why, in the very first decade of independence, the political leadership set out to abolish the inefficient, unproductive class of absentee landlords and rentiers and to give the actual cultivator a direct stake in the land, either through protected tenancy rights or outright ownership. In this exercise it very largely succeeded, and the success tasted sweeter for two additional reasons: this landlord class was largely pro-British and opposed to independence, and after 1947 it had begun to raise its head against the urban-industrial leaders of the freedom movement. In later years this leadership also succeeded in the second and last installment of its limited agrarian program to give to the new class of owner-cultivators sufficient incentives by way of assured prices, inputs, and infrastructure. The very welcome result was a strong thrust in agricultural production, and also some democratization of rural society, because economic, social, and gradually political power also descended in the village from the house of one or two big landlords to the houses of hundreds of medium-sized cultivators. As a consequence, peasant power became a very significant force in Indian politics within a decade and a half. But despite the rhetoric, which was mostly pretense, neither the aim nor the result was justice. Hence "land to the tiller" remained only a slogan. Laws were passed for lowering ceilings on land-holdings so that more surplus land might be distributed to the poor. But they were never implemented.

Since the rural poor have numbers on their side, according to the theory of democracy they should have been able to capture political power and use it to their own advantage. But in the Indian sociopolitical system this did not happen for many reasons.

The political leadership worked out a remarkable way of pulling the poor vote in on the coattails of the richer peasants of the same caste: The voting power of the rural poor is very fragmented because small and marginal landowning farmers, however poor they may be, and often they are as poor as landless labor, generally belong to the same caste as, and prefer to identify and vote with, the richer landowning peasants than with the landless, who generally belong to lower castes. In economic terms, the marginal farmers in fact have more in common with the landless than with the richer landowners.

The political culture bred by the leadership was liberal, not radical, and yet, while avoiding radical reform, it was able to make very good use of radical rhetoric and to keep the poor in a state of quiet expectancy. The poorest among the voters could not see through the rhetoric because of: (a) their own political inexperience in earlier years; (b) the evidence they saw in later years (and the hope it raised among them) that justice was reaching down to people only a few rungs above them in the land hierarchy of the village; (c) the absence of any meaningful parties of the left; (*d*) in very recent years, the overhang of personal power in politics, which further weakened the workings of the theory of demo-cratic power.

Answering the Current Crisis

The resulting quiescence of the rural poor worked very well for nearly three decades, both for the older urban middle-class leadership and the more recently risen power of the richer peasantry. The two could amicably share political power and the economic cake in peace. The former got what it wanted, a rural hinterland that became steadily better as a source of low-cost supplies and an expanding market; the latter got greater prosperity than had appeared possible until very recent years.

But a severe crisis was building up beneath the surface and in the past few years has begun to boil. Unless it is controlled and begins to recede within this decade, it can cause a severe political as well as economic upset. This is cer-tainly one possibliity. But an alternative possibility is also now emerging, that the crisis will be controlled. Reasons for both possibilities lie within the unrest that is forming in rural India, the causes of which are economic and technological.

The current type of the so-called green revolution, which consists mainly of pumping in the material inputs required for improved agriculture, is running out of steam. The costs of the inputs are rising, and in order to maintain their profits the relatively richer peasants, who have been the main beneficiaries of the rising productivity, are demanding price increases for their products that the urban industrial leadership believes are difficult to concede. The resulting strains are threatening the partnership between the better-off industrial and rural interests. The slowing down of the prosperity of the richer peasants is also creating internal stresses within the urban and rural economies. Consumer industries, which have already more or less saturated the urban market, fear that the rural market of the richer peasants might also stop expanding. On their part, the richer peasants are also complaining that they are unable to meet the rising wage demands of farm labor and are resisting the demands with increas-ing ferocity except in those areas where the green revolution has been particu-larly successful.

But probably a stronger cause of the impending crisis is that the poor are running out of patience, a phenomenon whose potential is as vast as are its causes. The burden of their poverty is now recognized by everyone. So is the severity of the danger that might arise if the burden does not begin to lift quite soon. But state policies for lifting it are severely inhibited by fear of what it is thought the effort would cost. Resources for investment in future growth would dry up, it is feared, and the country would be swallowed by this morass if "development" got entangled in eliminating mass poverty. That the fear is un-founded is not as yet realized.

Estimates vary. But probably several hundred million people, mostly living on lands that have been degraded by environmental ravages, have had no share in the improvements experienced by the rural economy in the past decade and a half. State policies have either neglected them or have been frustrated by sociological and environmental factors and often by both. In fact, the poor have been adversely affected by policies that were said to have been carried out in their interest. This is as true of the abolition of the feudal system as it is of the advent of the new agriculture and even of such measures as laws fixing the minimum wages of rural labor. The pressure of their disappointments is now catching up alike with the poor and the nonpoor.

All answers to this triple crisis—between agriculture and industry and within each of them—exist within India. All of them are within India's existing financial and technological capabilities. What is lacking as yet is the will to use them. Neither the political nor the social system shows the determination to use the means that exist for resolving this crisis. But I believe it is more likely than not that the determination will grow with the awareness that the answers exist. It will become increasingly clear that the cost of using the answers is much less than of not using them, that the cost of removing poverty might in fact turn out to be negative.

The answer to the crisis facing new agriculture does not lie in pumping in more of the modern technologies and costly inputs without first ensuring efficient utilization. That is largely what is happening in many areas and has been happening for a long time regarding the use of water. Returns are diminishing as a consequence. Low-cost local alternatives, for example biological manures instead of only chemical fertilizers and modern adaptations of traditional energy sources, are not being developed on the scale that is required and is quite practicable, though commendable efforts have been made.

The physical structure of agriculture remains neglected in many large areas; holdings are not consolidated, land is not prepared in advance either for receiving water or other inputs, domestic storage is wasteful, commercial storage does not exist, and physical links with markets, which in the better organized areas have given farmers the single most important incentive for increasing production, have yet to be made or are bottlenecked by middlemen. It neither needs much money nor new technical know-how, only a determined administration, to overcome these handicaps. Only then will the cost of modern agriculture be justified by the benefits, and gains in production will give farmers the profits they are now seeking only through price increases and through their refusal to meet a fair part of the cost of agricultural development. The political and social system simply lacks the will to create such an administration.

More dangerous is the continuing neglect of the possibility of eliminating poverty. The extreme poverty of the Indian rural masses can become the largest single threat not only to development but to the stability of the whole social and political system. The fear of costs persists, in spite of any number of very significant experiments and demonstrations that are proving that poverty can be eliminated in ways that are an investment in growth, can pay for themselves many times over, and offer higher and quicker returns than many enterprises and amenities which are set up so readily for the benefit of the urban upper classes and the richer farmers. Eliminating poverty does not require expensive technologies and foreign exchange. It requires only three steps: recognition that even the poorest have a productive potential that needs only to be activated; identification of the means of activating it; giving the poor the tools so that through their own efforts and after an initial period of help they may become a permanently viable societal group.

What these experiments are demonstrating is that this is ever more possible. Economic details, methods of operation, and the means identified and adopted differ from one experiment to another because the essence of these programs is that each is small in scale (though collectively they can be very big) and each is tailor-made to suit the specific conditions of the community in which it works; many are tailored for the needs of the particular beneficiary. But the following have been proved over and over again:

First: At an expenditure of less than Rs 10,000 per family, spread over three years or more, each family now below the poverty line can be given the means that that will enable it to have a permanently recurring net income of at least Rs 6,000 a year. That would still be a poor income by world standards but by Indian standards would mean the banishment of mass poverty. It is not only above the poverty line but close to the average income per family. Therefore, in five years at most and often earlier, cash benefits alone, not to speak of the enormous social benefits, exceed the full cost, and this additional income puts the beneficiary permanently above the poverty line.

Second: Such nonincome benefits as family health can be ensured at costs that are so low that for a few years at least society can well afford to meet them, and thereafter the beneficiaries themselves can meet even at their very modest per capita viability.

Third: Staying well within the costs of the aid given to them and acting as part of the program of their own rehabilitation, the beneficiaries are able to create valuable and permanent social assets, in addition to the added income they annually harvest themselves. These assets include land reclaimed from or protected against ecological ravages, new forests or pastures, conservation of the soil and water, development of subsoil water resources through micro-sized projects, and the development and popularizing of alternative energy sources. No other investment pays back as much as quickly.

Fourth: When they are rejuvenated through these programs for the removal of poverty through social action, even very backward communities become more receptive to such ideas as family planning, personal and public sanitation, preventive health, and education—all elements, the absence of which makes poverty so dehumanizing.

For such a large-scale program of social transformation, the cash cost for society is nil. It recoups more than it spends, and eventually the government also recovers its costs in various ways. More important is the physical input that is needed—land. Some land, often as little as one acre for each family, is needed for most of these programs, especially for the largest, the most popular, and the most promising: animal husbandry, with a fodder back-up the beneficiary can call his own, a place for his dwelling, and cover for the animals. But land of the quality that will do is not as scarce as one might expect in such an overcrowded country.

The government's own estimates are that 40 million acres of surplus land would be available for distribution to the landless and marginal farmers if the laws on land ceilings were applied effectively. That by itself would give an acre each to most families below the poverty line. But even if that day is still far off, enough land can come out of the vast stretches owned by public authorities at the federal, state, district, and village levels. Much of this land is lying unused because it is not good enough for conventional agriculture. But it can be improved and made productive by the intensive application of manpower in the very innovative ways that have been developed by the more successful among the existing antipoverty programs.

The second physical input that is most needed is spare labor. Of that India has no shortage, given the millions of unemployed and many more millions who are underemployed as landless labor. Just as degraded land idly languishes for lack of enough labor to upgrade it, idle labor languishes for lack of land to work on. Therefore, what the opportunity for removing poverty awaits is an effective marriage between idle land and idle labor.

It also needs two intangibles of little cost but crucial importance. The first is suitable organizational structures. Because of their traditions, habits, methods, and main aims, government administrations are unable to mobilize social actions of an innovative kind, especially those requiring acute responsiveness to the many varied habitats of Indian poverty. Social action groups like nongovernmental voluntary agencies can do that much better. But the scale of action of each is very localized because each must respond to very specific conditions. Therefore, on the one hand, voluntary actions must be encouraged to proliferate as fast as they can without losing effectiveness; on the other hand, effective linkages must be made between them and modified governmental operations that can provide the scale required so that proven innovations and experiments may acquire a sufficient impact. These linkages are being made and proved in some, though too few, parts of India.

However, the cheapest input is the most essential: the will, upon which all else rests. Does the Indian society as a whole, and particularly the leadership, have the will? The evidence so far is discouraging. But the logic of the situation is more promising. There are compulsions of enlightened self-interest that can overcome the lethargy of Indian society and the ideological limitations of the leadership. It was precisely this self-interest, as perceived at the time by those who had the power to act upon it or to ignore it, that abolished the feudalism of the absentee landlord, protected the rights of the cultivator, sowed the seeds of the green revolution, and in the process gave the Indian social and political system far greater vigor and a much wider base than it had before. Now the same self-interest, if nothing else, must compel it to take the next step, of enfranchising in the real sense of the word the vast population of the rural poor that at present is enfranchised only in terms of the voting ritual. Only in this way can the existing system last long enough to evolve into something still more vigorous and with a still wider base. Otherwise, it will perish. The instinct of self-preservation will help it evolve through the constant interaction between the theory of democracy and the social and economic realities that has marked the history of independent India.

The Development Experience in Africa

Jonathan Chileshe

Africa has twenty of the world's thirty least developed countries, with five more African states anxious to be admitted to the club of the poorest nations, in the hope of getting more crumbs from the master's table. Africa holds the world record in adult illiteracy. Africa is perhaps the continent most dependent on external foreign technology, foreign capital, and foreign experts and know-how.[1] Africa's oil and food import bills have dangerously overdrained her already scarce foreign exchange reserves, making the continent increasingly dependent on the industrialized countries of Europe and America as well as other developing countries for cereals to feed her hungry and drought-stricken population. Virtually every African state has a substantially increased national debt burden. For a few countries, the children born during 1982 will grow up, go to school, take employment, earn income only to pay taxes to service and repay debts that were accumulated before they were born.

This background is useful to situate certain global development strategies, especially when the chosen litmus paper is the totality of Africa. The region's share of export trade of developing countries continues to decline, falling from 20.9 percent in 1970 to 14 percent in 1980. Similarly, the region's share—even taking into account oil-exporting countries—in total imports of developing countries has also continued to decline.[2] To this may be added the public debt, which doubled between 1970 and 1979 from 3.7 to 7.9 percent and similarly for the interest rate on total official debt, from 2 to 4.2 percent. Maturity offered on public debt declined from 24.4 in 1970 to 16.7 years in 1979. Thus continues a trend toward hardening terms of borrowing for sub-Saharan Africa.

Africa as a region and the individual states themselves are unmistakenly disenchanted with world economic trends. The unfulfilled promises provide the opening statements for the Lagos Plan of Action and exhibit this disenchantment. It is clear in the first preambular paragraph of the Lagos Plan of Action (LPA), which states:

> The effect of unfulfilled promises of global development strategies has been more sharply felt in Africa than in the other continents of the world. Indeed, rather than result in an improvement in the economic situation of the continent, successive strategies have made it stagnate and become more susceptible than other regions to the economic and social crisis suffered by the industrialized countries. Thus, Africa is un-

able to point to any significant growth rate, or satisfactory index of general well-being, in the past 20 years.[3]

The Second Extraordinary Session of the Assembly of Heads of State and Government of the OAU in April 1980 devoted its attention exclusively to consideration of African economic problems. By adopting the Lagos Plan of Action, African leaders had demonstrated, among other things, their desire for a far-reaching regional strategy, primarily based on collective self-reliance by its member states. The approach attempts to minimize the tendency for undue reliance on external assistance in future development strategies. However, Africa's adversaries have been watching to see the true logic of this new trend. Perhaps this could mark the beginning of a definite shift with regard to tackling development issues.

In the words of its architects, the Lagos Plan of Action is designed to restructure the African economies on the basis of twin principles: (a) national and collective self-reliance, and (b) self-reliant and self-sustaining development. Restructuring in the plan implies not only the need to change the composition of goods and services by gradually increasing the shares of industrial products in the national and regional basket of goods and services; it is also taken to mean internalizing the sources of the supply of producer goods (capital equipment, spare parts and machines, and raw material inputs), of high-level skills for natural resources exploration, evaluation, and extraction, of product and process design, and changing the ownership of enterprises, not only between the public and private sectors but also between indigenous and foreign owners.

The plan was conceived to be implemented in an integrated manner. It therefore defines the concepts of self-reliance and self-sustainment to imply increasing dependence of economic growth and development on internal demand stimuli and the gradual substitution of domestic for imported factor inputs, while collective self-reliance is akin to such approaches as the challenge of developing intra-African trade. The plan also implies the pooling of resources —manpower, markets, institutions, finance, etc.—at the subregional and other multinational levels so that certain set objectives could be achieved in such a way as to reflect genuine economic growth and development for the majority rather than the privileged few.

The strategy proposed in the plan is based, as the OAU, ECA, and ADB secretariats have pointed out, on a diagnosis of the economic situation of the sub-Saharan Africa as it has evolved over the past two decades. Thus, Africa (a) though not resource poor, is, relative to the economies, underdeveloped in the industrial and other sectors; (b) has witnessed a rather slow overall rate of economic growth; (c) has been subjected to tendencies of sluggish agricultural performance alongside rather rapid rates of population increases (d) has suffered from deepening balance-of-payments and physical crises; (e) has been a victim of tremendously overextended public sectors and scarcities of financial resources, skilled manpower, and organizational capabilities.

Regional Development in a Global Strategy

The World Bank report *Accelerated Development in Sub-Saharan Africa*[4] has been reviewed within Africa by, among others, a coordinated forum of the OAU, the ADB, the ECA, and the Association of African Central Banks (AACB), in addition to a meeting of governors of Central Banks in Africa.

The report was the end product of a specific request addressed to the World Bank in September 1979 by the African governors of the World Bank and the IMF. That request asked for the preparation of "a special paper on the economic development problems of these countries (sub-Saharan African countries in the 1980s and beyond) and an appropriate program for helping them."[5] By the time the report was published in 1981, the Lagos Plan of Action had already become an African household word. It is therefore not without reason that the authors of the World Bank report included a recognition of the existence of the former. Thus, the observed reiteration that "the Lagos Plan endorses objectives for the African states to achieve a more self-reliant, more economically integrated Africa by the year 2000."[6] The reader is immediately reminded, rather pointedly thereafter, of the report's manner and areas of concentration. The report is said to deal with short- to medium-term responses to Africa's current economic difficulties. Similarly, that attention is focused on how growth can be accelerated and how the resources to achieve the longer-term objectives set by the African governments could be generated, with the support of the international community.

There is no denying that there is ample evidence in the report of both internal and external causes for the observed deepening economic crisis against which the strategies for accelerated development are proposed. Internal factors comprise constraints of a structural nature, some of which emanate from the historical background of the countries. Others, however, are a result of their respective physical environments, for instance, having to live with underdeveloped human resources, economic disruption that accompanied decolonization, difficulties and cost of colonial consolidation (neocolonialism), climatic and geographical factors that are hostile to development and yet conducive to rapid increase of burdensome population. External factors, on the other hand, include the adverse trends in the international economy, for instance, those surrounding the adjustment in oil prices, imbalance in the balance of payments, escalation in world prices accompanied by depression in commodity prices.

The report puts strong accent on agriculture as a very important motor for development in the African economy. It therefore calls for specific appropriate action in this field and recommends the implementation of agriculture-based and export-oriented strategies. Three areas for major policy actions are emphasized: (*a*) suitable trade and exchange rate policies, (*b*) increased efficient use of resources in the public sectors, and (*c*) improvement in agricultural policies. Other equally important recommendations in the report on which the strategies are based include reducing the size of the public sectors, encouraging small-scale enterprise cooperatives, and promoting the participation of foreign private capital.

Regional vs. Global Action

Because Africa is the object of action in both the Lagos Plan of Action (an example of a regional development strategy) and the World Bank Report (a strategy prepared at global level), contrasting the two may well reveal the existence of interactive processes. At the same time, one cannot overlook the bias or tendency by the global architects to gloss over or treat lightly issues that at the regional level are considered to be of crucial importance. Developing Africa is indeed an integral part of the Third World, but remedies for her ills cannot be those based on the rule-of-averages often favored by authors with a global predisposition. Playing poor, as those at the global level would like to advocate, is a luxury that can be afforded only by those who are not poor. This one distinction separates the person who wears the shoe that pinches from the bystander to whom the account is told to fill time (a Zulu proverb).

Both the plan and the report are agreed on the main causes for the lack of development and economic growth in the African region. Both are also in agreement that action or strategies to accelerate development should be initiated and that the results are subject to short-, medium-, and long-term gestation periods. The most fundamental areas listed include population, urban growth, forest and soil conservation, land use and planning (which includes a fuller exploitation of the agriculture potential), regional economic cooperation and integration, structural reforms, industrialization, and external assistance.

There is also much concurrence between the two with regard to certain strategies that could be considered for adoption, and both stress agriculture as a priority area.

The two approaches differ in their global overview of causes, prescriptions, and timing as to when to begin treatment of the supposedly sick Africa. A few examples suffice to illustrate. The regional diagnosis of the plan places blame on external factors; conversely, the report lays a major part of the blame on internal factors. The plan sees the issue of targets and objectives in the light of national and collective self-reliance, especially the development of national, subregional, and regional markets. The report tends to advocate the idea of continuing to feed external markets. The plan views agriculture, as does the report, as a motor for development and economic growth. The former, however, sees it in a broader context and advocates that it be interrelated with other sectors in the economy. The report seems to concentrate more on agriculture to the neglect of other sectors. The issue of strategies in the plan stresses internally oriented and intersector development and economic growth. The report gives prominence to agriculture-based and export-oriented strategies in order to increase foreign exchange earnings.

Differences between the two also exist with regard to recommended strategies and their implementation. The plan's proposals are much concerned with trying to avoid giving the impression that the African region is for sale to the highest bidder. In other words, they do not wish to mortgage Africa a second time or return to economic colonialism through overreliance on external assistance. The report treats the subject of industry more as a marginal subject. There is also no mention in the report of the Industrial Development Decade for Africa.

Some of the recommendations in the report regarding reform of the African economic structures could be said to amount to exerting considerable pressures on recipients, particularly when African countries seeking external assistance are pressured, as a condition for its availability, into structural reforms that give the donor rather than the recipient a free hand in determining the economic policies in the latter. Analysis in the report of the issue of tied-aid and especially the extent to which it can adversely affect the rate of development and economic growth is rather scanty. Similarly, the effects that the recommended increases in external assistance will have on debt accumulation do not seem to have been adequately addressed. There is also no guarantee that the mechanical relationships between the reform and increased assistance indicated in the report would work.

The analysis of the above issue seems to have lost sight of the fact that all aid has eventually to be repaid. This is why today's Africa expresses disquiet about burdening its unborn generation with having to pay or service debts incurred before they are even born.

Implementing most of the strategies proposed in the report would require a heavy outlay in money and human resources. This to some extent does not tally with the observation made in the report that the present world setting is not conducive to the release of sufficient development resources. Trends beginning about 1973 confirm that Africa's chances of increasing export earnings are rather slim.

Concluding Observations

The Lagos Plan of Action attempts to treat the various issues in an integrated manner. The World Bank Report, on the other hand, tends to emphasize in a rather isolated manner most of the sectors. For instance, for agriculture, emphasis is laid on the export production component for purposes of increasing foreign exchange earnings. When oil prices increase, exporters of manufactures to Africa also increase the merchandise by margins higher than the increase in oil prices on the pretext that this is necessitated by the increase in the main input of their manufactures. The end result is that the African economy is hit on both sides: (a) having to pay for high import bills when it did not originate the crisis; (b) having to cope with depressed prices on commodity exports because of high import prices in the industrial countries. It is unlikely therefore that the recommendations in the report are the type that really tackle this issue well enough to justify any optimism about accelerated development in sub-Saharan Africa, especially for both the least developed among the developing countries and the non-oil-producing countries.

Because the relevance of global vis-à-vis regional development strategies on the basis of these two examples has been summarized in an assessment made by the OAU, ECA, and ADB secretariats, we have made only passing reference to certain inconsistencies between the two. In particular, we have focused on the selection of goals and the characteristics of the proposed strategies. The Lagos Plan of Action attaches greater importance to increased production from all economic sectors as well as to the interrelationships among those sectors as a means of achieving faster growth and accelerated development. It advocates greater exploitation of domestic factor inputs with the aim of satisfying internal demand. However, we are not told how this is to be done, except in general terms. On the other hand, the report, while not totally rejecting this concept, seems to emphasize production intended to feed external markets in order to earn foreign exchange. Apparently, the lack of foreign exchange is what seems to have been at the root of the present crisis of the balance of payments in the African economies. The report also tends to underplay the tremendous influence and unpredictability of external forces on the rate of development in Africa.

The 1980s conjure up a pattern that makes it quite evident that the success of any strategy will depend to a large extent on a mix of the main ideas expressed in the Lagos Plan of Action and the World Bank Report. Raising self-confidence is crucial; so is self-reliance. However, it would be fruitless to wage a war of words over which is the most appropriate of the two. A true test of any development strategy must be its ability to enable all of us "to pursue relentlessly and with single-minded determination the objectives of establishing a new national and regional economic order in Africa based on an increasing measure of national and collective self-reliance and dedicated to the task of achieving an equitable distribution of the products of development among the African peoples."[7]

Notes

1. See also Jonathan H. Chileshe, "Aid: The Amorphous African Development Catalyst," *Symposium on African Perspectives on the New International Economic Order* (The United Nations University in collaboration with Addis Ababa University, Addis Ababa, 3–9 May 1981).

2. U.N. Economic Commission for Africa, "A Review of the Developing International Crisis and its Implications for Africa," Eighth Meeting of the Conference of Ministers, Tripoli, 27–30 Apr. 1982 (Document E/ECA/CM.8/15), para. 2.

3. Organization of African Unity, *Lagos Plan of Action for the Economic Development of Africa, 1980–2000*, p. 5, para. 1.

4. The World Bank, *Accelerated Development in Sub-Saharan Africa: An Agenda for Action* (Washington, D.C., 1981).

5. *Accelerated Development in Sub-Saharan Africa: An Assessment by the OAU, ECA and ADB Secretariat*, E/ECA/CM.8/16 (ECA edited version), para. 3.

6. World Bank, *Accelerated Development in Sub-Saharan Africa*, p. 1.

7. AdebayoAdedeji, "The Economic Commission for Africa: Its Origin, Development, Problems and Prospects" (address to the 14th session of the Commission and the 5th Meeting of the Conference of Ministers, Rabat, Morocco, 20–28, Mar. 1979), p. 40.

Arab National Economic Plans: A Look at Some of the Imbalances

J. M. Hashim

The Arab world consists of twenty-one countries spread over an area of 13 million square kilometers with a total population of 163 million inhabitants which, given its average growth rate of 3.2 percent per annum, is expected to double by the year 2000. By virtue of the structure and composition of the Arab world, economic divergence among the member countries does exist, and in some cases and areas it is acute. In reality, the Arab world is an aggregation of twenty-one national economies and different levels of economic and social development. Consequently, an analysis expressed in terms of means and averages must not be construed to represent a unified development pattern in the whole region.

The Arab region occupies a strategic position in the international geo-economic and political setting. This is the result of its vital exports, particularly oil, and its ever-increasing imports of industrial goods as well as agricultural products. In the field of finance, the Arab world commands a unique position in the international monetary system and its various institutions. The development pattern in the region over the last two decades has therefore been interactive with international economic trends taking place during that time.

Planning for Development

Development planning has been an accepted concept and an instrument for economic and social progress for a relatively long time. In certain Arab countries national economic plans were devised and implemented in the early 1920s. The first three-year Iraqi plan was implemented between 1927 and 1930, and the Development Board was created in 1950. Syria and Morocco started their first plans in 1947 and 1949, respectively. Today almost all Arab countries implement development programs and monitor their progress through national plans. In this sense, the pattern of sectoral development—its impact on the respective national economies as well as its imbalances—is easily traceable in most Arab Countries.

Tremendous efforts have been made during the last three decades, particularly during the 1970s, to improve the performance of the Arab economy. During the last decade two important developments took place in the structure of the economy of the Arab region.

First, the recuperation of Arab natural resources, particularly oil, was completed by the mid-1970s. This operation had a triple effect: (*a*) It gave Arab planners a more comprehensive view and command of their respective economies. Consequently, they attempted to integrate the oil sector into the structure of the Arab economy. More thorough plans could be worked out. (*b*) The recuperation process meant larger financial resources which, in most Arab countries, removed the foreign exchange constraint that Arab planners have always lived with. This has had a tremendous impact on the development programs of the region. (*c*) The recuperation of Arab oil has put the Arab world in the limelight and, therefore, at the crossroads of international interferences and interventions that are likely to affect Arab expectations as expressed by economic plans. Furthermore, the continuous external control on oil transportation and distribution maintains an unbalanced pattern of economic relationships between the Arab world and the rest of the world.

The second important development in the Arab economy has been the increased interest in the development of Arab human resources. This was reflected in the national plans by way of expanded expenditure on educational, cultural, and scientific programs and in the determined effort to exterminate illiteracy in certain Arab countries.

In terms of national development effort, there has been a tremendous increase in allocations for development plans in the last decade. The total allocation in the Arab world amounted to approximately $338 thousand million, while allocations for the second half of that decade (1975–80) amounted to $226 thousand million. In 1980 fixed capital formation amounted to $98 thousand million, which represented 23.9 percent of GNP in the Arab world for the same year.

When compared with that of the developing countries, the rate of growth in the Arab region was comparatively high at 7.3 percent per annum for 1980. However, this does not necessarily reflect good economic performance from the productive sectors. Implicit in this high level of growth are the effects of the quick utilization of resources and the world inflationary effects reflected in the high prices developing countries have to pay for their imports.

In its attempt to realize a high level of development growth in the shortest possible time, the Arab development pattern in the 1970s witnessed imbalances in the growth of productive sectors in the economy.

A Look at Sectoral Performances

Industrial Sector. Arab national plans were committed to a process of wide and ambitious industrialization with the expectation that this would broaden the national economic base through forward and backward linkage effects, create gainful employment opportunities, increase foreign exchange earnings and, in general, favorably change the patterns of social development. However, the industrial sector has in fact failed to achieve the objectives set for it. For instance, in spite of a comparatively high rate of growth (about 8.2 percent per annum during the 1975–80 period), the contribution of manufacturing industries to the Arab GNP was only 5.9 percent in 1980 compared with 8.8 percent in 1978. In contrast, the contribution made to the Arab GNP by the extractive and quarrying subsector has increased from 48.6 percent in 1978 to 51.5 percent in 1980. No diversification has yet taken place. Arab economies continue to be "mono-productive economies" since they are still based on a handful of primary products, particularly crude oil, phosphates, and cotton. Furthermore, because of the availability of labor, transportation, and other facilities, industrial projects were set up almost exclusively in urban areas, thus creating, in individual Arab countries, regional imbalances at the expense of the countryside.

Agricultural Sector. The picture in agriculture is quite illustrative. Agriculture contributed to about 6.5 percent of the GNP in 1980 compared with 8.6 percent in 1978. Recognizing that this sector has traditionally been labor intensive (employing about 50 percent of the Arab labor force), one realizes that underemployment and underdeveloped production techniques led to the obvious low level of productivity in this sector.

In 1970 there was more or less a balanced situation between domestic demand for and production of agricultural products. This position was drastically changed over a period of ten years. Self-sufficiency in grain production, for example, decreased from 85 percent in the early 1970s to 60 percent in the early 1980s. The ratio of agricultural exports to agricultural imports declined from 94 percent in 1970 to 20 percent at the end of the decade. The cost to the national economy of the imbalance in the agricultural sector increased in terms of net imports of agricultural products: from $100 million in 1970 to $5.5 thousand million in the 1974–78 period, finally reaching a staggering $11.5 thousand million in 1979.

Human Resources. In some Arab countries the development effort, and particularly the industrial drive, could not have taken place without recourse to a massive foreign labor force, which has come to constitute the largest share of current labor. In other words, there is a quantitative imbalance between the supply and demand of the labor force. Moreover, in some cases the expatriate population constitutes the majority of the total population. This situation has created a dangerous social imbalance which, in the future, could lead to political imbalances or disturbances. The Arab world is also characterized by a qualitative imbalance when it comes to its labor force. In some cases, nonnational scientists and engineers constitute more than 90 percent of the total stock of scientists and engineers. A similar situation exists in the proportion of nonnational R&D scientists and engineers. This is largely the result of three factors: (a) Illiteracy rates are high and school enrollments are low, which is characteristic of the developing countries. (b) The output of the educational system does not correspond to the needs of the economy. A 1976 UNESCO study of national science and technology policies in the Arab states concluded that "The figures show a preponderance of students in humanities, education, arts, social sci-

Table 1. Structure of Production and Employment in Sixteen Arab Countries in 1979 (%)

	Agriculture		Industry		Manufacturing		Services	
	Contribution to GDP	Employment	Contribution to GDP	Employment	Contribution to GDP	Employment	Contribution to GDP	Employment
Somalia	60	84	11	8	7		29	8
Mauritania	27	85	33	5	8		40	10
Sudan	38	78	13	10	6		49	12
North Yemen	32	76	—	11	5		—	13
Egypt	23	50	35	29	28		42	21
South Yemen	13	47	26	15	11		61	38
Morocco	19	53	32	12	17		49	26
Syria	16	32	22	31	—	—	62	37
Tunisia	16	35	33	32	12		51	33
Jordan	8	21	32	19	16		60	60
Lebanon	—	12	—	26	—		—	62
Algeria	7	32	58	24	11		35	44
Iraq	8	43	73	26	6		19	31
Saudi Arabia	1	62	74	14	5		25	24
Libya	2	20	73	27	3		25	53
Kuwait	0	2	81	34	5		19	64

SOURCE: *World Bank Report* (1981).

ences and law." This has led to an imbalance at the expense of graduates in natural sciences, technology, and agriculture, and, consequently, to a shortage of trained manpower in the productive sector. (c) Brain drain is the third contributing factor to the imbalance between the supply and demand of the labor force. For instance, between 1962 and 1967 more than 5,000 professional and technical workers emigrated from five Arab countries (Egypt, Lebanon, Syria, Iraq, and Jordan) to the United States and Canada, and one Arab country (Jordan) lost to the United States and Canada about one-third of its stock of natural scientists. Arab countries have sought to reverse this regrettable trend through combined actions to restructure and refurbish their educational systems, increase spending on education, and introduce and implement plans specifically designed for the development of human resources.

Employment. There is an imbalance between the structure of production and that of employment. The agricultural sector's contribution to the economy is the highest in terms of employment and the lowest in terms of GDP. When it comes to the industrial sector, we have the opposite situation. The implication of such an imbalance is an inequitable income distribution (see table 1).

All these factors contributed to an imbalance in the development of the national economies of Arab oil-producing and non-oil-producing countries. The role and importance of the oil-producing countries in the Arab economy took on an unprecedented status. Its share in the Arab GDP increased from 71.6 percent in 1978 to 82 percent in 1980. In growth terms, Arab oil-producing countries achieved a real rate of growth of about 8.5 percent in 1980, while in the same year the rate of growth of the least developed Arab countries did not exceed 1 percent.

On the generation of income and capital utilization, the situation reveals no less of an imbalance. While it is estimated that the accumulated capital reserve of some Arab countries invested in the international markets was about $330 thousand million by the end of 1981, other Arab countries had to turn to the international money markets in order to borrow—frequently under unfavorable terms. The volume of these borrowings was declared at $16.5 thousand million in the period 1971–78. It is not unreasonable to assume that at least part, if not a substantial part, of this available capital is of Arab origin.

Planning and Social Change

The development of social change in the Arab world, taken as a whole, suffered substantially during the past decade. In qualitative terms, the migration from the rural to urban areas not only diminished the role of the former in social change but also brought added burdens to urban centers. More and more bottlenecks appeared in the process of managing and servicing the economy. The technological gap became more and more widespread, and the structure of the national economy became increasingly dependent upon that of the industrialized Western world. Quick and easy "solutions" further aggravated the already existing imbalance.

In our observations, we have concentrated on the imbalances in the Arab national economy without analyzing the causes and the economic patterns responsible for them. However, we might point out one singularly important cause of these imbalances, that is, the persistent subordination of our national economy to the economies of the more industrialized countries. This is by far the most damaging aspect of the negative circumstances affecting our development effort.

Our dependence on foreign technology is undoubtedly going to increase. But the pattern of technology transfer of the last two decades must change in favor of a technology that can be appropriately adapted to the local situation and then indigenously developed. Further, the increasing role of the multinationals in development projects is making worse the dependence of our development on external parameters. And finally, the current process of recycling our financial resources and investing them in foreign markets is giving greater control and power to external agencies not concerned with the needs of our countries.

By the year 2000 the Arab world will be dependent on outside sources to satisfy its demand for meat (41.8 percent), sugar (44.3 percent), wheat (42.1 percent), and rice (43.8 percent). This high rate of dependence, especially in strategic food items, constitutes a severe threat for the Arab world in the economic, political, and security fields. What more effective weapon can be used against a developing nation than to control its means to feed its population?

Another facet of our economic subordination lies in the domain of energy supply. That may sound peculiar, but as an illustration, while Arab oil constitutes no more than 9 percent of the world energy reserves, Arab countries presently supply between 40 and 50 percent of the total energy requirement worldwide. In other words, the present favorable position the Arab countries enjoy is highly marginal and quite tentative. Estimates indicate that the Arab oil resources will be depleted in a matter of twenty-five years or so, at the most, in forty years' time (assuming the most favorable conditions of production and utilization). I hesitate to speculate on the added pressures such a crisis would create on the economy, especially in those non-oil-producing Arab countries like South Yemen and the Sudan, where income per capita in 1980 was a mere $280 and $500, respectively, and which are classified by the United Nations as least-developed countries.

The Future: An Exciting Challenge

By pointedly discussing imbalances in Arab national development plans, no one should assume that there is no other side to the coin. The Arab investment program in the 1970s has been phenomenal; consequently, the expansion of the Arab GDP has been very marked. The non-oil GDP jumped from $29.6 thousand million in 1970 to over $372 thousand million in 1980. The efforts made to expand the oil-based industries in Saudi Arabia, Iraq, and in the Gulf are exciting both physically and conceptually. Expansions in infrastructure, in transportation, road networks, housing, communication, and education are milestones in the development program of the past two decades.

What is most promising is that these efforts, both at the investment and the implementation level, are continuing into the 1980s with greater intensity and commitment. The imbalances mentioned are the challenges we have to face in the 1980s from a sense of responsibility and commitment—commitment to our people and our region in its drive to achieve progress and development. Moreover, some of the imbalances such as in food and human resources require regional action and therefore provide one more very good reason for cooperation and integration within the Arab community. We also face our challenges out of a sense of responsibility to the world community as equal partners with us in the development process.

Population and Development

Rafael M. Salas

If we look at the world today we will find that there definitely is a decline in the population growth rate. From an estimated 1.9 percent two or three decades ago, current population growth rate is now down to 1.7 percent. This is a remarkable achievement because the decline in the growth rate comes primarily from the developing countries and is partly due to the extensive efforts of governments in undertaking population programs that started only fifteen to twenty years ago.

The first country to advocate the inclusion of population programs in its development plans was India, which began doing so in the 1950s. But it was not until about the late 1960s that developing countries as a whole began to integrate population programs in their development plans. The growth rate of 1.7 percent is expected to go down even further, to 1.5 percent by the year 2000. This does not suggest, however, that there will be no growth in absolute numbers because world population continues to increase at a rate of about 80 million per annum. This means that by the turn of the century we would have a global population of about 6.1 thousand million.

Developing countries have intensified efforts to look at their population problems from the perspective of their development programs. The approaches vary. Not always do the countries advocate the limitation of fertility or reduction of the growth rate. Some countries, as a matter of fact, want to increase fertility rates and population growth rates. As it stands now the governments of about 80 percent of the population of the developing countries wish to reduce fertility, governments of 3 percent wish to increase their population growth rates, while the remaining 17 percent are quite satisfied with their present growth rates.

A regional perspective reveals that the bulk of the countries in Asia would wish to reduce growth rates simply because of the pressure of population—an extremely burdensome reality for most countries—and that those countries in Africa south of the Sahara would opt to maintain present rates of growth. Latin America is a mix between these two types of activity: there are some countries that because of population pressure, particularly in Central America and the Caribbean, would like in fact to reduce growth rates; however, the temperate areas of South America want to increase population growth. The Middle East is equally a mixed area for population policies. Some countries would like to increase population to increase the labor supply, while other countries, like Egypt, have launched programs to reduce fertility.

Where there is the capacity to innovate and the technical and financial resources to do so, even rapid population growth can be accommodated by an
increase in the supply of food and other necessities. The question is how long
such increases can continue. This is not simply a matter of carrying capacity in
terms of theoretical yields. There are allied concerns about the long-term effects of fertilizers and pesticides, and about water-logging and salinity where
irrigation is needed. More information is needed on these points, particularly
as they affect societies in the process of modernization.

The industrialized countries of the world now have an average growth rate of
about 0.6 percent to 0.7 percent, which means that, more or less, there is
stability in that part of the world. Their concern is not primarily the growth
rates but emerging problems such as the aging of their populations and, to a
degree, the urbanization that is still occurring. Today's developing countries are
also firmly set on the path to urbanization, but the industrial base to provide
employment and sustain vastly increased population is not yet in place. We
need now consider means to relieve the pressure on major cities, what consumption patterns and population trends would best assist this process, and
how the necessities of urban development may be brought into line with the
demands of a secure and undamaged natural environment.

There are several things that must be underlined in all the developments in
the past decade and a half, the first of which is to realize that countries today
have found the capacity for action in the population sphere. This is quite a
different perspective from that of ten or fifteen years ago, when countries looked
at populations purely as underlying variables, meaning that they undertook to
study population because of the impact of numbers on other programs. For
instance, population growth was examined to determine how many schoolchil-
dren there would be in order to know how many schoolhouses to build. It was
never before thought that as a programmatic thrust something could be done to
lower fertility and thus effect some correlation with economic development
plans. This perception by governments of the population concept and the capacity to act appropriately represents the big difference in attitudes and policies
that has been evident over the past ten years.

Today when we speak of population, we include not just family planning but
also the collection of basic data that relates population to development plans,
including such things as censuses, surveys, population dynamics (relating economic and social variables with population), population education, and communication to disseminate information, both formally through educational institutions and the media as well as one-to-one relationships on the importance of the
concept with regard to individual and family behavior. Another factor that has
emerged in the course of these past years is that population must always be
linked with socioeconomic factors such as the economic participation of women,
the high illiteracy rate prevailing in many countries, better distribution of
income, equal rights, and opportunities for women. The gross disparities that
now exist between and within countries deny to many—among them the poorest groups, women, and the elderly—the opportunity to make their fullest

contribution. Maximizing the contribution to development of a nation's greatest resource, its people, demands the maximum opportunity for each individual and community. Population policy must therefore be shaped to give the fullest expression to these demands.

Finally, in considering population, we must also make the necessary connections with ongoing environmental studies. Population policies must relate to the environmental efforts that today are being undertaken by so many countries. Maintaining a balance between population, resources, and the environment, while at the same time pursuing overall development goals, depends to a great extent on how quickly population growth rates can be brought down. But it also depends on expansion of the resource base—irrigation, reforestation, planned land use, for example. These will, by producing a decline in death rates, eventually affect fertility also. The combined efforts of a number of disciplines will help in defining what combinations of population and other development inputs will be most effective in shaping appropriate policies.

Index

About the Authors

Ismail Sabri Abdalla is President of SID, Chairman of the Third World Forum, and a former Minister of Planning, Egypt.

Michael Allen is a graduate student at the London School of Economics and former lecturer, University of the West Indies, Jamaica.

Jeffrey Ashe is Associate Director, Accion International.

Dragoslav Avramoric is Adviser to the Secretary General, UNCTAD.

Munir Benjenk is Vice President for External Affairs at the World Bank.

Lee Bloom is President of UNILEVER U.S., Inc.

Elisabeth Mann Borgese is Advisor to the Austrian Delegation to the Law of the Sea Conference and Chairperson, Planning Council, International Ocean Institute.

Jonathan Chileshe is President of the Ethiopian Chapter, SID, and is with the U.N. Economic Commission for Africa.

Pran Chopra is a Fellow, Centre for Policy Studies, New Delhi.

William Cline is Senior Fellow, Institute for International Economics.

Luigi Coccioli is President, Banco San Paolo di Torino, Italy.

Emilio Colombo is Minister of Foreign Affairs, Italy.

Javier Perez de Cuellar is Secretary General of the United Nations.

Kenneth Dadzie is High Commissioner of Ghana to the United Kingdom.

Francis Mading Deng is Ambassador of the Sudan to Canada.

Clarence Dias is President of the International Centre for Law and Development (ICLD).

Mahdi El-Manjra is a professor at University Mohammed 5, Morocco, and has served as an adviser to the Intergovernmental Bureau of Informatics.

Frank Feather is President, Global Futures Network.

David Gill is director, Capital Markets Department, International Finance Corporation, Washington, D.C.

James Grant is Executive Director of UNICEF and immediate past President of SID.

Mahbub ul Haq is Chairman of SID's North-South Round Table and Minister for Planning and Development, Pakistan.

J. M. Hashim is a former President of the Arab Monetary Fund and Minister of Planning, Iraq.

S. N. Leela is with the Department of Economics, Millersville State College, Millersville, Pennsylvania.

Ronald Leger is the Director, International Non-Governmental Organisation Division, Canadian International Development Agency (CIDA).

Mark Leland is Assistant Secretary for Monetary Affairs, U.S. Treasury Department.

Joan Lestor is a member of the British Parliament.

Mark MacGuigan is Minister of Foreign Affairs, Canada.

Alister McIntyre is Deputy Secretary General, UNCTAD.

Martin McLaughlin is Vice President, Overseas Development Council.

Robert McNamara was from 1968 to 1981 President of the World Bank. He presently chairs the Overseas Development Council.

Peter McPherson is Administrator, United States Agency for International Development (USAID).

Ann Mattis is Research Consultant with the Society for International Development.

Simon May is Foreign Affairs Adviser to former British Prime Minister Edward Heath, M. P.

Donald Mills was formerly Jamaican Ambassador to the United Nations and Chairman of the Group of 77.

Robert Moore was formerly High Commissioner of Guyana to Canada.

Olof Murelius is Special Advisor, Energy Planning, Natural Resources and Energy Division, United Nations.

Ulla Olin is principal officer in charge of policies and programs, U. N. Development Program (UNDP).

Ricardo Palma-Valderrama is assistant general manager, Arab–Latin American Bank, Lima, Peru.

Rafael Salas is Executive Director, U. N. Fund for Population Activities (UNFPA).

Soedjatmoko is rector of the United Nations University.

Inga Thorsson is Under Secretary of State for Foreign Affairs, Sweden.

Cesar Virata is Prime Minister, Republic of the Philippines.

Tarzie Vittachi is Deputy Executive Director of External Relations, UNICEF.

Andrew Young is Mayor of Atlanta, Georgia, and former United States Ambassador to the United Nations.

Muhammad Yunus is a former university professor of economics. He now directs the Grameen Bank Project, which he established.

The Society for International Development

The Society for International Development is an independent nongovernmental organization whose purposes are to provide a forum for collective reflection and to encourage a mutually educating dialogue on development at all levels.

The Society was founded in 1957 and has evolved into several interlocking networks—including its membership and chapter organizations—that link individuals and institutions in different ways around a varied range of activities.

SID's major programs include: the North-South Round Table, an intervention at the international level; the Alternative Development Strategies program, together with the Society's journal, *Development: Seeds of Change, Village through Global Order*, acting as catalysts in the dialogue at national levels; and the Grass Roots Initiatives and Strategies program, which will attempt to pool the knowledge and technology emanating from spontaneous people-oriented activities in industrialized and Third World countries at the local level.